A PASSION
TO LEAD

A PASSION TO LEAD

Seven Leadership Secrets for Success in Business, Sports, and Life

JIM CALHOUN WITH RICHARD ERNSBERGER, JR.

ST. MARTIN'S PRESS ⚘ NEW YORK

To my parents, James A. and Katherine M. Calhoun, who are my inspiration and reason for this book in my life; and to my six grandchildren, Emily, Katie, Sam, Avery, Reese, and Peyton, the stars in my eyes and our future.

www.stmartins.com

Design by Jamie Kerner-Scott

Library of Congress Cataloging-in-Publication Data

Calhoun, Jim.
    A passion to lead : seven leadership secrets for success in business, sports, and life / Jim Calhoun with Richard Ernsberger, Jr.—1st ed.
        p. cm.
    ISBN-13: 978-0-312-36271-3
    ISBN-10: 0-312-36271-4
    1. Leadership. 2. Success. 3. Motivation (Psychology)   I. Ernsberger, Richard. II. Title.
    BF637.L4C28 2007
    158'.4—dc22

                                                                    2007023532

First Edition: October 2007

10 9 8 7 6 5 4 3 2 1

CONTENTS

ACKNOWLEDGMENTS

My success as a basketball coach has been dependent on the great support I've received over the years from, first, the administration at Northeastern University and, more recently, the administration at the University of Connecticut. I owe both schools a great debt of gratitude. No coach can win consistently without consistent encouragement and commitment from a university's president, athletic director, athletic staff, faculty, students, and fans, and I certainly am fortunate in that regard. The current and former University of Connecticut presidents: President Philip Austin; my dear friend Dr. Harry Hartley; and the man who hired me and helped start the whole journey here at UConn, Dr. John Casteen. And, everybody associated with the university's athletic department, starting with the AD who hired me, John Toner, who is a great friend and a man of incredible intelligence; followed by Todd Turner; to Lew Perkins, who not only developed a terrific Athletic Department for me and everyone associated with UConn but also became a great friend; and finally Athletic Director Jeff Hathaway, also a personal friend. All are passionate about building great sports programs, across the board, and they share my dedication to not just winning games but, more important, turning young student-athletes into rock-solid American citizens.

I want to thank my wife, Pat, for her constant love and support over the years. She truly is a special person who has not only made my career special but most important, made my life a great journey. It's not easy being the wife of a coach, but Pat's steady personality and commitment to our family has been a source of strength for me ever since we got married. I may suffer through every win and loss, but she always keeps our life in perspective. My sisters—Rose, Kathy, Joan, and Margaret—along with my brother, Bill, have always been loyal and loving, and a great source of inspiration for me. The same holds true for my sons, James and Jeff, their wives, Jennifer and Amy, and their six wonderful gifts, their six children (three for each couple) Emily, Katie, Sam, Avery, Reese, and Peyton. My sons are my unofficial basketball sounding boards. I solicit their advice and respect their opinions (even they don't always realize it).

Whatever success I've had as a coach is directly attributable to the able men who've worked with me over the years. I want to thank my current coaching staff for their dedication and friendship—George Blaney, Andre LaFleur, Patrick Sellers, and Beau Archibald. I've had an amazing group of assistant coaches during my career, and many of them have gone on to become accomplished head coaches. Dave Leitao, head coach at the University if Virginia; Karl Hobbs, head coach at George Washington University; Howie Dickenman, head coach at Central Connecticut State University; Glen Miller, head coach at the University of Pennsylvania; Steve Pikiell, head coach at Stony Brook University; and Ted Woodward, head coach at the University of Maine. Tom Moore, who was a key assistant for thirteen years for leaving UConn last year to be the head coach at Quinnipiac University, will be especially missed. They all had great passion for building a great program here with the student-athlete always coming first. I thank all the coaches, past and present, for their total commitment to their jobs and the basketball programs at Northeastern and Connecticut. They were, and remain, dear friends.

Thanks to Ted (Doc) Taigen for his counseling work with the basketball team. His wise counsel, and sense of humor, are a great asset to Connecticut basketball. His incredible passion for our kids is like none other I have ever seen, and each and every player comes away a better person and player. I also want to acknowledge Dee Rowe, special adviser, athletics, who urged me to accept the Connecticut job more than twenty-five years ago and has been a dear friend ever since. *Dave Gavitt has performed the role of mentor to me for all these years.* I would be remiss if I didn't mention our associate athletic director and former SID, Tim Tolokan, who is the best at what he does and clearly and definitively is my best friend at UConn and a man who truly bleeds Huskie blue and white. A special thanks to Joe Sharpe, who is now the head trainer for the NBA Charlotte Bobcats and whom I view as a son. Thanks, also, to Jeff Anderson, M.D., director of sports medicine at the University of Connecticut; (remove Dr. Trojian); James Doran, assistant athletic trainer; Chris West, strength and conditioning coordinator; Christina Buccheri, our program assistant; and Kathy Swanson, my administrative assistant. Kathy handles a thousand and one details so that I can concentrate on what I do best—teach young men how to get better at basketball and the game of life. She truly is someone special and everyone who comes into contact with her realizes it.

And last and most important, what makes the most sense and makes all this complete, my players of thirty-five years. They have made us successful with their play, and on a daily basis, taught me so many things. When I finish my career, I would hope that the lasting tribute that I would receive is that I made a difference in each and every one of their lives.

Introduction

ABOVE THE RIM

WE ALL STRIVE TO be successful in our careers and in our lives. And when success comes in the form of recognition by your peers, the moment is special.

On September 9, 2005, I was inducted into the Naismith Memorial Basketball Hall of Fame in Springfield, Massachusetts. It was a great day for me, to say the least. I grew up in Massachusetts and graduated from American International College (AIC), which is located in Springfield. I played basketball for AIC—well enough to get a tryout after graduation with the Boston Celtics, the team I idolized when growing up.

While I was in college, I visited the original Hall of Fame a few times. Like everybody else, the busts and plaques commemorating the game's legendary coaches and players from both the professional and college ranks dazzled me. Many of them were heroes of mine.

When I was young, I never thought seriously of getting into the Hall of Fame myself. For a kid in his late teens and early twenties, the idea was too farfetched. At that age I was just wondering where I'd find the money for my next meal. But, subconsciously, I'm sure it made a bigger impression on me than I realized.

For one thing, I loved sports, and especially basketball—I went on to become a coach. And thirty-three years later, there I was on that

September day, standing in the hallowed place myself, accepting my ring as a member of the class of 2005. Bob Cousy, the great Boston Celtic guard, presented me to the Hall of Fame. That was a tremendous honor. Jim Boeheim, my friend, competitor, and fellow Big East coach at Syracuse University, was also inducted, as was the late coach of the LSU women's basketball program, Sue Gunter, among others.

About eighty supporters cheered as my plaque was unveiled. My wife Pat, who has supported me with loyalty and love since our marriage in 1966, was by my side. So were my sons Jim and Jeff, who are both married with children of their own. Scores of friends and associates from my athletic career also came to Springfield to help me celebrate, including fifty of my former players, which made me feel very proud. There were ten guys from the Dedham (MA) High School team I coached between 1971 and 1972, one of my first jobs; five players from Northeastern University, where I coached between 1972 and 1986; and thirty-five players from the University of Connecticut, where I've coached for the last twenty-two years. As Pat said with a smile, "Honey, this is a great tribute to you—and at three hundred and fifty dollars per ticket for eighty guests, a very expensive one!"

Truthfully, it was a tremendous honor. I had been voted into the world's most exclusive basketball fraternity—one that includes former Celtics coach Red Auerbach (who didn't waste much time cutting me from his star-studded team in 1967) along with such college coaching greats such Hank Iba, Dean Smith, and Bob Knight. I felt like an astronaut who, after decades of training, finally gets a chance to climb aboard a rocket ship and fly off into space. That's what getting elected to the Hall of Fame was for me—a trip to the stars.

Some guys downplay big honors. They say it's nice, but they don't want to make a big deal about it. Not me. Getting elected to the Hall was very special for me. It was meaningful. My late parents used to tell me all the time: "You're known by the company you keep." Well, the Hall of Fame is very good company.

When I got the call telling me I'd been voted into the Hall of

Fame, what do you think I was doing? Coaching. I was in St. Louis at the Final Four. I was the head coach for the NABC All-Stars Team that was about to play the Harlem Globetrotters. We were in about our third day of practice.

The phone call from the Hall of Fame actually made me numb for a few seconds. It unleashed a wave of memories. An image flashed in my mind: I saw a passionate and demanding coach standing in a gym, wearing a gray T-shirt, beige shorts, and white sneakers, a silver whistle hanging around his neck. He was teaching a group of attentive, sweaty young players the fundamentals of a game—basketball. He showed them how to pass a basketball properly, how to block out an opponent and get a rebound, how to set a pick, how to run a fast break, how to beat a press, how to attack a zone defense, how to shoot a jump shot. That coach was me—and every other coach past and present.

I was reminded in an instant that we coaches are, above all, teachers, and that we coach because we love to teach. Coaches may be minor celebrities in this sports-crazy country, and we certainly can't avoid the glare of the media spotlight when the games begin. But that's not why I got into coaching. And it's not why I've remained a coach for all of my adult life, thirty-five years now. I coach because I love to help transform impressionable kids into responsible young adults. And I coach because I love the challenge of building a new team every year—taking a new collection of kids and trying to turn them into winners. Those are the two things that get me excited every year.

In my Hall of Fame reverie, I thought of my lifelong love for sports—the many summers when I played baseball during the day and then basketball at night, under the lights, on asphalt courts in Braintree, Massachusetts, and surrounding towns. We'd often play until ten at night. Those were fun, carefree days.

I recalled my early coaching career and the many bumpy bus rides I took to towns big and small throughout the northeast—Worcester, Philly, Providence, and many others. There were memories of late-night coaches' meetings, a million and one afternoon practices, the collective "squeak" from basketball shoes changing direction on a polished hardwood floor, the thump, thump, thump of basketballs echoing off of empty bleachers. Sometimes when I go to sleep at night, I can hear that thump.

I thought of the great Big East coaches whom I battled during my first few years at UConn—Lou Carnesecca at St. John's, John Thompson at Georgetown, Rollie Massimino at Villanova. Lou and John have retired, while Rollie, who along with John won a national title, is coaching again at Northwood College in West Palm Beach, Florida. Not so long ago, it seemed Jim Boeheim and I were the young turks in the Big East Conference. Now we're the league's graybeards.

I thought of the many players I've prodded, cajoled, and taught over the years, trying to make them better basketball players and better people. Nearly all of them have succeeded. Over the past eighteen years, twenty-one former UConn standouts have been selected in the NBA draft, including fourteen in the first round. Entering the 2006–2007 season, fifteen former Connecticut players were on NBA rosters. No other university could boast as many. They included perennial all-star Ray Allen, along with Richard Hamilton, Donyell Marshall, Cliff Robinson (the oldest player in the NBA), Caron Butler, Ben Gordon, Emeka Okafor, Kevin Ollie, and most recently Rudy Gay, Hilton Armstrong, Josh Boone, and Marcus Williams. I'm proud of all of them.

Ben and Emeka were the second and third picks in the 2004 NBA draft. Meka (our nickname for him) was the NBA's Rookie of the Year in 2005, playing for the Charlotte Bobcats. Ben, playing for the Chicago Bulls, won the award as the league's best "sixth man" (meaning top substitute). He's now a key player on the Chicago Bulls.

Those awards were recognition of the character and skills of those two young men—and also positive reflections on the Connecticut basketball program. In 2006 we had a record five players drafted by NBA teams, including four in the first round—small forward Rudy Gay at

Number 8, center Hilton Armstrong at Number 12, strong forward Josh Boone at 23, and point guard Marcus Williams at 22. Guard/ swing man Denham Brown was taken in the second round by Seattle. And another Huskie player on the 2005–2006 team, Rashad Anderson, is playing pro basketball in Greece. They were all key players on our 2005–2006 team, which barely missed making it to the Final Four.

Up by My Bootstraps

IN THE SPAN OF a few seconds after I got the Hall of Fame news, I couldn't help taking stock of how far I'd come in my life. Braintree was a working-class, Irish Catholic neighborhood. Nobody was wealthy in a monetary sense, but the town was rich in family values. My parents, Kathleen and Jim, created a loving home for me and my five siblings, one brother and four sisters. My dad, like most of his generation, was strong, hardworking, and stoic. A classic man of few words, he led by example. He died when I was fifteen. I was playing centerfield in a All-Star baseball game in the summer when a guy just yelled out at me: "Hey, Jimmy, you'd better get home, your dad just died."

What a terrifying, awful way to learn that the person I loved most in life was gone. That moment deeply changed me. After a prolonged period of sadness, it would come to transform my life. It made me grow up in a hurry.

Suddenly, I wasn't a carefree teenager anymore. I had to help take care of my mother, who, despite some health problems, was always perky and optimistic—a bit like the actress Goldie Hawn. I delayed college to go to work and make money to help support her. I took a bunch of tough jobs. I worked at a gas station, and for an electronics distribution company. Later, I got up at four thirty in the morning to work as a stonecutter at a granite monument company in Quiacy, Massachusetts. It was grueling work—a grind—but it made me a strong man, emotionally and psychologically. It built my character.

My parents instilled in me a collection of values that I cherish—to be honest and moral, to be loyal, to care for others, to work hard. And, you may have noticed, I have a rather intense desire to succeed. That's evident to anyone who's seen me pacing the sidelines at Connecticut basketball games over the years—shirt wrinkled and tie askew, hands up in the hair, cursing at anybody within earshot.

When asked why I'm so intense and animated, I sometimes quip: "I yell because I care." It's a joke, but it's true. I've spent most of my life in a basketball gym. Coaching college basketball is not the most important occupation in the world. I'm damn sure not a diplomat or an engineer, or a cardiologist like my brother, Bill.

But it's an honor and a responsibility to coach, because every year I get to shape the lives of fifteen or so impressionable young men making the tricky transition from youth to adulthood. If you coach long enough, you touch a lot of young lives, and hopefully shape them in a positive way.

I think I have, and I'm not just talking about turning a raw athlete into a polished performer who will go on to live large in the NBA. I mean teaching young men how to be mature, responsible adults who make good life decisions and are accountable for their actions.

Athletic skills have a short shelf life. Most professional athletes are back in the real world by age thirty or thirty-five, and basketball skills don't help much then. What does is the character of the individuals, and the life lessons they acquired when younger. Character and judgment will shape the rest of their lives. In the end everyone is judged by what kind of people they are, not how much money they have or the quality of their jump shot.

The vast majority of the players I've coached did not go on to play pro basketball. They didn't sign multimillion-dollar contracts. They got their degrees and stepped out into the real world like everybody else. They found jobs, worked hard, raised families, and became good citizens. They are working as lawyers, dentists, doctors, college presidents, high school teachers, salesmen, store managers, and coaches.

Good citizenship is a responsibility we all share, and building awareness of that in my student athletes has been, and remains, one of my priorities. Phil Gamble, who was one the best players on my first UConn team, grew up in the projects in Washington, D.C. After graduating from UConn, he played pro basketball in Europe for several years. He's now teaching kindergarten in D.C. and coaching a middle-school basketball team in the city. As he said recently, "I'm giving back to the community, and teaching kids about life as I was taught." That's good citizenship.

It's my job to ensure that every UConn basketball player sees the "big picture" of life. I want every kid, first, to value himself and his potential as a human being. I want him to learn that getting a good education is important; that being dependable and responsible to yourself and your family, friends, and teammates is vital; that there is no substitute for hard work; and that the need to broaden yourself never ends. And believe it or not, there *are* virtues more important than jamming a basketball through the net.

As I frequently tell my players, *life is a do-it-yourself proposition.*

Talent determines what you can do in life. Motivation determines what you decide to do. And attitude determines how well you do it.

Life *is* a journey, and it is full of opportunities. But you have to be ready and willing to grab them. As I wrote in my first book, *Dare to Dream:* Strive to be special, not ordinary. Kevin Ollie, who played point guard for us in the early to mid-1990s, has been cut by eight NBA teams in his career. Eight. But he's *still* in the league and getting well paid for his efforts. There is a guy who has dared to dream. Most guys would have quit the game after getting released the second or third time. Kevin kept at it—he never gave up. That's a can-do attitude, a person who *made* himself special by choice.

It's my job to build my program from the outside in. That means paying almost as much attention to the walk-on player at the end of the bench as the star player sitting next to me. Why? Because the walk-on's role, while less visible, may be just as important to the team's success.

As I said in my Hall of Fame acceptance speech, the game of basketball offers much to the people who play it. The game has no prejudices, and neither do I. But I insist that my players give something back to the game as well. I want each player to work to improve himself and his teammates. If they do that, the team benefits, and that is my chief concern.

I've been the basketball coach for the University of Connecticut Huskies since 1986. During that time, we've won a league record sixteen Big East Conference championships—ten regular season crowns and six tournament titles. We've made the NCAA tournament fourteen of the last eighteen years. We've won thirty-seven NCAA tournament games, and made eleven appearances in the coveted Sweet Sixteen over the last seventeen years. We've also won two NCAA championships, in 1999 and 2004. Since 1990, only Duke's Mike Krzyzewski and North Carolina's Roy Williams have won more NCAA tournament games than we have.

With the help of many people—assistant coaches, administrative personnel, trainers, academic advisers, managers, fans, and of course the many talented and dedicated kids who've played for me at both Northeastern University and Connecticut—I had won 750 Division I games in my coaching career entering the 2007–2008 season. That placed me fourteenth on the list for all-time wins. By the end of 2007 I moved into the twelfth position, passing the coaching greats John Chaney of Temple and Phog Allen, the legendary Kansas leader from 1920 to 1956. (In 2007, Bob Knight passed Dean Smith's 879 victory total and become the all-time leader for Division I wins.)

The victory numbers are nice. If you coach long enough, they'll grow. But what I'm really proud of is the simple fact that, with lots of old-fashioned hard work and dedication, my UConn colleagues and I have transformed a modest New England basketball team into one of the premier programs in the country. Connecticut may not yet be mentioned in the same breath as, say, North Carolina, Kentucky, or Duke, the traditionally elite college basketball schools in America. But as I think my friends in Chapel Hill and Lexington and Durham would admit, we are closing in on them. We've beaten Duke the last two times we've played the Blue Devils in the NCAA Final Four. Trust me, that's not easy to do.

Jim Boeheim, the great Syracuse coach and a man for whom I have a huge amount of respect, paid me a very nice compliment recently. He said: "Jim Calhoun has done as good a job as has ever been done in college basketball history, by taking over a program that was at one level and taking it to a totally different place. A lot of coaches have been able to take good programs, or even really good programs, and keep them at that level or make them a little better. But Jim has done something at Connecticut that I really don't think anybody has ever done anyplace else."

I think Jim said that after his Syracuse team beat us in the Big East tournament quarterfinal game in 2006, when he was in a very good mood! Seriously, coming from a peer and fellow Hall of Fame coach, that's a genuinely humbling comment. And Jim Boeheim and his staff have accomplished as much at Syracuse as we have at UConn, as any fan of the Orangemen would attest.

Our success has been a wonderful thing for the state of Connecticut, for the University of Connecticut, and for me. The university is located in Storrs, Connecticut, about thirty minutes from Hartford, the "insurance capital" of America. UConn was founded in 1881 as an agricultural school but is much more than that today. It comprises fourteen schools and universities and 25,000 students. Most of them are big fans of UConn basketball. Thank goodness we've been very good in recent years. For sports entertainment, UConn is the only game in town. The state has no professional sports teams.

Fans, acquaintances, and people in the business world often ask me how I've managed to win so many games so consistently. How have I managed to get ahead and create a first-tier basketball program that I hope and expect will keep rolling along long after I retire, much like Kentucky and North Carolina have rolled on after the retirements of coaches Adolph Rupp and Dean Smith, respectively?

One thing good managers learn is this: There is a big difference between having one outstanding team (or one hot product or one successful sales year) and building an organization that succeeds consistently over time. In sports, think of the Boston Celtics under Auerbach, or the Vince Lombardi-led Green Bay Packers, or the New York Yankees.

It's not hard to put together one good, or even great, year. For some organizations, it's lightning in a bottle, a one-time thing. It's a matter of good timing and good luck.

But strong legacy organizations are different. They capture lightning in a bottle almost *every year,* because they have people and values that perpetuate their success—year after year after year. They have tradition and imbedded institutional qualities that don't diminish over time. They've also got committed, demanding senior managers who make the strategic and tactical adjustments necessary to maintain a high level of success.

Think of great U.S. corporations like General Electric, IBM, Intel, Coca-Cola, and Johnson & Johnson. They've always seemed big and profitable, but their management never takes success for granted. They know that times change, that customer preferences change, that technology changes—and that the competition is always coming after you. That means that they must constantly be ready to alter their strategies and personnel to maintain their competitive advantages.

Sports teams do the same. Just as Dean Smith developed the "North Carolina style" of playing basketball, so am I trying to create a Connecticut basketball tradition. Chris Smith, the school's all-time leading scorer, recently came back to play in an alumni game, and he said to me: "What made it so fun at UConn when I was here was the camaraderie. There was togetherness, both on and off the court, because you always wanted your team to be a family."

Sharing Goals

"WHAT CHRIS SAID WAS valid. Coaching sports is ultimately about bonding with a relatively small group of people who spend *a lot* of time together. We share an identity, and we share the same goals: to improve individually, to work hard, to act responsibly, and to value the team's success more than any individual accomplishments. Those are good life lessons, I think."

And I am lucky: The University of Connecticut is a great place to work. It truly is a community—and as led by Dr. Philip Austin, Dr. Harry Hartley, and Dr. John Casteen (presently the president of the University of Virginia) it's just hitting its stride. President Austin has led the school through a period of unprecedented academic improvement and physical growth. The university is revitalizing its campus through a $2.3 billion, twenty-year state investment in infrastructure, including new buildings for the chemistry, business, biology and physics, information technology and engineering, and agricultural biology departments. The UConn Health Center is getting a $300 million makeover. Thanks to these initiatives, the university is enjoying remarkable success in student recruitment and retention. Out-of-state applications have skyrocketed. And there is a major plan on the drawing board to revitalize the town of Storrs, which has everybody excited.

The university has made a major commitment to men's and women's athletics, because athletic competition is not only good for student development, but also good for the institution. Nowadays, sports are an important marketing vehicle for almost every Division I university.

Some people might lament that fact. Using sports to sell an academic institution is putting the cart ahead of the horse, critics of major college athletics argue. And they are half right. But it's also the reality. We live in a sports-crazy country, and like it or not, sports programs and sports results affect the public's perception of universities. We in sports are nothing but the front porch of the University. Our visibility has allowed people to see what a great institution UConn is. In turn, those perceptions affect the vitality of universities. That's why almost every university—big and small—recognizes the importance of having vital athletic programs for their men and women.

President Austin, who holds a Ph.D. in economics, is of course focused on making UConn the best academic institution it can be. But he and and the rest of the administration take great interest in our athletic programs—all of them, men and women. In the eleven years he's been president, UConn's men's and women's basketball teams have been enormously successful. Geno Aureimma, the women's basketball coach at UConn, has built a powerhouse program of his own, winning five national titles. Our men's and women's soccer teams each won the Big East Conference title in 2006. And the football program has moved into the Big East as a 1-A program.

Meanwhile, our basketball success has generated pride in our alumni and in the residents of the State of Connecticut. Many of our most avid fans didn't even attend the university. The positive publicity generated by our men's and women's basketball programs has helped to boost contributions to the athletic department and the general scholarship fund. They are one small reason why the university is thriving.

I'M A FIRM BELIEVER in philanthropy. The Connecticut community has been good to my family and me, and we like giving back to it. Both Pat and I are deeply involved with numerous charitable causes. We care deeply about the disadvantaged in our society. We feel that every person should try to help others, in ways large and small.

Both of us have lost parents to heart disease, so we've made a sizeable personal and financial commitment to support the cardiology research at the University of Connecticut Health Center. I'm proud to say that the Pat and Jim Calhoun Cardiology Center provides not only excellent care for its patients, but is a leading research center, as well.

I host an annual golf tourney to support our cardiology research foundation—The Jim Calhoun Celebrity Classic Golf Tournament. It has raised more than $3 million over the last six years. It's been wonderful to be associated with such a caring and professional institution. In addition, for the past twelve years I've served as honorary chairman of the Juvenile Diabetes Foundation, helping to raise some $5 million for research over that period. Pat and I also have a longstanding involvement with the Franciscan Life Center, a counseling and education center operated in Meriden, Connecticut, by the Franciscan Sisters of the Eucharist. In 2003 and 2004, I was a host of "Coaches versus Cancer," a series of black-tie galas for the American Cancer Society. We raised about $400,000 for the cause in those two years. And every year the Huskies basketball team has taken part in food drives over the Thanksgiving and Christmas holidays—giving out turkeys and other food products to needy families in our state and provided over 100,000 meals.

OVER MY CAREER, I'VE developed a lot of ideas about leadership. In this book, I'll outline some of them and offer my thoughts on how you can lead a successful life, have a winning career, and become a strong and effective leader. I'll explain how I've built a winning organization at the University of Connecticut, and how some of the management principles I use every day might be applied to your life or your business, whether it's large or small. And I'll offer a few ideas about how managers and CEOs can keep their organizations on top once success has been achieved. As hard as it is to build a winner, staying on top of the mountain is even tougher.

Twenty years ago, Connecticut basketball wasn't taken very seriously. Our rivals didn't fear us and our fans, frankly, were a little apathetic. It was understandable—UConn wasn't very good. Years ago, winning twenty games was a major achievement for the Huskies.

Nobody here thought much about making the NCAA tournament, much less winning it.

But that's not the case now. Nowadays, playing Connecticut is a big deal for every team in the country. And in Storrs, as at any college with a winning tradition, expectations have been raised. Win one title and fans will want a second; win two and they ask when you might get that third one. Now, local columnists wonder why we're only 16-4 after twenty games, or why the team lost in the third round of the NCAA tournament. Once you make a great leap forward, everybody expects you to jump at least as far, if not farther, the following year. The competition gets harder. There is more pressure.

We felt it two years ago. We won thirty games, lost four. By almost any standard, it was a great season. And yet everybody associated with UConn basketball was disappointed with the way the season ended, starting with me. We were upset by George Mason (the giant killer) in the NCAA regional championship, a defeat that kept us from going to the Final Four.

We were the top ranked team in the country for part of that year, and we had an experienced and talented group of players. Many basketball analysts picked us to win our third national championship. Some of my veteran players, who'd won a national title as sophomores, anticipated winning another. Maybe that was a problem. My guys' concentration seemed to wander in the NCAA tournament, despite the best effort of our coaches. Some were thinking about three letters—NBA—before their four-letter NCAA career was over. Others, I think, were getting antsy about leaving college. Uncertainty is never a good thing, especially when you're in the NCAA tournament. In the end, we simply didn't play as well in the NCAA tourney as we did during the season, and I take responsibility for that. The buck always stops with me.

I thought that, with luck, we could win it all again. But I also recognized that we had weaknesses that my two previous championship teams did not have; and believe me, while you need star players to win a national title, you also need a favorable nod or two from Dame Fortune to win six tournament games in a row.

It's a tough row to hoe, no matter how good you are. We won three tough NCAA games before the Patriots of George Mason got the best of us. They were the tournament's Cinderella story, but make no mistake, they were also good. The Patriots knocked off three premier programs on their way to the Final Four—North Carolina, Michigan State, and us—and you don't do that without having some kids who can play.

My point is simply that prolonged success creates higher standards. The bar gets raised, and jumping over it gets tougher. But I wouldn't have it any other way. My coaches and I enjoy the pressure. We like challenges. The tougher the game, the more adverse the circumstances, the more excited we get.

For many years, I coached underdog teams. I thought of myself as a Don Quixote type, riding on my trusty, if aging, steed, holding my sword, a few loyal assistants at my side, trying to slay bigger opponents. It was a nice motivational idea. It helped to drive me as a coach, and in turn I used the underdog role to fire up my Northeastern and Connecticut teams.

We can't play that role anymore, however. Now the Huskies are a big dog, and lots of other coaches are on their horses, swords out, charging at us. And, as anybody who saw us play last year knows, we got knocked off our own horse once or twice. I'm not whining, but in some ways it's tougher to remain a elite program than it is to become one in the first place. Who doesn't want to be the king? All managers, whether the sales chief at an insurance company, the creative director at an advertising agency, or the CEO of a multinational, should feel the same way.

I'm not at all suggesting that Connecticut stands in a class by itself. We don't. We never, ever, think of ourselves as "better" than other teams or programs. We aren't. We just want to be special in our own way. We want to create our own standard of excellence. That's the distinction.

Humility is a very important quality to me. There are many good basketball programs in the country, all trying every year to win the NCAA title. Doing so requires a lot of talent and a helluva lot of hard work.

I'm a coach, so ultimately this book is about winning at the game of life—and there is no more important game. It's also a book about beating the odds and defying conventional wisdom. I've got a *lot* of experience doing both. Everybody, in my estimation, can improve—get up over that rim, and achieve much more than he or she might expect. But you've got to *want* to make the leap, because getting ahead is hard work.

Those outside a successful organization don't see the blood, sweat, and tears that go into achieving goals. On the day I was inducted into the Basketball Hall of Fame, I'm sure some people who don't follow basketball too closely might have heard a news blurb and thought: "Oh, Jim Calhoun. I've heard of him. Intense guy. Yells a lot. Tie's always crooked. Good basketball team at UConn. Won a couple of national championships."

It's the type of tidy assessment we all use to pigeonhole people. People just assume that, because you or your organization have been on top for a while, it's always been that way. Or that getting to the top was preordained somehow.

Wrong. Winning, in the general sense, is a lifelong process. It's a learning process, and for most people, it never stops. There are setbacks along the way—failures. You exert great effort, start rolling the rock—your goals—up the hill, then watch in horror when you lose your grip and the boulder goes tumbling back down the incline. You're lucky it didn't roll over you.

Then what do you do? Give up? Run away? Or do you walk back down the hill, grab hold of that damn rock, and start pushing it up the hill again—redoubling your effort because getting it up and over the ridge means something to you?

Those who succeed in life—on the job and at home—have a strong sense of themselves. They have a sense of purpose. They know what they want, and they are passionate about getting it. And they are smart enough and tough enough to push past the adversity that inevitably blocks the way. If you want to achieve, to lead, to succeed, some of the ideas I write about in subsequent chapters might provide a spark.

1

WINNING EVERY DAY

'M OFTEN ASKED TWO related questions: How did I build the University of Connecticut basketball team into a top national program, and what's made me a successful coach?

My first response is always that I alone haven't built Connecticut into a "name" program. It's been a group effort, to say the least. I haven't scored a single point or grabbed any rebounds. The players have, and we've had some exceptionally talented and dedicated student athletes. In addition, I've been very fortunate to have, over the years, a tremendous collection of assistant coaches who've spared no effort to help us win. Some are still with me, and others have moved on to coach at other schools where, to a man, each is doing an outstanding job.

As to what makes a coach successful, I confess that I've never discovered any mysterious secrets for building great basketball teams. There are no magic formulas that, if found, will lead to market dominance, a corner office, great wealth, or, in my case, an NCAA championship.

Winning lives are not built easily or quickly. Nor are first-rate organizations. Sure, some Internet entrepreneur might hit on an idea that catches on and makes a pile of money. But the vast majority of successful companies are built painstakingly—with blood, sweat, and tears. They are made successful over time by people who are strong, productive, creative. People who burn with a passion for what they are doing and what they want to achieve. In turn, the founders or original leaders hire others who are talented and share the boss's enthusiasm for the business.

I'VE ALWAYS BEEN A pretty intense man. Ask people who know me, and they'll say I'm an emotional, two-fisted Irish Catholic guy with the personality of a bulldog. That's pretty much true. Maybe it comes from my roots in a working-class suburb of Boston. George Blaney, one of my assistants at UConn, says that I wake up intense. Others joke that I get out of bed looking for a fight.

I don't disagree. No question, I've got a lot of inner drive, and I've benefited from it. It's my nature. I can't wait to get up in the morning. I curse the fact that there aren't enough hours in the day to get done all that I want to do. I love spending time with my family, watching movies, reading novels, going to the theatre, and riding my bike. Friends joke that I can get excited about eating lunch. Hey, in the past, I *did* look forward to eating a meat loaf sandwich for lunch—it was my favorite. I don't eat meat loaf much any more—too fatty. But I still look forward to just about everything on my schedule. How many other veteran leaders can say that?

It's trite but it's true: If you do not have a great passion for your job, or your life, the odds are high that you will *not* be successful at either of them. It's my job coaching, and that's where you can see the intensity. Here's what I've told my players countless times over the years, and a point that I make in almost all my speeches to outside groups: *Find your passion.*

Nothing Great Is Ever Accomplished Without Enthusiasm

PASSION IS ANOTHER WORD for enthusiasm, which translates into energy, which in turn produces action. The more passion and energy you have, the more things you're likely to get done in the course of a day or a week or a year—and the better off you and your organization will be. It's called being productive—and it means that you're working harder than your competitors, whether you're flipping pancakes in a New Mexico diner or trading bonds in Manhattan.

I ask our players all the time: "How did you feel at six this morning?"

My players *don't* get up at six in the morning. How many teenagers do you know who do? The question is rhetorical—my way of letting the student athletes know that *every* day is full of great possibilities, if you have an optimistic attitude. What I'm really suggesting is that they take an aggressive, can-do approach to life.

SUCCESS STARTS WITH WANTING to be successful.

Forget about reaching goals. You can't even set goals if you don't have an inner drive to succeed. I do. As long as I can remember, I wanted to be special and make a mark in life. Like most people, when I was young I didn't have any idea what I might be good at, or how I'd succeed. But I *wanted* to get ahead in life. As I tell our players and others: *Begin with an end in mind.*

When you get up in the morning, you should have a pretty good idea of what you want to get accomplished that day. Think about what you want to get done this week, this year. Think about what you want to be doing in three years, or five years. Think ahead. Plan. Set goals, and then start to chase them.

Some people are born with drive. It's in their genes. Others aren't natural strivers and never seem motivated to do anything. Getting out of bed is a big deal for them. They don't care a lot about challenging themselves. They're lazy or unmotivated. It's just the way some people are. Whenever my dad thought I was loafing, often when I was raking leaves in our yard, he'd fix his gaze on me and say: "Laziness, dare not I offend thee." It was his way of reminding me not to take shortcuts in life.

A lot of people do, but I also believe that people can develop a desire to achieve.

O   O   O

PEOPLE CAN BE TAUGHT to think big.

For starters, they can be taught good personal habits that will help them realize their potential. They can be taught to set goals and not settle for what they *are*, but instead set their sights on what they might *become*—with more work and passion.

Why wouldn't I think that way? I'm a coach. I'm in the business of motivating kids—and, importantly, *trying to teach my student athletes to motivate themselves,* so that after a year or two, perhaps, I can stop yelling at them.

In the late summer of 2006, we brought eight freshman players into the Connecticut program. That was the most new players we'd ever had. They came to Storrs from all over—Alabama, Arizona, Georgia, Maryland, New York, and Connecticut. One was a seven foot, three inch player from Tanzania, who'd moved to America three years earlier, when he was sixteen. Another kid, Ben Eaves, grew up in England and represented his country three times in international basketball competitions. Ben spent a year at Worcester Academy in Massachusetts, which is where we first saw him play. (He has since transferred to the University of Rhode Island.) Meanwhile, freshman guard Doug Wiggins grew up in East Hartford, about a half hour drive away.

They were a diverse group, each unique in his own way. But in one respect they were no different than every other group of first-year players we've had: They all thought, when they arrived, that they were good basketball players. They all thought, when they arrived, that they understood the meaning of hard work. They all thought they knew a lot about basketball, and school.

They were all wrong. They all *do* have athletic potential. They're all good kids who certainly energized the coaching staff last year. And many of them have good study habits. But college is a major adjustment for everybody, and most students don't realize that until their heads are spinning after week one.

That's especially true for freshman basketball players at UConn. Quite frankly, they don't have a clue about how challenging their new lives will be. They don't realize how busy they will be. They don't understand yet how hard we will work them—and how much we expect them to work on their own.

As I tell the players: *To whom much is given, much is expected.*

The freshmen don't know yet how tough it is to become a good player in the Big East Conference. They don't comprehend how organized they'll need to be to handle the many new demands on their time—academic, athletic, and social. They are starting an entirely new phase in their lives, heading in a new direction, and they need a few people with compasses to point the way.

That's where the coaches come in. We are teachers, first and foremost, and our first task is to let the new student athletes know immediately that things will change. *Life will be different.*

COLLEGE LIFE IS MORE demanding than high school life. Before, the players were living at home, maybe coddled by their friends and parents. They were fawned over, given things. If they messed up, Mom or Dad would be there to clean things up. In college, nothing will be given to them. The freshmen are away from home for the first time, and will have to solve problems on their own. They can still talk to Mom or Dad on the phone, but they aren't around anymore to fix their mistakes.

A lot of freshmen student athletes come to college with a sense of entitlement. That's a bad thing. My coaches and I try to get rid of that attitude, but you can't change an eighteen-year-old mind-set in six months. It takes longer than that.

Going to college is all about learning how to become a responsible adult. I tell my players constantly: You are accountable for your actions. Before, schoolwork may not have been really challenging. In college, the academic requirements are more rigorous. Before, athletic success came pretty easily, and everybody adored these players. In college, the competition will be much tougher, and the kids will have to work far harder to earn accolades from me or the other coaches.

The faster the freshmen get the message that being a student athlete will not be a stroll in the park—that they've got *responsibilities*—the better off they and our team will be.

The transition to college can be a jarring experience. Even the most confident or headstrong student athletes can seem a little confused. There is uncertainty, lots of it. The players are suddenly immersed in an entirely new environment: new school, new scenery, new teachers, new coaches, new responsibilities, new and better competition on the basketball court. It can be overwhelming, especially for kids who have had things easy for a while, and it can chip away at the self-esteem of an eighteen-year-old.

I do not want that to happen.

I tell our young players all the time that they wouldn't be wearing a Connecticut basketball jersey if they weren't special players and special people. I tell them they wouldn't have been offered a scholarship if we didn't have confidence in them, as students and as athletes.

I want every kid who plays for us to believe in himself—totally—even as we break him down a bit to start the process of making him stronger. My message is this: "I know you want to be special, and you will be. But you've got to be willing to sacrifice to reach your goals." As the sign reads in our locker room: *Connecticut basketball is a commitment.*

The golfer V. J. Singh wasn't exactly teeming with confidence when he was a poor young man growing up on the Pacific island of Fiji. But he had an absolute passion for golf, and an equally strong desire to be good at it. The locals don't play much golf in Fiji, and for a long time the people there couldn't watch the Masters or any other golf tournaments live on TV. Singh would ask friends in other countries to send him videotapes of the Masters and other tournaments, and then watch them.

For years he dreamed of winning on the famed Augusta, Georgia, golf course. He knew that there was only one thing he could do to make it happen—practice. No, more than that: Practice like a man possessed.

When he was in his twenties, Singh spent hours every day hitting golf balls on the practice range. In ninety-five-degree heat, he'd hit hundreds if not thousands of balls. He was fanatical about practice, even after coming to America to play in the mid-1980s. At tournaments, Singh's competitors would hit balls for an hour after a round and then go out to dinner. Singh hit for two or three hours, until it was too dark to see, and skipped dinner. Commitment.

In 1999, after being on the PGA tour for a few years, Singh decided to get even more serious about winning the Masters. He got in better shape, started eating healthier food. He also watched tapes of himself hitting golf shots in tournaments. He analyzed his game completely—and kept practicing. Commitment.

The following year, he won the tournament that meant the most to him—the Master's. Asked how he accomplished the feat, Singh replied, "I wanted it badly that year and was prepared to pay the price. That is what made me a champion. It was not luck." He's been one of the world's best golfers for the last decade, and has now won three major tournaments—all because he was willing to sacrifice to fulfill his dream. As he said, it was not luck. It was commitment.

Is It in You?

ENTHUSIASM AND PASSION FOR what you do are the first stage of a process I call *"winning every day."*

Former U.S. Chief Justice Oliver Wendell Holmes once said: "What lies behind you and what lies ahead of you is of very little importance compared to what lies within you. If love, trust, and commitment lie within you, yours will be a happier, more productive life. No matter what obstacles you confront, you will find a way to win every day."

Boiled down, winning every day means trying to accomplish a few positive things *every day*. As I tell my players: *Make every day your minor masterpiece.*

They can be little things, minor achievements, that put you in a position to achieve bigger things later on. I'm not talking about making a $100,000 sale every day, or winning a big consulting contract, or getting a promotion at NASA. I'm not talking about marrying the prettiest woman in your college, or winning your first World Series start as a pitcher. Those are once-in-a-lifetime breaks, and they don't happen at all unless you've done some work—put in the time, effort, and planning necessary to reach a goal.

Boeing, for example, doesn't just sell 777s to Japan Air Lines or Southern Airlines in China. The company spends years laying the groundwork for future sales, by working with current or potential customers on airline designs, by establishing relations with key government figures, by subcontracting work out to Asian manufacturers to establish good will and cement long-term business partnerships.

Before my knees got balky, I used to run a lot. When I coached at Northeastern University in Boston, I used to run along the Charles River with my players. I also ran six marathons, three in Boston and three in New York. Trust me, you don't just hop out of bed on the day of a marathon and run 26.2 miles. You can do that if you want to flop down at the halfway mark, dehydrated and in pain, and get carted off to the hospital.

Better to train heavily before trying to run a long race. You start out by running relatively short distances—for days or weeks—then gradually stretch out the length and duration of your workouts. You learn to run three miles comfortably, then five miles, then ten miles, and then twenty miles. You expand your lungs, improve your pace, learn to adjust psychologically to the physical demands of running long distances. That's how you prepare for a major endurance test.

It's a basic idea: *Make incremental progress.*

Building a company or career is a bit like a getting over a high-jump bar: You set the bar at one height, preferably one that is reachable, then start working on technique. With luck and determination, you leap over the bar. Then you move the bar a little higher, start training again, and test yourself against the new height. You're not sure if you can clear it—but you do. And when you do, you feel good about yourself—and move the bar still higher.

You won't keep clearing new heights. Eventually, you'll reach your limit—in athletics, in your career. But you don't know what your limits are unless you test them—unless you keep raising the bar.

Try to make regularly incremental progress in your life—at the office, in your work habits, in your business and personal relationships— and you might surprise yourself. You might go higher and farther than you think.

What is a basketball game? It's really a long series of little battles played out over forty minutes, hundreds of momentary skirmishes— battles for loose balls and rebounds, one-on-one matchups between a guy who, with the shot clock running down, is going to shoot the ball and a defender who must keep him from putting it in the basket. Win enough of those little fights and you win the game. You've got a few more points on the scoreboard than your opponent when the final horn sounds. By doing lots of little things well, you've accomplished a very big goal.

Winning in Life Is a Process

IN COLLEGE BASKETBALL, WE don't just give kids Connecticut uniforms, teach them a few plays, and then push them out on the court, hoping they'll score eighty points and win a game. We spend months recruiting talented kids, cultivating relationships with their parents, just to get them to the University of Connecticut. That's step one.

Then, after they get here, we encourage the players do a lot of running and conditioning work on their own, prior to the official start of practice in mid-October. It's psychological and physical prep time for the grind that lies ahead. That's step two.

The night before our first practice, we have our "Basketball Madness" celebration, also known as First Night. We've got great fans at UConn, and last year 9,000 of them gathered in Gampel Pavilion to greet the new team, cheer, and have a little fun. We do it every year. The players were introduced individually, and some grabbed the chance to perform for the crowd. Freshman Stanley Robinson buffed the Huskie logo with a towel. Fellow freshman Curtis Kelly did a little dance. The fans roared, the players laughed. The coaches cringed.

We had a dunk contest and a three-point shooting competition. While guard A. J. Price was shooting threes, I could hear his mom, Inga, screaming encouragement to him above the din. She's got a lively personality and loves to talk. Her husband was taking pictures. It was nice to see A. J., a player we were counting on a lot, finally on our basketball court. He'd missed the previous two years of basketball with first a serious health issue, and then legal problems. But they were behind him. A. J. felt good, and both his parents and I were thrilled that he was ready to start his UConn career.

First Night is fun for everybody. But the next day, the mood shifts. It's time to get down to business. The laugh quotient is greatly reduced. The work quotient is greatly increased. It has to be that way: Our first game, usually an exhibition, is in two weeks. Last year our first real game was on November 10. With a frighteningly inexperienced team, we needed three months of practice to get ready. We had three weeks.

Every year, we start with lots of running and physical conditioning to build the stamina necessary to play basketball at a high level for forty minutes. We then focus on basketball fundamentals—playing hardnosed defense, making good passes, shooting free throws—and learning proper techniques, such as how to move your feet properly when playing defense, or how to pivot in the post after getting the basketball.

Basketball is, fundamentally, a simple sport: You move the ball around, try to find an open shot, and get the ball in the basket. Defensively, you try to stop your opponents from putting the ball in the basket. But individually, the sport can be very complex. There are, for example, many fundamental techniques that each position player must learn to become proficient both offensively and defensively. These techniques vary by position and must be taught to the players, and reinforced in practice, practically every day.

For example, a center, or post player, must master *many* different techniques to become a good offensive player. A post player must learn how to read a defense; must learn to shoot the ball off the glass, or backboard; must learn how to bend his knees and make himself a wide target for a teammate who wants to pass him the ball; must learn how to establish proper position in the low post (by keeping contact with the man defending him); must learn how to power up when shooting the basketball; must learn how to catch the ball properly; must learn how to chin the ball after catching a pass or grapping a re-bound (a term that means protecting the basketball by putting it under your chin, hands on either side of the ball, elbows out, thereby keeping the ball up and away from smaller players); must learn how to create space near the basket; and must know how to seal defenders (by using his backside to put a defender in a weak defensive position). And those are just a few of the offensive techniques a center must learn. There are more, and there's an entirely different set to learn for defense. And guards and forwards have completely separate skill sets.

When you've got a very young team, as we did last year, you spend even more time on the basics. Our first practice of last season lasted three hours and forty minutes. That's about an hour longer than we practice once the season is underway. I told the players during the workout that they were in bad shape, physically and mentally: "We've got our work cut out for us."

When we've got a decent foundation for the fundamentals, we push ahead and teach the players more specialized team tactics. We show the kids, among other things, how to play a three-quarter-court trap defense; how to attack a 1-3-1 zone defense; how to beat a full-court press; how to pull back from a fast break (if opposing players have gotten back to defend it); and transition into what we call our "secondary offense."

Learning how to do execute well as a team takes a *lot* of practice time and a huge amount of repetition. We run the same plays, the same drills, over and over again. Good basketball teams have chemistry. Each player has certain skills and a certain role, and over time most players develop an innate sense of their teammates' basketball style. A good point guard, when racing down the court on a fast break, will know, almost without looking, which of his teammates is hustling down the sidelines and ready to catch a pass. And the point guard also will know where that guy likes to receive the ball—with a bounce pass, say, no more than three strides from the basket. That is chemistry, and it takes time to develop.

Trust me, I know. We didn't have much chemistry last year. Young players tend to make mistakes, and the only way to eliminate them is to make the kids practice until execution becomes second nature to them. We work on the basics constantly—team defense, rebounding, and getting the ball down the court quickly on offense after we get a rebound.

Either before or after practice, we hold meetings and watch videotapes to reinforce the instructions the coaches give on the court. The tape sessions allow us, as a group, to ask and answer questions. We analyze our play, individually and as a team—point out mistakes, hand out a few compliments. Only after weeks of practice and preparation are we ready to play our first game.

My point is, we spend a ton of time honing basic skills, learning plays, and developing good habits to help train the team to win. There is a lot of physical and mental preparation.

There is a tendency to think of sports as merely physical competition—a collective test of strength and shooting touch and quickness. But the mental aspect of sports is huge. Even the best athletes have fragile egos, and the confidence of a team ebbs and flows as well. What it means is that the coaches, like all organizational leaders, must spend a lot of time getting players in a winning frame of mind—building confidence and, importantly, toughness; motivating the players to work hard to improve. It's almost a 24/7 job, and nearly as important as the physical aspect of the game.

Why? Because a kid can practice shooting fifteen-foot jump shots for a week, and even make them consistently. But if his confidence level is not right come game time, if the tiniest doubt creeps into his head after the opening whistle, for whatever reason—and there can be many—he'll start clanking shots and then we've got problems. Trust me, I know. We clanked a lot of shots last year. I touch on mind games and motivation in a subsequent chapter.

Concentrate on the Basics

To BE PRODUCTIVE IN life, to make progress toward a goal, you have to perceive every hour of every day as important.

How to do that? In a word, *structure*. One of the nice things about college life and college sports is that they are both highly structured. Students have multiple classes every day, and they start and end at precise times. There isn't any variance. And after a day of classes, there are study requirements at night.

Sports is the same way. Take a look at the Connecticut practice schedule on the following page. It will give you a sense of how structured we are. We typically practice somewhere between two hours and three hours every day. Before a practice starts, my staff and I have mapped out precisely what we intend to work on, and for how long, during that practice. We script our practices every day, down to the minute.

Thought of the day: "I will get ready, and then perhaps my chance will
                           come."—Abraham Lincoln
Emphasis of the day: Defense: Change from offense to defense quicker
                           Offense: Continued emphasis on good passing

DATE: 10/28/06	CONNECTICUT BASKETBALL PRACTICE SCHEDULE	PRACTICE # 13

Time	Activity	Point of Emphasis		Duration
8:30	Foul Shots	- Foul Shooting		31 mins
		- Scrimmages		
9:01	Talk	- #2 Press back to #6		2 mins
9:03	4 minute shooting teams	- Shell Stagger		6 mins
		Double-Down Screens		
9:09	5 on 0			4 mins
9:13	Split the post			4 mins
9:17	Man offense vs yellow			15 mins
9:32	Stretch			7 mins
9:39	2 on 0 (Pleasant Valley)			7 mins
9:46	throwouts			2 mins
9:48	3 on 2 continuous	Jerome	Marcus	6 mins
9:54	5 on 5 #2 to #6	Doug	Jeff	6 mins
		Pit	Bulls	
10:00	Bigs -			7 mins
	Littles - 3 on 3 weave			
10:07	1 on 1 zig zag			4 mins
10:11	2 on 2 box			2 mins
10:13	water			1 min
10:14	Shell with officials			15 mins
	Stagger to Down			
	Screens			
10:29	Diamond ??			31 mins
	#6 Scrimmage			
11:02	#5 scrimmage			15 mins
11:17	4 minute shooting teams			6 mins
11:23	3 man 6 layups			22 mins
11:45	foul shots			4 mins
11:49	talk			2 mins
11:51	3 minute shooting			3 mins
11:54	end/weights			

WHO WE ARE	COACHES' REMINDER	TOTAL MIN
1. Fast Break 2. Defend-Full/Half 3. Rebound 4. Execute Offense 5. Play Hard and Together		204 mins 3 hrs. 24 mins

Post Practice Notes
Practice #13
10/28/06

—Great intensity & energy for the entire practice

—"All Day Jeff" played great again today
- ○ Needs to practice vs. Big to Big

—Guards need to make better use of screens when running pick and roll.

—Guards must utilize their five-second count while we are getting into an offensive set. We are still starting the play before guys get into position.

—Stanley
- ○ Needs to work on his footwork on the wing
- ○ Was he at practice today?

—Guards need to learn the plays all the way through—not just learn their position.

—"2" to "6" and "2" to "5" looked good today.
- ○ Blue team panicked against the press in best vs. best (Diamond).

—AJ, Jerome, Doug, and Marcus J. were all terrific today.

—Hasheem had a very good day.

—We need more work with secondary zone.
- ○ Trailing big man reversing the ball and diving
- ○ X Cuts
- ○ Guards giving the bigs a look when the X cut

Free Throws		Practice # 13	
	Made	Attempted	%
Jeff	57	72	79.17
Craig	69	72	95.83
Jerome	68	83	81.93
Ben	60	75	80.00
Gavin	44	72	61.11
Rob	65	71	91.55
Marcus	62	72	86.11
Curtis	54	82	65.85
Jonathan	60	82	73.17
AJ	39	56	69.64
Stanely	60	78	76.92
Hasheem	34	54	62.96
Dougie	68	78	87.18
Team Total	740	947	78.14

As you can see, on October 28, our thirteenth practice of the 2006–2007 season, we decided that the entire practice would last exactly 204 minutes, or three hours and twenty-four minutes. Within that three-hour, twenty-four-minute period, we broke up the practice into specific, stand-alone practice drills lasting anywhere from two minutes—for my talks to the team to open and end the session—to thirty-one minutes for both foul-shot practice and a five-on-five scrimmage.

I start every practice with what we call the "thought of the day." It's an inspirational message of one kind or another. I read it to the team and let them think about it for a few seconds. Coaches are pack rats when it comes to finding motivational messages or stories that we use to fire up the troops. We all collect them for years. My assistant coach, George Blaney, keeps a large book in his office full of inspirational lines uttered by famous people. He pulls one out, and it becomes our thought of the day. I've heard or read most of them many times, but I don't tire of hearing them. Believe it or not, they still move and motivate me.

The thought of the day for Practice Thirteen came from former President Abraham Lincoln, who said before his election: "I will get ready, and then perhaps my chance will come."

As you can see from the practice schedule, we have an "emphasis of the day" for every practice, too. During Practice Thirteen, we wanted to focus on our so-called transition defense—changing more quickly from an offensive team to a defensive team (which is a constant in basketball). And we wanted to focus again on improving our passing skills.

At the bottom of the practice sheet, I noted other practice points that I felt would help define us as a team. For Practice Thirteen, I wanted to see improvement in our fast break, in our full- and half-court defense, in our rebounding, and in our offensive execution. And I wanted us to play hard and play together. I have to admit, that covers just about everything that's important in basketball!

A team manager, holding a watch, begins and ends each practice period by sounding a horn. On October 28, we stretched for seven minutes—no more or less. We practiced "splitting the post"—which involves peremiter players cutting to the basket after the ball has been passed in to the center—for four minutes. We practiced fast breaks and layups, three kids running the length of the court, for twenty-two minutes. At the sound of the horn, we end one drill and start another, and so on.

Everything is precisely scripted to boost our productivity. It's all about being efficient and accomplishing as much as we can in a short period of time. There is no wasted time, no standing around. It's nothing more than an athletic "to do" list.

Most everything we practice is related to boosting our fundamental basketball skills. We work constantly on shooting jump shots and free throws, on passing and defending—all integral parts of the game.

Responsibility and Trust

I'LL BE THE FIRST to admit it: Running a major college basketball program is not rocket science. It's not the same as running, say, Motorola, Aetna, or Procter & Gamble. It's not the same as running a nonprofit organization like the Red Cross or a major urban hospital. Not hardly.

But it *is* a pretty big deal.

Why? Not because the world will stop on its axis if UConn doesn't win its next basketball game. I understand that. But we do value sports competition in America. It's entertaining, yes. But at a more basic level, sports is a great way to build character in young people in their formative years. Sports helped me tremendously in life. It kept me off the streets. It taught me the importance of being competitive—not just on a basketball court or a baseball field, but in life generally. It toughened me up, in a good way. It put me through college.

Universities benefit tangibly from having vibrant sports programs. That being the case, lots of people depend on me, directly and indirectly, to make the University of Connecticut men's basketball program the best that it can be.

The university president, Philip Austin, depends on me and my staff to field a basketball team that reflects well on the school and the state. That means the players must be more than athletes. They have to be responsible students with solid values, who aim to obtain their degrees.

The athletic director, Jeff Hathaway, depends on me to field a basketball team that is competitive not just in the Big East Conference, but also nationally. Our success on the basketball court helps boost financial donations to the athletic and academic departments, which of course benefits the university. Last year donors contributed about $17 million to the University of Connecticut athletic department. A sizeable chunk of that amount came from fans of the men's basketball program.

UConn students, fans, and alums depend on me, too. They depend on me to win games—a lot of them! They expect us to beat Villanova, Georgetown, Syracuse, Seton Hall, Louisville, Marquette, and the other nine teams in what is now the oversized Big East.

In addition, I'm also largely responsible for the well-being of three assistant coaches, a dozen or more managers, several medical trainers, and about ten administrative personnel in the basketball department. If the program were to falter under me, they'd all feel the negative affects.

And perhaps most important, I'm responsible to the roughly fifteen players on my team, along with their parents. The parents have given me their kids and their trust—a bond that was sealed when the players signed their "letters of intent" and committed to attend the University of Connecticut in exchange for an athletic scholarship. Their parents expect me to help their sons become better people and, yes, better basketball players.

Some of the players want me to help them get into the NBA. That's fine—so long as they come to understand that they won't get there without a helluva lot of hard work, dedication, intelligence, and passion. Without saying so, they want me to help them to grow up. College is a transition from boyhood to manhood. My job is to make the bumpy process of gaining maturity as smooth as possible.

And I enjoy it. I like teaching kids about life and basketball. We get a lot of kids from tough backgrounds. They haven't had a lot of positive role models in their lives. I am their role model, and so are my assistants. I'm happy to help the kids chase their dreams, so long as they work as hard and selflessly as the other coaches and I do for the Connecticut basketball program. I don't slack off at any time, and I don't expect my players to, either. We think of the program as a big family, and that means we support each other and we each do what we can, every day, to keep it successful.

Bootstraps and Basketball

I'VE BEEN CALLED MANY things, but "complacent" is never one of them. I think it's because I've had to earn my success the hard way. I didn't grow up in a privileged background. I've pulled myself up by my bootstraps. Former UConn coach Dee Rowe puts it another way. He says I didn't have a rabbi early in my career.

I'm Catholic, but he's right. I didn't have a coaching mentor who got me an assistant's job at a prominent basketball school while I was relatively young, as some guys do. I started my career at the bottom—coaching at three different high schools in New England, two of which couldn't have cared less about basketball.

I was lucky to get my collegiate head coaching jobs, first at Northeastern, and later at Connecticut. I have been extremely proud to be associated with each university. They were good opportunities for me, but it's fair to say that they weren't the most prestigious jobs in college basketball at the time I took them. Each program was a little shaky when I took over—that's why I was hired. And in those early years, I was an unknown quality, too. So there was nothing to do but set high standards and work like hell to reach them.

Obviously, no one wins at everything they do every day. We all deal with a lot of failures in our lives—small mistakes or disappointments, and large ones. Some screwups are our fault. Others may be twists of fate—bad luck, unfortunate circumstances, whatever. When bad things happen—you're late for an important meeting with the boss, you lose an important client, or miss a deadline—nobody is happy.

That's to be expected. Stuff happens. But don't dwell on mistakes or failure. What's important is that you take responsibility and move on. If you are part of a group failure, it's important that the group take collective responsibility.

When we win games, everybody shares in the victories—the play ers, coaches, walk-ons, trainers, managers, office staff, everybody. When we lose a basketball game, it's everybody's fault, starting with me. Accountability is a big deal with me. So when we get beat, I don't have a problem taking responsibility for the loss. I don't like hiding behind the players and calling the team out for a bad performance. Coaches, generally, should shoulder losses.

Last year we played our first eleven games at home against relatively easy competition. We won them all. Then we played two away games in succession, against good basketball teams, first West Virginia, a Big East rival, and then LSU in Baton Rouge.

The results were not pretty. We had a very young team—eight freshmen and four sophomores. You can't get much younger, and our inexperience showed. We got thumped twice. West Virginia beat us by ten points in Morgantown and then LSU beat us 66–49. The spicy food we ate in Louisiana was the highlight of that trip. It was the first time we'd scored less than fifty points in four years. (We were even more futile in our last Big East game of the season against Georgetown, when we scored forty-six points.)

Neither loss totally surprised me, but I was disappointed by our lack of aggressiveness against LSU. The one thing our teams usually have is swagger, but that's hard to have when almost everybody is wet behind the ears. We suffered through a lot of growing pains last year. It was the price we paid for having zero returning starters. I am not a patient man, but we were in a rebuilding mode, and I knew going into the season we'd play some ugly games. Still, I took responsibility for all our losses, and so did the players. When we lose, everybody associated with the team takes the hit, and we all vow to work harder and do better the next time. That's the way you develop trust and get better.

When everybody takes responsibility for a loss, the group can begin to make changes and move on. That's the way to win, in a sense, after you've lost. Whenever someone in a group or organization wants to dodge his role in a failure, wants to blame others and play the role of victim, that person is essentially saying: "Don't blame me. I had nothing to do with this. It was beyond my control." With such an attitude, that person is essentially refusing an opportunity to make any changes that will benefit the group. That's not what a leader wants to see in his people.

Sure, it's easy to get sidetracked by some problem—a negative comment from your boss, a decision that doesn't go your way, or a personal issue at home. Life is full of disappointments. The way to get ahead is to jump over them and keep running.

You're Doing *What?!*

TWO YEARS AGO WE signed a bright, seven-foot, 280-pound center out of high school named Andrew Bynam. The kid was built like a truck, and had loads of potential: amazing size, surprising athleticism, good hands, lots of confidence. He was an excellent prospect. I helped him get an invitation to play in the McDonald's All-American Game, which is a showcase for the best high school prospects in the country. Andrew played in it, and performed pretty well.

And then he called and gave me some shocking news. He told me that he'd decided to declare himself eligible for the NBA draft. He wanted to skip college and go straight to the pros.

I was stunned. It was like a slap in the face. Andrew was one of top recruits in America that year. At the time, I didn't think he was making a prudent decision, and I still don't. But he and his parents made it, and there was no changing the big kid's mind. It was a blow to our recruiting effort—it was too late to find another top center to replace him—but we moved on. And I have to say, Andrew, who's about to begin his third season with the Los Angeles Lakers, is developing into a good NBA player.

As I tell groups regularly, when things go wrong, try to fix them and move on.

**Accept things you can't change, change the things
you can—and have the wisdom to know the difference.**

The Lay of the Land

THINK ABOUT THIS: AFTER the 2005–2006 season, we lost our top six players to graduation and the NBA. Three seniors graduated, and three undergraduate players decided to give up their remaining collegiate eligibility and turn pro. My two best players, Rudy Gay and Marcus Williams, were in that second group. Rudy could have played for two more years; Marcus, one. Instead, each declared for the NBA draft.

I'm a little ambivalent about losing good players to the pros. On the one hand, I'm truly happy when my players are talented enough to be drafted in the first round. It's the culmination of a dream for them, and a good reflection on our program. And, of course, they will make a lot of money—millions annually, tens of millions over the course of their careers.

I will encourage my best players to leave if it's clear that they'll be drafted high. Rudy and Marcus each could have benefited from another year of college basketball—Rudy to get stronger and improve his ball handling, and Marcus to improve his defense and leadership skills. At the same time, they were both talented enough to be drafted in the first round, and they were, so they probably made the right decisions.

Certainly, we would have had a *much* better team last year had they opted to stay in school. They would have given us some experience, some linkage between classes. But a lot of other college coaches lose so-called early-entry players, too, so I can't complain. It's the lay of the land in basketball right now. If a kid can be a first-round pick, I don't try to talk him out of turning pro. I want my kids to stay in school and earn their degrees. But it's also true that a twenty-year-old man has a lot of time to earn an academic degree, and usually only one chance to get drafted in the first round and, in doing so, achieve financial security for the rest of his life. And we do urge all our players who leave school early to return to Storrs, as time allows, and earn their degrees. That's important to me and to the university.

Early-entry players are part of the college game now. The best college players almost never stay in school for four years. Hell, they often don't stay in school *two* years. The best player in college basketball last year was an eighteen-year-old freshman, Kevin Durant of Texas. He's an amazing player, six feet, eleven inches, incredibly long, and with dazzling offensive skills. He can dribble and go to the basket, he can shoot the three. He was practically unstoppable last year around the basket. He played one year at Texas and left for the NBA, as he should have, because he was destined to be the number-one or -two pick. (By the way, the 2006 collegiate freshman class was phenomenal, one of the best ever. And watch: There will be a raft of kids turning pro early this year and next.)

Last year we had two, maybe three players on our team with long-term NBA potential. Before the season started I said five, but some of our top young players struggled more than I expected, and going into the 2007–2008 season, we don't have anybody who's close to ready for professional basketball. Top 10 Hasheem Thabeet of the 2010 class has NBA shot-blocking skills, but he's got to improve his offensive skills and get stronger so that he can hold his position in the post. We've got a few of other guys—Jeff Adrian, Jerome Dyson, and Stanley Robinson—who could become NBA players, but after last year I'd be upset to hear any of my kids talking about an NBA career. Put it this way: We don't have any Kevin Durant–type of players on our team at the moment—and nobody outside of Austin, Texas, does either. What we have are a lot of guys who might be good, but have a helluva lot of work to do first.

Ironically, the allure of the NBA is leveling the playing field in college basketball. Because I coach at an elite program, we now recruit some of the better high school prospects in America—kids like Rudy Gay, who has a feathery jump shot and can jump out of the gym. Rudy's also got a million-dollar smile and, now that he's playing professionally in Memphis, he has a bank account to go with it. Then there's Hasheem Thabeet. He's seven feet, three inches and as a freshman for us last year, he weighed 265 pounds. A native of Tanzania, Hasheem migrated to the United States and played his final year of high school basketball in Houston. He's played only three years of organized basketball, but for someone with his immense size, he's a pretty good athlete. He can run the floor, and is already a big-time shot blocker.

Hasheem was raw—a project. He needs to learn some offensive moves. But he's got some major upside. Right now, he's strictly a defensive stopper. But that's okay. Dikembe Mutombo, another seven-foot African who played for Georgetown in the early 1990s, was the same way. He never really learned to make baskets, but he's been in the NBA for fifteen years. That's the beauty of coaching—you never know!

There are obvious downsides when players leave college prematurely. For one thing, they may never earn their degrees, although we have had at least twelve kids come back to earn a degree. That's the academic issue. There's also a basketball issue, and that is that the best college programs in America seldom have experienced teams anymore. That's because their best players are constantly leaving. It's ironic. We can and do recruit the best high school talent in America, kids with NBA potential. And many of them come to UConn precisely *because* we can help them get to the pros. But we cannibalize ourselves in the process, because these talented kids end up spending too little time on campus.

The increased turnover means that my staff and I have a smaller window in which to make hay—meaning to win championships. Because Rudy Gay only played for us for two years, we had very little time to utilize his talent. He was good as a freshman, but clearly needed time to adjust to the college game and develop some confidence. Last year, when Rudy was a sophomore and on a team with some veteran talent, we had a shot to win the national title. It didn't happen, mostly because late in the year we allowed our team weaknesses to become more prominent than our strengths. If my best players stay for three years, then we have a year or two to put together a special team. But that's it.

Losing kids to the NBA regularly means that we've got to bring in more new players every year. That, in turn, increases the teaching load for the coaches. So the NBA is truly a double-edged sword for college programs.

One reason we lost to George Mason last year in the regional final was that the two best players for the Patriots were seniors, while my two best players were a sophomore and a junior, respectively. North Carolina won the national title two years ago with three or four talented underclassmen. But it's not easy to do, as I think UNC coach Roy Williams would acknowledge. It's nice to have both talented and experienced players on your roster, but it doesn't happen much anymore.

The NBA has instituted a new rule that may help a little. The league now requires players to be at least nineteen years old before they're eligible for the draft. That is forcing most of the best prospects to attend college, at least for a little while. Greg Oden, a mobile seven-foot manchild, was the top high school prospect in America last year. He would have been a top-five NBA pick coming out of high school, had he been eligible for the draft. But the new age limit kept him out of the pros for a year, so instead he signed to play for Ohio State. Like Durant, he played for one year and then entered the draft.

One year of college is better than no years of college, in my opinion. But I'd like to see the age rule raised to twenty years old. That would provide an even stronger incentive for kids to attend college—and stay there for at least two years.

My point is, simply, it would have been easy for me to get discouraged after watching three good underclass players leave early. But I didn't, because I'd be doing a disservice to the many good players still on our team. Coaches are always dealing with change, anyway. Only now, with so many kids eyeing the NBA, the process is accelerated. It can be frustrating at times, but I was truly excited about coaching last year simply because I knew it would be a challenge to turn such a young group into a good team. We didn't quite get there, but we will.

A big part of my job, and this is true for every manager, is getting our players to handle adversity. We faced a lot of it last year. We lost five games in a row at one point. But even within games themselves, all players must deal with minor failures. Whenever we lose the ball on a turnover, or allow the other team to score, or commit a foul, we've failed in a tiny way. Those things happen almost every minute of every game, and they bother me.

But not for long. No leader can afford to let minor mistakes get him down. If we are struggling in a game, I make adjustments—consult with my assistant coaches, substitute players—and stay focused on the big picture, which is having more points than our opponents when the clock runs out.

If I sank into a funk every time we fell behind in a game, or lost a prospect, or we were on the wrong end of an official's call, I'd be a lousy leader and a lousy coach. My negativity would infect the players and they would dwell on their mistakes—making it very likely that they'll make more mistakes because they've lost their concentration and confidence. That's no good. To be successful, both individuals and organizations have to be resilient.

My 2005–2006 team didn't face too much hardship. It was older, more experienced, more talented. We won thirty games. Late in the year, we heard the pundits talk about how UConn should win the national title. We were the favorite. I didn't really agree with that assessment, but I certainly didn't run from it. We had a good team, sometimes very good, but as I told people before the NCAA tournament, we had obvious weaknesses. We weren't as good as my 2004 title team. I've always said that you need a couple of great players to win a championship. We had two great players in 2004—Emeka Okafor and Ben Gordon. But we didn't have any great players in 2006, yet Rudy Gay and Marcus Williams would become top NBA draft picks in one more year. We had half a dozen good players. And we had only one player who could consistently beat his defender off the dribble.

Basketball is a game that often comes down to one player with the ball, trying to beat a defender and score. Great teams usually have at least a couple of guys who can do that. But the talent issue aside, my team seemed to play with the weight of high expectations late in the year, especially in the NCAA tourney. I don't care how good you are, it's not easy to play when everybody is telling you for six months how great you are—or should be.

Know Yourself

I'M LUCKY: I ALWAYS wanted to play basketball—and found coaching was just as exciting and worthwhile. I played basketball in college and started my coaching career even before I got my degree. While wrapping up my degree work and starting grad school, I became a graduate assistant coach at American International. I never looked back.

Four years later, I got the biggest break in my career when the interim basketball coach at Northeastern quit to join the FBI. That was his dream job, and when he left, he created an opening for me to pursue my dream of coaching college ball.

Call it serendipity. But I'd also put myself in a position to get lucky by having a great season as a high school coach the year before Northeastern hired me. And I think my passion for basketball, and winning, came through in my interview for the Northeastern job. It also helped that the first six candidates the college tried to hire all turned down the job!

But I wanted the job, and that raises an important point: *Know yourself.*

It's easy to trudge through life, putting in time and making enough money to pay the bills and go to dinner once a week. A lot of people do that, but aren't happy. And often it affects their work. You can't be successful if you're distracted, unhappy, or always wondering in the back of your mind if you made the right career choice.

My suggestion is this: If your current job doesn't excite you, spend some time thinking seriously about what truly does puts a twinkle in your eye. Chase your dream. You won't be happy if you don't. If you're an accountant who's always wanted to be a financial adviser, go be a financial advisor. Take the courses and the tests you need to make the switch. If you're a lab technician who's always wanted to be a chef, get yourself into a cooking school and start the transition. If you're a store manager who is intrigued by sales, go find a sales job.

Change is unsettling. Changing careers is especially hard if you're older and have a family. Can you really quit your restaurant job and become a software developer? I realize that changing careers is a difficult thing.

In the end, you'll have to weigh your desire for change against your need for stability and financial security, and go from there. Maybe you can start the transition by doing some part-time work in the field you love. But if an opportunity to pursue a dream job arises, how can you not go for it? The passion will kick in, the adrenaline will flow, and that can only mean great things for you in the long run.

I'VE BEEN COACHING BASKETBALL for forty years, thirty-five of those as a head coach in college basketball. And I can truthfully say I still get excited every year when a new season rolls around. That's because every season is different—kind of like a new season of the TV show *24*, but with fewer terrorist attacks. I have a new cast of players every year, and so does every other team in America. The team that I knew so well at the end of the last year is gone—poof. The new team is a blank slate, and I have very little idea how it will evolve. I don't know how the freshman players will perform, or my more experienced players, for that matter. Every year I'm pleasantly surprised by the development of some players, and sometimes disappointed that others are still struggling. There is lots of unpredictability.

Before a season starts, I seldom know exactly who will play regularly, or at which positions. I don't know how the kids will interact—will they all get along? There are many questions and few answers. But I also know that there will be many positive surprises.

I coached for a long time with a chip on my shoulder. I like my kids to play the same way. I want them to play every night like they've got something to prove—and they do, to me and the other coaches. I demand that my players and my staff share my passion for preparation, for winning, and for Connecticut basketball. Almost everyone does, which is why we've been successful.

I think that one of the things that separates good leaders from lesser ones is this: *attention to detail.*

Strong leaders never leave work undone, and never assume that important tasks will get done. They make sure that the organization's ducks are in a row every day.

From the start of practice in late September to the end of the NCAA tournament in March, the *official* college basketball season lasts about six months. But in reality it's a 365-day-a-year deal. Because after the season, there is a block of time that must be devoted to recruiting, and another stretch of time devoted to the team's off-season conditioning, and then in the summer and fall there are coaching clinics and basketball camps for kids and high school players.

They are all important. In fact, everything I do outside my personal life is important to Connecticut basketball—every phone call I make to a recruit, every conversation I have with a trainer or academic adviser, every meeting with my coaches, every chat I have with a player. Everything I do—every detail—will either contribute to or detract from the success of my basketball team.

We've all heard the expression "the devil is in the details." I turn it around and say: Success is in the details—not the devil. Master the details you need to stay on top of your organization, your people, your industry, your meetings, your day. You can't just decide you'll concentrate on the big tasks and then slough off other things because they seem trivial, assuming somebody else will take care of them. That's how organizational performance begins to slide.

I don't micromanage, but I do demand that my staff keep me updated on everything—recruiting, stats, opposition scouting reports, practice drills, the whole nine yards. Even now, after more than three decades of coaching, I still like to watch a lot of college and pro basketball games on TV when I have some free time. Sometimes I watch to scout teams we're playing later in the year, or might play in the tournament. Sometimes I watch to see what tactics other coaches are using. Sometimes I watch just because I love basketball.

Some nights I'll call George Blaney, one of my assistants, at 11:00 P.M. and ask him if he's been watching a particular game on TV. He usually is, and we'll chat about what each of us has noticed: some young kid who looks to be an emerging star; the performance of the team. Last year we noticed early in the season that Boston College played a hard-nosed brand of basketball. It was not a spectacular insight, just an early thought on a rival that we stashed in our mental briefcase.

Hands-on Leadership

I HAVE A VACATION house on Hilton Head Island in South Carolina. It's a wonderful place, right on the beach. Every summer I go down there for a few weeks to spend time with my family—my wife, my two sons and their wives, and our six grandchildren. My wife Pat prefers to sit on the beach and read books. I play golf and hang out with the kids.

It's wonderful. But while my body is far away from Storrs, my mind seldom strays very far from Connecticut basketball, which Pat would tell you. July and August are key recruiting months. There are Amateur Athletic Union (AAU) tournaments all around the country for some of the best high school sophomores and juniors, as well as basketball camps sponsored by Adidas and Nike. My assistant coaches fan out to watch games and scout the players, and I go to most of the tournaments, too—about five or six every summer. That is my vacation.

At the same time, our incoming freshmen, who were recruited a year earlier, typically enroll and start a six-week summer semester on campus in Storrs in July. The NCAA allows incoming freshmen to start classes in the summer, and it's a good idea. It gives them a chance to get their college experience started as early as possible, so they can begin to make the big adjustment from high school to college.

The freshmen can take a couple of classes in the summer and get a head start on their academics without the distraction of basketball. Then, in the fall, when practice starts and the demands on their time become intense, they can better juggle their academic and athletic responsibilities without feeling overwhelmed.

I want to be on campus to greet the new student athletes, so every year I fly from Hilton Head to Storrs. I know the kids, because I recruited them, but it's important for me to be on campus when they start this new phase in their lives. It's a chance to get to know the new players a little better. Great teams of any kind are built on solid relationships. I always want the freshmen to get off on the right foot. I set the tone for the program, and first impressions are crucial. First, I want the new players to know that I care about them, and that I'll help them in any way that I can. I've got their backs.

Second, I want to give the new players a sense of my ground rules—what I expect from them, what their new responsibilities are. For starters, I expect them to attend their summer classses. Colleges are a microcosm of our society. Put a large number of eighteen- to twenty-two-year-old guys together and you've got a combustible environment. Things happen, especially in the summer when the campus is relatively quiet and some kids get bored.

In the summer of 2005, two of our players, A. J. Price and Marcus Williams, got caught accepting stolen merchandise—laptop computers pilfered from dorm rooms. It was a black eye for the university, the basketball program, and the kids, who had never been in trouble before. A. J.'s parents are both college graduates; his dad played at Penn and works on Wall Street. They are great people. Both A. J. and Marcus are good kids. I think they were bored, fooling around, and somebody they knew came around looking for ways to get money. In any case, the courts took care of the problem, the kids got suspended, and did about four hundred hours of community service each.

Of all the challenges managing a major college basketball program, the biggest may be keeping the kids away from bad characters.

Hangers-on can be a problem, and when I hear about "friends" hanging out with the players, I want to know who they are and why they are on campus. I tell my players to stay away from people with shady reputations.

My point is, the university has rules, standards, and moral values, and so do I. And I want to make sure all new UConn players know what they are from day one. A team's strength derives from the contributions every individual makes to the group. Every player is accountable for his actions, starting the moment he signs a letter of intent to be a Connecticut student athlete.

Over the years we've developed a "Connecticut way." Boiled down, it means that I want our values as a program to be passed along from player to player, from team to team. I tell the freshmen: "We've had a lot of great players come through here over the years. Most have won Big East Conference titles. Some have won national titles. Many of them are playing in the NBA and having great careers. All of them followed my rules, which start with staying out of trouble and going to class. If my rules were good enough for Richard Hamilton, now with the Detroit Pistons, and Ray Allen of the Seattle Supersonics and Emeka Okafor of the Charlotte Bobcats, and hundreds of others, they are good enough for you." They get the message.

Two summers ago, when I was in Hilton Head, I spent a lot of time working on recruiting. It was a vital recruiting year, because after the 2005–2006 season, we figured to lose a lot of players and so would need to sign a large contingent of freshmen. That meant that we were under more pressure than usual to find a large number of prospects.

While in Hilton Head, I was on the phone several nights talking to recruits and their parents. In the morning, I'd have a 7:00 A.M. conference call with our chief recruiters, Tom Moore and Andre LaFleur. We reviewed our progress with various prospects: Is this kid responding to our interest? Who are his favorite teams? Can we get him on campus for a visit? Would it be good if I called him?

In short, though I was supposed to be on vacation, I was working.

One night at about eleven, I was chatting with the parent of a kid we were recruiting from California. The father told me that he was sitting on the porch having a beer. "I'm envious," I told him. "I'd rather be doing that than talking to teenagers." He laughed.

One weekend in July, I flew to Los Angeles to watch an AAU tournament with Tom Moore. We saw the kids we wanted to see play on Friday, then tried to figure out our Saturday and Sunday schedule. One player we were interested in was playing in a tourney in Trenton, New Jersey, on Saturday. Another prospect, a kid named Spencer Hawes, was playing in Seattle on Sunday.

That presented a dilemma. I wanted to see both kids play, but how could I manage to do that, given that they were playing at opposite ends of the country? It would have been logical for me to fly from L.A. to Seattle to watch one kid, and then send Tom to Trenton to check out the other one. I'm a guy who does delegate, and I greatly value Tom's judgment and skills as a talent evaluator.

But in that instance, I was determined to see both kids in person. So here's what I did: I caught a red-eye flight from L.A. to Philadelphia, arrived Saturday morning, rented a car, drove to Trenton, and watched the first prospect play. Immediately after the game, I drove back to Philly and caught a 9:00 P.M. flight to Seattle. I arrived on Saturday night in time to watch Dawes play the next morning. By Sunday at 3:00 P.M., I was on another flight back to Newark. I got back to my home in Connecticut at three Monday morning.

I'd traveled 9,000 miles in forty-eight hours to see a couple of young guys play basketball games. And here's the sad kicker: Neither one signed with us. (Dawes plays for the University of Washington.) I didn't have to make those trips, and, quite frankly, a lot of head coaches wouldn't have. But I wanted to because prospects and their families are impressed when the head coach shows up at a tournament to watch them play. If I think a prospect is special and we have even a slight chance of landing him, I'll watch him play myself. It can make a difference.

One day, before leaving Hilton Head for a flight back to Hartford, Pat said to me: "You love it, don't you?"

The comment stung a little. I replied, "No, I don't love leaving you, Pat, the beach and the golf course and the grandchildren in the middle of my vacation to return to work. But if I'm going to lead the program and keep it successful, this is the only way to do it." Pat understood. My point was, simply, that I don't cut corners. My dad taught me not to, and I never have. I don't intend to start now. It's one reason I've been successful as a coach.

GOOD LEADERS AREN'T JUST passionate. They're also good at spreading their zeal down through the organization—from the board room to the senior executives, then to senior, middle, and junior managers, and eventually to the rank and file. Look at Microsoft: Bill Gates was always obsessed with the success of his company. He's got an almost maniacal desire to win. Steve Ballmer, Microsoft's CEO, who has worked with Gates almost from the beginning, is the same way. Can you imagine anyone taking over from Gates as the company's day-to-day leader who isn't fanatical about kicking the competition's ass?

And just about everybody at Microsoft is the same way: They're all true believers. They've bought wholeheartedly into Gates's vision for Microsoft, and the products the company develops. Google employees are the same way. So are Apple Computer employees—they share Steve Jobs's passion for technology and innovation. Result: the iPod and Pixar movies, two of the biggest commercial success stories of the last decade.

Jack Welch, whom I've met a couple of times, was a passionate and demanding guy when he led General Electric. The people who worked for him said that they never felt like they pleased him. So they always tried to do more. Welch was very good at getting the people who ran his operating units motivated to reach specific financial targets—revenues, return on investment, a cost cut—and once it was achieved, he'd downplay the accomplishment and set the bars a little higher, sometimes a lot higher. Failure was not an option. My coaching philosophy is very much the same, though I don't think about it consciously.

I'm never satisfied. You never hear anybody around the UConn basketball program use the word "content." Do we feel good when we win a big game or a tournament? Sure. We celebrate every win, but we also recognize, always, that there is more to do. And I make sure everybody knows it. There is always room for improvement. I've never known a player or team that couldn't get better—and that holds true for some of the All-Americans we've had, and some of the national championship teams. The same applies to me: I can always be a better coach.

So if you want to be a leader, and a success, *find your passion*.

After the passion comes everything else. You set the strategic goals, build a management team, identify and implement effective tactics, and search for competitive advantages. In other words, after the passion comes the hard work and the details. All the titles and victories that we've achieved have been wonderful. But they're not why I've been a college coach since 1972. I coach because I love the game of basketball; because I love teaching and leading young men; and because I love competing and testing my coaching skills—and above all, my passion for winning—against others.

Character Is the Core

I'M OFTEN ASKED WHERE my passion comes from. It's not easy to pinpoint. Certainly one source was my parents. I grew up in a large Irish-Catholic family, one of six children. My father, Jim, was my hero. He was a bright, hardworking, tough leader with a great sense of humor. Like most men of his generation, his life was influenced by war. He was a Merchant Marine in his youth. He sailed the world five times, and I used to sit mesmerized as he told me stories about London, Paris, and the Orient. He was bitten by a camel in Egypt.

In east Braintree, a suburb of Boston, my dad was a supervisor for the local gas company and he did his job well. And he was involved in the community. He was president of the Knights of Columbus and president of the Fraternal Order of Eagles in Weymouth, Massachusetts, the town next to Braintree.

My father was a leader himself, in an understated way. He understood the value of hard work—rolling up your sleeves and setting an example and taking care of your responsibilities without complaint. He was both tough and easygoing, a no-nonsense guy. For those who remember old movie stars, he was a bit like Gary Cooper, the strong, silent type. He loved his children, and we'd often run out to Weymouth Landing to meet him on his way home from work. He was a terrific, terrific father.

I played a lot of baseball, and he came to most of my summer league and high school games. Dad didn't like sitting in the bleachers with the other parents. He didn't want me to feel pressure to play well just because he was watching the game. And he wasn't entirely comfortable jawing with other fathers, some of whom got too caught up in the games and their kids. Dad preferred to stand out beyond the centerfield fence by himself and watch me play, far away from the action. My dad believed that if you took care of yourself and your business, everything else in life would fall into place. Don't worry about what other people do, he'd tell me. Don't get frazzled by things that are beyond your control.

My father wasn't easy to please, so when he praised me it always meant something. He didn't often raise his voice if I ever got out of line. A stern look from him would usually set me straight. He was tall (six feet three inches), athletic, loved football and baseball, but not, ironically, basketball. That's because they didn't play much basketball in the Boston area when he was young.

Like all great fathers, mine used to take me places with him. In those days the Weymouth High School football team, in the next town over, was a powerhouse. We'd go watch Weymouth play games on Friday nights or Saturday afternoons. My dad also took me to Fenway Park to watch the Red Sox. To sit with my father, eating peanuts and watching the Sox play at Fenway, well, it didn't get any better than that. I cherished all of those trips. I idolized my dad.

I had two older sisters, Rose and Margaret, but I was the oldest boy in the family. My sisters called me "the king," and my brother Billy, who was eleven years younger, was "the prince." The nickname was an Irish thing. My family was comfortable financially, though like most everybody in the 1950s, we lived conservatively. We were frugal. Growing up, we certainly didn't have a lot in the way of material possessions, but we were a close-knit and happy family. My mother, who had a wonderful sense of humor, kept our family talk light and optimistic. She doted on me, and so did my sisters.

But much was expected of me. I knew that, and then felt it firsthand in 1957, when my dad died suddenly of a heart attack. He was fifty-three. (My grandfather had died of a heart attack, too, at age forty-five. And like me, my father was fifteen when it happened.) I was playing baseball when I got the news. I walked home in a daze, unable to comprehend what it meant. There were people at the house. According to my sisters, I walked up to my mother and said to her, "Don't worry, I'll take care of you." I don't remember saying that. All I remember is being totally devastated by my father's death.

But to a certain degree, I did start taking care of my mother and the family. She had a heart condition, and my father's death left us vulnerable financially. My two sisters were still in high school, and so was I. My brother was only five. I was busy playing three sports at the time—football, baseball, and basketball. I liked them all, and was pretty good at all three. The *Quincy Patriot Ledger,* the newspaper for the South Shore, named me All Scholastic in football. But basketball was becoming my favorite sport: I was growing, on my way to my eventual height of six feet five inches tall, and I had a good jump shot.

My high school years flew by, because in addition to playing sports nearly every day, I began working to make money for the family. I was seldom at home, except to grab a meal and go to sleep. I took various jobs—separating scrap metal at the Fore River Shipyard, tending animals in the paddock area for the Marshfield Fair. On Saturday mornings, from 6:00 to 10:00 A.M., I worked at a local gas station, pumping fuel and cleaning windshields. After my shift, somebody picked me up and I scooted off to play basketball. Work and sports, to a large degree, were my life.

I was a shy kid, and my father's death made me more so. I clammed up, internalized my feelings. My grades fell. But I continued to improve at basketball, thanks to my high school coach, Fred Herget. After my dad's death, Fred was the father figure in my life. He looked after me. He was a small man, about five feet nine inches—but like a lot of men of that era, a very tough guy. He served in the army, fought in World War II, and afterward worked at night to make ends meet. He was an elementary school teacher and also the basketball coach at Braintree High School. He also worked as the town's summer parks and recreation director.

Fred was cagey. He kept an eye out for tall, coordinated kids in the fifth and sixth grades, and then encouraged them to play basketball. I was one such guy. He made sure we all played in the outdoor summer leagues; he'd come turn on the court lights at 8:00 P.M., and we'd play until late. He worked year-round creating a feeder system for Braintree High School, and it paid dividends. He won two state championships and was elected into the Massachusetts Hall of Fame.

Fred liked to wear red socks. It's rare to find any men these days who wear red socks—especially tough guys—but Fred loved them. We certainly never made jokes about them. Fred kept us on the straight and narrow. When I played for him at the high school, he did whatever it took to get his message across. He'd instruct, he'd yell, and he'd physically move us if necessary. When practicing foul shots, if one of us missed a shot and failed to follow the ball to the basket for a possible rebound, he'd come up, push us in the back, and yell, "Go get the rebound!" As crusty has he was, he was the first guy to arrive at special moments, such as my high school graduation.

After high school, I didn't go straight to college. I didn't feel like I could. I kept working to help support my mother. I worked first for an electronics distribution company in Quincy, then for Settimelli Stonecutters in the same town. While many of my friends were going to college classes, I was cutting and sandblasting stone—granite—starting at five in the morning. It was nasty work, and I came home covered in dust. I gave half my paycheck to my mother.

I didn't like most of those jobs, but I didn't mind the work because I saw that it had value. It enabled me to assist my mother financially. There's no question that my strong work ethic was forged at the shipyard and the gas station, and by cutting stone before dawn. That kind of work will either build your character or destroy it. It built mine—and my strong work ethic has served both my career and my teams well. Cutting stones might even have made me smarter, for I learned something from the job—that if I didn't get my butt off to college, I'd be stuck sandblasting for the rest of my life. I sure as hell didn't want that.

I had scholarship offers in high school. While I was working, I played basketball for various club teams in the area, and Fred Herget kept prodding me to go to college. He told me I had to do something more with my life. Talk about loyalty: I didn't play for the man anymore, but he still cared about my future.

As it turned out, I got lucky. I was playing in a weekend basketball tournament in Holyoke, Massachusetts, when I was nineteen, and in one game I scored forty points. The coach at American International College, Bill Callahan, happened to see the game. He took an interest in me and offered me a scholarship. I was interested, but I told him I had to work. "No problem," he said. "We'll get you a job at Milton Bradley, making toys. You can work there during the day and start classes at AIC at night. We'll go from there." So off I went to college—to go to class, play basketball, and make toys.

I had a good experience at AIC. You've heard the joke, "College was the happiest five years of my life." Well, if you count the year I spent as a graduate assistant coach at AIC, I was in college for six years. I played forward, and started for three years. I averaged fourteen points as a sophomore, twenty-one points as a junior, and fourteen as a senior. I joined a fraternity, made friends for life, and began to find myself after the trauma of my father's death. I lost most of my earlier insecurities.

Bob Samuelson, my roommate and teammate at AIC, has described me as "very self-assured, very confident. Jim wanted to be the leader of the pack, king of the hill, but not to the point of being arrogant." He jokes now that I never played defense, that I shot the ball every time I got it, and that on those rare occasions when I passed the ball to him, it would hit him in the head because he wasn't expecting it. Like I said, he's a joker. Bob also said of me: "I'm sure down in those dark places he had the same insecurities that we all have, but he didn't show them."

I worked all through college, too. In addition to working at Milton Bradley, I worked other jobs Callahan helped me get. One of them was doing the laundry for the AIC athletic teams. After our games, I would gather all the uniforms—including socks and jocks—and dump them in the washing machines. Talk about a humbling experience.

AIC was a small school, and in the sixties there was no distinction between Division I, Division II, and Divison III schools. There was the university division and the college division. AIC was in the college division. One year, we played Walt Frazier's team, Southern Illinois. We lost. I've always felt that I could have played in the NBA, but there were only twelve teams in the league in those days, and the opportunities to break in were far fewer than there are today.

But things turned out all right. After my senior year, I hadn't quite finished my course work. Callahan suggested that I spend a year as a graduate assistant coach, so that I could get my degree and start graduate studies if I wanted. Good idea. I took the coaching job and put a whistle around my neck for the first time. Nothing ever felt better to me in my life. I knew at our first practice that I wanted to be a coach.

That year, 1967, was important in another way. It was the year Pat and I got married. We met while I was in college. She was a Weymouth Landing girl, living in the town next to my hometown of Braintree. She was the first girlfriend I had who was a real friend. That was big. We talked a lot, about everything, and fell in love. We couldn't understand how we failed to run into each other as kids.

Turns out, we were close. While Pat went to Catholic schools and I attended public schools, our families were members of the same church, Sacred Heart. We joked that we might have received First Communion together, on the same day. Guess what? We had. Pat's father had filmed the event, and we watched it. There was Pat, at the front of the line, a beautiful girl in a white dress and veil. And near the back of line, there was this tall, gawky kid in a white suit, hands folded. Sixteen years later, we got married in the same church. Pat took a job with AT&T in Springfield, and I started my coaching career—happy and ready to tackle the world.

2

STANDARDS, THEN VICTORIES

As older New Englanders who follow basketball know, Connecticut was a pretty good regional basketball school for a long time, starting in the 1940s. Coach Hugh Greer won 286 games and lost only 112 between 1946 and 1963—a winning percentage of seventy-two percent. UConn dominated the old New England–based Yankee Conference for most of the 1950s and 1960s.

The Huskies got to the NCAA tournament a few times by virtue of winning the Yankee Conference and got to the Elite Eight in 1963–1964. But most of the time, the team lost in the first round of the NCAA tournament. Like a horse with a modest pedigree, every time Connecticut tried to step up in class, it got beat.

In the first eighty-nine years of the program, from 1900 to 1989, Connecticut won four NCAA games. Led by former Coach Dee Rowe, the Huskies got to the Sweet Sixteen in the 1975–1976 season, and then lost to Rutgers. But the team could never really parlay its regional success into a national profile.

The program hit a rough patch in the 1980s after joining the Big East Conference. It wasn't surprising. The university wanted to create a national name for itself by moving into a prominent conference.

Great idea, but the program got bruised making the transition. In those days, the Big East was much like it is today—tough and highly competitive. It was loaded with top teams and elite coaches. George-town, led by John Thompson, won a national title in 1984, two years before I took over at Connecticut. Villanova, coached by Rollie Massimino, won the NCAA championship the following year. St. John's, coached by Lou Carnesecca, was very good. A guy named Rick Pitino was coaching Providence, and Jim Boeheim was at Syracuse. He'd take the Orangemen to the Final Four at the end of my first season in Storrs. And P. J. Carlesimo had it going at Seton Hall—they stormed into the Final Four in 1989.

It was not a league for the fainthearted, and Connecticut took its lumps. It wasn't stated, but the school's goal for a few years was to finish fifth in the conference. The team also hoped to avoid playing the infamous "eight-nine" play-in game in the Big East tournament. That's when the two worst teams in the league played a qualifying game to see which would qualify for the eight-team tourney field. The winner earned a chance to play the top seed—essentially meaning you lost and went home.

In those days, Connecticut played all its home games either in the Hartford Coliseum or in the Field House on campus. Hartford has 16,000 seats and didn't always sell out. The Field House held about 4,500 people, and the home crowds were typically under 3,000. No question, there was some fan apathy. We weren't exactly Duke with its boisterous Cameron Crazies.

Connecticut is a small, wealthy state, but it's got a lot of good high school basketball talent. Trouble was, in the early 1980s all the best players were shunning UConn and leaving the state. Charles Smith, a great player from Bridgeport, went to Pittsburgh and then to the NBA; Harold Jenson from Trumbell and Harold Pressley from Montville went to Villanova and played on the Wildcats' national championship team in 1985. Jay Murphy, John Bagley, Michael Adams, and John Garris, all from Connecticut, all went to Boston College, and all later played in the NBA. Ouch.

UConn had four straight losing seasons before I grabbed the reins in 1985–1986. The school's Big East record the year before was 3-13. The school wanted a coach who could turn things around, somebody who had some attitude and intensity—a chip on his shoulder—somebody who wouldn't be intimidated by stout competition, and who wouldn't be satisfied coming in second in the conference, much less fifth.

In all those respects, they had me pegged.

I'm not somebody who likes being mediocre, or even reasonably good. My attitude has always been: Let's get after it. Let's be the best. Why can't this organization, this team, be special?

The answer is, there's no reason why any organization can't be successful—provided that the owners and top management are committed to winning. Success starts with the attitude of the person leading an organization, and the institutional culture that he or she creates.

I've always believed this:

If you want to build a winning organization, you must first establish a culture of winning. To do that, set high standards for yourself and your colleagues in every aspect of the operation. Make everyone accountable. Out of high standards come victories.

The knowledge that the top management of a sports franchise is truly focused on winning will energize an entire organization. And the same is true of any business. You might own a cheese factory in Wisconsin. Nice spread, plenty of cows, smell of fresh coffee and whole wheat pancakes on a country morning. It all sounds delightful—except for the fact that you inherited the farm from your parents, and you hate farming. It's too much damn work. You hate mucking out stalls. Truth be known, you'd rather be living in a high-rise in Chicago. You aren't happy, the cows aren't happy, and your cheese isn't so great.

Like I said, attitude is a powerful force!

Over the last ten years or so, the fans of the Kansas City Royals baseball team have surely questioned the commitment of the franchise's owner to winning. Kansas City is a relatively small market, and clearly the team doesn't get the big TV broadcast contracts that the New York Yankees and Los Angeles Dodgers and other big clubs get.

Still, Kansas City had a very good baseball team for at least a decade, from the mid-1980s to the mid-1990s. They won six division titles and one World Series. There was a culture of winning. Owner Ewing Kauffman invested in good players, and General Manager John Schuerholtz ran the team astutely, making some savvy trades. The fans supported the team.

Then it all fell apart. Kaufmann died in 1993 and Schuerholtz left to join the Atlanta Braves, where he would make his name as one of the best GMs in baseball. Kansas City's new owner, David Glass, was an executive at Wal-Mart—surely a bad sign, given that company's obsession with cost-cutting.

Sure enough, the Royals started slashing the payroll budget. It fell from $41 million in 1994 to $19 million in 1996. The team traded its best players, including Johnny Damon and Jermaine Dye. The Royals started losing—badly.

The culture of winning had disappeared. The team lost 100 games in 2002 and 104 games in 2004. In 2005, the Royals and Tampa Bay Devil Rays had the two lowest payrolls in major league baseball, and arguably the two worst teams. Glass decided to spend more money on talent last year, but the Royals still ranked twenty-sixth in the league in player spending, and still had a weak team.

My point is, you don't win without good players, and if you aren't willing to invest in your product, you are not committed to winning.

I'm not suggesting that every team owner spend money like a drunken sailor. The New York Yankees have a payroll of more than $200 million—the highest in baseball. George Steinbrenner likes trying to buy championships. He hasn't done so lately, but his heavy spending pretty much guarantees the Yankees a play-off spot every year.

Those owners who take the opposite approach, who are excessively frugal, are almost guaranteed to lose. The worst teams in professional baseball the last few years—the Royals, the Devil Rays, the Florida Marlins, the Pittsburgh Pirates—have all been at the bottom of the league in player spending.

The Detroit Tigers were a cheap club for many years, and they played like one. Between 1994 and 2005, they didn't post a winning record. The last two or three years, owner Mike Ilitch has opened up his wallet, brought in some established players, and guess what: the Tigers were in the World Series last year.

The "lightning in a bottle" strategy almost never works. You don't win with mediocre talent, and any owner or organizational leader who thinks otherwise is only deluding himself. In a competitive environment, you have to be committed to winning—and it's usually pretty obvious when you aren't.

When Ted Turner, the founder of CNN and the Turner Broadcasting Company, owned the Atlanta Braves baseball club, it was obvious he wanted to win. Turner was a sportsman and a competitor—he'd won the America's Cup yacht race. Turner spent money on the Braves. His enthusiasm for the club was obvious and trickled down to the club president and the general manager, the on-field manager and the players, and also the fans. And the Braves won.

In the 1990s, Turner sold his company, which included the Atlanta Braves, to Time Warner. Things slowly changed. Time Warner is a huge, New York-based media conglomerate, and its top brass clearly didn't care much about a baseball franchise in Atlanta that's nothing more than a minor asset for a major company. Time Warner, in recent years, has cut the Braves' payroll. The Braves don't get involved much in the free-agent market. The result is the team's performance has been slipping. After winning a phenomenal sixteen straight division titles, the Braves missed the play-offs last year.

Time Warner recently sold the team to Liberty Media, which is controlled by mogul John Malone. I don't think he's another Ted Turner. Malone bought the Braves as part of a stock transfer arrangement with Time Warner—he owned a big chunk of Time Warner stock—and from what I read, the deal gave him a serious tax break. I don't think Malone bought the Braves because he loves baseball or Atlanta.

My point is, not everybody is as committed to winning as you might think, especially when corporations are moving assets around like pieces on a Monopoly board. I've got nothing against tax write-offs, but who wants to work for an owner that values his company for that reason?

Some organizations have a winning culture and maintain it for years. Other organizations are just the opposite. It's been a long time since the Atlanta Hawks or Los Angeles Clippers had a good basketball team. And as happened to the Royals, some organizations can have a winning culture but then lose it. The commitment to winning ebbs, standards fall, and the losses start to mount.

College athletic departments don't have to worry about player payrolls, thank goodness. But a commitment to winning is crucial. Critics argue that major college athletics has gotten out of hand. The competition is excessive, they argue. There is too much emphasis on the second word in the term "student athlete."

But like it or not, college sports are a big deal in America. The NCAA basketball tournament is a monster event. What sports fan doesn't get fired up for March Madness? There isn't a Division I program in the country that doesn't want badly to be in the NCAA tournament. Television coverage of basketball and football has expanded dramatically. With certain cable or satellite TV packages, a fan can watch half a dozen games every night. People pay attention to college sports. They know who's winning and who's losing—and right or wrong, win-loss records shape the public's perception of schools.

Every sports program must uphold the academic integrity of its university. So long as we do that, I think most college administrators would admit that winning is better than losing. Winning brings benefits. The University of Connecticut has benefited from the success of our basketball teams, both men's and women's. The school has gotten lots of exposure and positive publicity, and they have carry-on effects. Donations to the university and the athletic department have risen. A lot of the money comes from people who take great pride in the university's academic and athletic achievements. Students and faculty feel the same.

UConn is committed to having strong sports programs. Over the last five years, the university has taken major steps to improve the football program. Obviously, college football is hugely popular, and yet the Huskie football program, until recently, was in much the same position as the basketball program twenty years ago. It's been a minor player on the national stage.

Now that's beginning to change. The university has just spent $150 million on a new football stadium and practice facility. The athletic department wants to put the football program on a par with the basketball program, and everybody associated with UConn basketball supports the effort.

As the competition in college athletics has increased, so has what I call the facilities arms race. Schools are constantly upgrading their stadiums, locker rooms, life skills centers, and practice facilities. If one school adds luxury boxes to its football stadium to enhance revenues, or builds a new indoor practice facility, or a nice new weight room, other schools in the same conference take notice and follow suit.

One reason is recruiting. When a prospect visits a school, he wants to see nice facilities. If Marquette or Louisville builds a state-of-the-art basketball complex, they've got something the rest of us don't have. The complex wows recruits and becomes a competitive advantage. Nobody wants to ride in a Buick if a Mercedes is available down the street.

In addition, as women's sports have grown, schools have sometimes struggled to find adequate practice space. In my opinion, UConn's basketball facilities are beginning to show their age, and we've got to do something about it. We need a new basketball practice facility, which might cost about $25 million. That money will have to be raised privately, and our first priority will be to find an anchor donor— somebody who will contribute a major chunk of money in exchange for having the building named after him or her. Twenty years ago, the late Harry Gampel gave the university $1 million for our new basketball arena, and the school named it after him. That's walking-around money these days. We'll need to find a donor willing to give at least $5 million for naming rights, just to get the project off the ground. We're in the process of recruiting some fund-raising prospects now.

Perception . . . and Reality

PERCEPTION AND REALITY ARE two different things, of course. But it's also true that what others think of you or your organization can affect how your group thinks, acts, and performs. You might run a very solid company, but if stock market analysts conclude that your firm's growth prospects are blah, you've got problems. Investors will sour on your stock. And that perception can have some real, and negative, repercussions.

Perceptions *are* reality. I have managed a lot of people for a lot of years, and one of the things I've learned is this: *Whatever you are in life starts with what you think you are.*

Your perception of yourself and others becomes reality. Isn't it true? If you think you are not worthy of success, you're doomed. Self-doubt is corrosive. On the other hand, self-confidence can enhance your performance and help you get through rough patches.

Richard "Rip" Hamilton, Ray Allen, Ben Gordon: Each of those great UConn players questioned their abilities at one time in his career. Each guy had a ton of talent, but each went through periods of self-doubt. When each of those guys came to believe what my coaches and I were telling him—that he was special—the change was dramatic. Thanks to an injection of desire and self-belief, each of those guys morphed from an Audi into a Ferrari.

Here's something else I tell my players:

Talent determines what you can do in life.
Motivation determines what you're willing to do.
Attitude determines how well you will do it.

Each of us is born with certain skills. They vary from person to person. Some people have a knack for sinking twenty-foot jump shots. A lot of other people don't. Some people have a natural ability to draw, or fix cars, or solve math problems. Others don't. But no matter where your talent can be found, whether you're crazy about horseshoes or bond trading, you can probably get better at it if you're determined to do so.

I like golf. I play it during the summer when I take a little vacation. I knock the ball around at various corporate and charity events. I'm not a hugely talented golfer, mostly because I only play it sporadically. Like a lot of people, the more I play it, the lower my score. Like a lot of sports, it's a game that rewards practice and repetition. If I practiced a lot more, I'd be a better golfer—so long as I maintained a positive attitude about my game and didn't start taking it too seriously.

If I did start to obsess about my game, my handicap would probably plateau pretty quickly, or even rise. Why? Because golf is a difficult game to master, no matter how much time you devote to it, and my expectations would start to get the best of me. I'd get down on myself after bad shots—fume, throw clubs, lose concentration.

Now, what if I were a very good golfer, with professional-level talent and PGA Tour aspirations? What if I chose golf as my career? Then my motivation level would obviously play a major factor in whether I maximized my potential as a golfer or not, whether I was making cuts, and money, or missing cuts and scrambling to hold on to my PGA card. I'd have to be out on the driving range and chipping green every day, working on my game; if not, I'd be cheating my potential.

We all like the professional golfer John Daley because he looks, and sometimes acts, like an average hacker even though his natural talent level is *much* higher. He's won two majors, made millions, but it's pretty clear that he's squandered some of his potential. He's clearly not the most disciplined guy on the PGA tour—he's overweight and he smokes. He's on his fourth marriage. I think, at times, he's let personal demons and distractions get the best of him. I'm not criticizing Daley—he's a likeable guy. The fans love him, because he's an Everyman. I just think he's an example of somebody who's left some of his potential in his golf bag.

Davis Love III, the outstanding pro golfer, once told me a story about Daley at a pro-am event. He said that a few years ago, Daley and Tiger Woods played a practice round together, and after the round Daley asked Tiger to join him in the clubhouse for a meal and a beer. Tiger declined, saying he wanted to go hit balls. Daley tried to change Tiger's mind. Tiger again said no. When Daley persisted, asking Tiger one last time to join him, Tiger fixed his eyes on Daley and said, "John, if *I* had your talent, I'd probably be inside having a beer." And with that, Tiger left to go outside and practice.

In my opinion, successful people are not necessarily the best and the brightest in their business. You need skills and intelligence to get ahead in life, now more than ever. But success is not always a function of pure talent or technical expertise. A master's degree in business—an MBA—is valuable in the corporate world. And yet, many CEOs in America don't have one.

Rip Hamilton, who has been an exceptional player in the NBA for years, is not the most physically gifted guard in the game by a long shot. He's skinny and not very tall. But what he does have is a winning personality, which I define as a combination of talent, drive, and ambition. And because he's got those qualities, he's won two championships—one with us and one with the Detroit Pistons.

Technically, there are probably coaches who have bigger playbooks than I do, or more complex schemes. But complexity doesn't always translate into wins. The biggest, fastest players don't always make the best football players—not if their talent is not accompanied by a strong will to win. The smartest people don't always do the best job of managing people. To be a good manager, you need to communicate well with others. You also need to be creative and single-minded. Intelligence alone doesn't build great organizations.

Pulling a Mule Train out of the Mud

I GOT MY FIRST college coaching job in 1972, when I took over the Northeastern University basketball program. A large commuter college in Boston, with roughly 19,000 undergrads, Northeastern has never been an athletic powerhouse and probably never will be. But over the course of my fourteen years there, I was able to turn NU into something it had never been—a successful midmajor program. We went to the NCAA tournament four out of my last five years at the school. We went to the second round of the Big Dance three times.

We didn't have the most talented team in America by any stretch, but we had some good athletes and we focused on fundamentals. I knew Reggie Lewis had great potential when he started playing for us in 1983, and by combining his athleticism with a strong work ethic, he really found himself as a player. My teams, collectively, did the same. We had some talent, but most important, we played *hard* every game. Real hard. We didn't back down from anybody. We had a fierce desire to compete, and we made it difficult for teams to beat us.

Turing a mediocre enterprise into a winner is like trying to pull a mule train out of the mud. The mules are stamping and snorting, but the wagons just keep sinking deeper into the muck. It takes work, salesmanship, and will power—from everybody—to get the group moving forward again.

But, as I said, it all starts with the attitude of the head man, which trickles down throughout the enterprise. His values and standards become the group's values and standards. I've always had sky-high standards.

My attitude and intensity are my biggest assets as a coach. Starting out in the business, I never entertained the idea that I wouldn't win and achieve my goals. I saw no reason whatsoever why Northeastern couldn't be the best team in our conference, and win enough games to qualify for the NCAA tournament.

Was I crazy? No, just a stubborn optimist—and a competitor. I'm an optimist by nature. My family sometimes teases me because I like just about everything. They say I'm the last person anybody should ask for a movie or restaurant critique.

If we go to a movie, one of my sons might say afterwards: "Whew, that was lousy. The plot was thin, the acting was weak." And my response usually is: "You know what, I thought it was pretty good. It wasn't great, but it was okay. For an hour and forty-five minutes, I was entertained. I didn't think of anything else." Give me a microwaved meal and I'll say: "You know what, that wasn't bad. I was hungry, now I'm full; it wasn't bad."

I am the same way about most things in life: I see the upside, the potential, the possibility for good things to happen.

I build my programs around the concept of *family and togetherness.*

It's a corny idea, but I believe in it. At UConn, it is one of our organizational standards. Never underestimate the importance of unity—everybody sharing the same goals and pushing in the same direction. You've heard the cliché: *There is no I in team.* Championship teams take that adage to heart.

Basketball teams, including the support staff, are pretty small in number—about twenty-five people. That's a good thing. It makes it easier to promote camaraderie and to function like a family. Khalid el-Amin, the point guard on our 1999 national championship team, said this about that title-winning team: "What we had at UConn was a special bond. I've been on lots of teams, but at UConn we had more than just the traditional player-coach roles. We were a tight-knit family."

The same was true five years later. Immediately after we'd beaten Georgia Tech to win the 2004 national title game, swingman Rashad Anderson found himself holding the game basketball as the buzzer sounded. He took the ball into the locker room and then gave it to Emeka Okafor, our All-American center. But it wasn't just a gift; Rashad wanted something in return—Meka's shoes. He got them, and Meka's championship sneakers now sit in a trophy case in the Florida home of Rashad's parents. That little trade said a lot about the closeness of the guys on that team.

Togetherness doesn't always occur organically. It has to be culti-vated. As the leader of the program, I demand that my players, and everybody else on the staff, get along. I don't ask them to get along, I *insist* on it.

I want my players and coaches to care about one another, and to help one another when needed. During games, I tell the guys all the time: "Don't save your breath." What I mean is, be an enthusiastic teammate at all times. If you're in the game, give encouragement to your teammates as you're running up and down the floor. Let the other guys know you're fighting along with them. If you're on the bench, don't be selfish or quiet—cheer on the team.

When we do things as a team—go to a meal on the road, visit the Liberty Bell in Philadelphia on the day before a game, watch a UConn football game in the fall—we all do it together. Nobody is allowed to miss group activities unless he has a very good excuse. We meet to-gether, we eat together, we play together. That's not a negotiable point. It's one of our standards.

In last summer's World Cup, I was struck by how close the play-ers on the two finalist teams, Italy and France, were. They spoke frequently about the unity of their teams. For an organization to succeed, individuals must suppress their own egos and personal goals for the good of the group.

Every individual has obligations to the team.

That's an idea I stress constantly, and it's been crucial to our success. I demand that everybody associated with UConn basketball conform to my standards, expectations, and rules. That means that when we have a meeting at 2:00 P.M., every player and staffer is expected to be there at two or a little earlier. No exceptions. It means that every player and staffer conducts himself or herself responsibly, on and off the court. I don't, for example, tolerate my players complaining about foul calls or yelling at officials. That's my job—and some people say I'm pretty good at it.

I don't expect my players to be lemmings. Every person has a distinct personality, and I want to see it. But at the same time, if you as a leader accept too much individuality, you put the cohesiveness of the group at risk. There's a chance cracks will appear in the foundation.

That's one reason why my players aren't allowed to wear hats during team meetings. If I see a player wearing a hat inside our basketball complex, I will ask him, "Is it raining in here?" The hat comes off. I don't want players wearing iPod earphones or chatting on a cell phone in the locker room or in the basketball offices. I don't want players who bicker or complain—that's an invitation to disaster.

I tell the kids all the time, if they have any questions or concerns, come talk to me. And they often do.

There is more to the idea of camaraderie than just togetherness. Good organizations, whether big or small, have lots of people who are not only energetic, but who are also willing *to sacrifice and give of themselves* for the good of the enterprise. At UConn, that means everybody does whatever is needed to help us remain an elite basketball program. That is one of our standards.

During recruiting season, my assistants Tom Moore and Andre LaFleur put in long hours selling top prospects on the idea of coming to play for us. They travel a lot, work the phones until late at night. Often, I do the same. We don't go home or stop calling recruits when the clock strikes five. Just the opposite.

I'd like to think that everybody associated with the program is just as dedicated. We have student managers who often sacrifice their free time to help our players improve their skills. If a player wants to practice his shooting at night in the gym, typically a manager will go with him to retrieve the basketballs and pass them back out to him. He or she might also chart the player's shots—keep track of where he's shooting from and how accurate he is from different spots on the floor. It's a little contribution, but in the long run little things mean a lot.

Everyday Victories

WHEN A PLAYER PUTS in extra time to sharpen his game, that's what I call an everyday victory—and I like to reward the effort. If guard Craig Austrie was in the gym the night before, working to get better, I'll give him a pat on the back for his extra effort—and I might let the team know, as well. If somebody on the team is getting great grades, I'll congratulate him in front of the team. I want everybody to know. I regularly make a point of thanking our secretaries, administrative assistants, media relations folks, trainers, and managers for their good work. I let them know they are appreciated and that they're important to the program. It's not just a cheap attempt to boost morale. I mean what I say.

Just as good attitudes can propel an organization forward, so can bad attitudes act as a drag on team progress. Leadership IQ Study, a leadership training and research company, recently conducted a comprehensive study of corporate attitudes and productivity, interviewing more than 70,000 employees, managers, and executives from private, public, business, and health-care organizations. The survey found that poor performers are often thought, erroneously, to lack "skills" of some kind. Mark Murphy, the CEO of Leadership IQ, said that while a skills problem can sometimes be a factor, "most low performers are so identified because of a difficult attitude."

The study found that poor producers tend to have a negative attitude, stir up trouble, blame others, lack initiative, and can be incompetent. Result: "Low performers can feel like emotional vampires, sucking the energy out of everyone around them."

They hurt the productivity of a group's best employees, and make them want to quit. According to the study, only 14 percent of senior executives said that their organization effectively manages low performers, and only 17 percent of middle managers said they feel comfortable improving or removing a low performer. The study concluded that though it may sound paradoxical, you have to get rid of your worst employees to keep your best employees.

In my business, a low performer might be a guy whose basketball career hasn't progressed as he thought it might. Maybe he's not playing a lot and that makes him unhappy. He develops a bad attitude, then starts griping to his teammates and criticizing the coaches. Suddenly, there is a divisive element on the team. If we can't find a way to bring some peace of mind to the malcontent, he could corrupt the attitude of the best players. And that can royally screw up a team.

I've had a few bad apples over thirty years, but not many—partly because I make it clear from the get-go, every year, that I'm the boss, that we stick together, and that bad attitudes won't be tolerated. If a kid has a persistently bad attitude, I kick him off the team. But it's a pretty rare thing at UConn.

ANOTHER VALUE THAT IS important to me is *pride*.

I want everybody associated with UConn basketball to be proud of their efforts and those of the team. One thing we have in common is a collective pride—it's part of having a championship mindset.

It's certainly true in sports, and no doubt very important in the business world as well: *You have to find and cultivate internal leaders.*

In my case, I pick player captains every year—typically, one or more of my experienced players who have set high standards for themselves, who play regularly, who are respected by their teammates, and who can be counted on to buck up a teammate who's going through a rough patch, whether it's a stretch of poor play or some outside problem or distraction.

I want and expect my older players to "spread the gospel," as we call it—impart to the younger players the expectations and responsibilities that they have as Connecticut basketball players.

In 2005–2006, my captains were Rashad Anderson and Denham Brown. Both were seniors who'd played for me for three years. I was confident that they could function as my voice, to a certain extent, when I wasn't around. We need that. Experienced players don't buy everything I tell them—and my assistants and I don't buy everything we hear from the players. It's a kind of mutual respect, in a perverse way.

But players almost always listen to their peers. Neither Denham nor Rashad was especially vocal, but they were good about speaking up when our play got sloppy. Denham, in particular, was tough and respected by the other players. Off the court, Rashad was easy to be around. He had a good sense of humor, but was also serious enough so that when he had a point to make to the team, they listened.

You'll never have a really strong organization if you, as leader, have to apply all the performance pressure yourself—shouting down from the mountaintop, as it were. Ultimately, your core people have to want to win as much as you do. They are the ones in the trenches, and they have to set high standards for themselves and the group, and then quietly enforce those standards.

When you get that, you've generally got a very cohesive organization.

The Big Break

I WAS LUCKY TO get the Northeastern basketball job in 1972. At that time, more than thirty years ago, I was in the coaching minor leagues, to be sure. I was preparing to start my second year as the coach at Dedham High School, in Massachusetts. We'd had a great season the year before, compiling a 21-1 record, and I'd been named the Massachusetts High School Coach of the Year.

An assistant football coach at Dedham, Jerry Varnum, was a graduate of Northeastern, and he was still involved with the school's athletic program. One day he told me that Northeastern had a problem: The school needed a basketball coach, and fast.

The Northeastern coach, Dick Dukeshire, had taken a sabbatical the year before to coach the Greek national team. He was scheduled to return to his Northeastern job, but had contracted an illness in Greece and was too sick to coach. It seemed natural that the interim coach, Jim Bowman, who'd filled in for Dukeshire the previous year, would retain the job for another year. But there was a fly in the ointment: Bowman had a dream of working for the FBI, and had already turned down two previous job offers from the feds. He wasn't going to pass up his last chance, so he resigned from Northeastern.

That left Northeastern in a major fix. With about two months before practice was to start, they had no basketball coach. And that wasn't all: Northeastern had just taken a major step up the athletic ladder—it had moved from being a Division IAA basketball program to Division IA. That's like a theatrical troupe moving from dinner theater performances in Indiana to Broadway. Division I is the collegiate big show. Northeastern would be playing bigger schools, with better basketball programs—if they could find a coach.

The school's athletic department quickly offered the job to half a dozen other coaches, including Rollie Massimino, who was then the coach at Stony Brook University. At Varnum's suggestion, I applied for the job. I wasn't optimistic about getting it, but the Northeastern football coach, Joe Zabilski, gave me some help. He knew that I'd had a great year at Dedham, which didn't have much of a reputation for good basketball before I got there. He talked me up to the Northeastern athletic director, Herb Gallagher, and told him that I had some college experience as well, since I'd been an assistant at American International College.

Gallagher offered me the job. I accepted it on September 26, less than a month before practice was to start. I was twenty-nine, perhaps the youngest coach in Division I. My salary was $13,800—less than I was making at Dedham High School. Be careful what you wish for.

Needless to say, I wanted to succeed as a college coach. But the distance between wanting something and getting it can be long. At Northeastern, we had only five basketball scholarships and a paltry $10,000 recruiting budget. Not exactly a recipe for success.

I won my first collegiate game on December 9, 1972, when Northeastern beat St. Michael's 82–66. It was a good feeling, and the first season went much better than I'd expected. We finished with a 19-7 record. But after that we struggled for a few years. I didn't recruit quite as well as I'd hoped, and we just didn't have the budget or the players to win consistently.

But then, starting in 1979, I started to bring in more athletic players who fit my style of play, and we got on a roll. My best recruit ever at NU was Reggie Lewis, a shy superstar who grew up in Baltimore. Reggie was six feet seven inches, mobile, and he could shoot. He was a key member of the Dunbar High School team that went 50-0 and also included future NBA players Reggie Williams, David Wingate, and Tyrone "Muggsy" Bogues.

Reggie didn't start as a freshman for me. He was a reserved young man, but he let me know that he was not happy with that decision. I didn't blame him; he certainly could have started, but I loved his role as our sixth man. He was my first substitute, played a lot, and averaged eighteen points a game his first year.

The next three years, Reggie started and lit up the league. He averaged more than twenty-two points a game over his Northeastern career from 1983–1987, and became the school's all-time leading scorer.

But here's the stat to remember: Reggie took 2,098 shots in four years and made half of them. He shot 49.7 percent from the floor for his career. That is an unheard number for a player who's not a big man.

The Celtics drafted Reggie with their first pick, and he flourished on a great team. Reggie played with Celtic legends Larry Bird, Kevin McHale, and Robert Parish. He became the sixth captain of the Celtics, taking over that role from Bird. He was an NBA All Star in 1991–1992. He was the only player in the history of the Celtics to register more than 100 rebounds, 100 assists, 100 steals, and 100 blocked shots in a single season.

In 1993, tragedy struck. While practicing during the off-season, Reggie collapsed on a basketball court and died of a heart attack. He was twenty-six. He was not just a tremendous basketball player, but a devoted father and friend. There was a quiet grace about him. Both Northeastern and Boston retired Reggie's number, 35.

I also recruited Andre LaFleur, who's now one of my assistant coaches at UConn. Andre was my starting point guard at Northeastern for four years in the 1990s. He was a gifted ball handler and passer—one of the best assist men in college basketball history. Andre's got a great understanding of the game.

Like a lot of smaller schools, we fed off the idea of being an underdog at Northeastern, especially on the national stage. Even when we were dominating the East Coast Athletic Conference, or the ECAC, regularly, we never took winning for granted. Anybody who played us in those days knew they were in for a dogfight. My guys always played tough defense, and they always rebounded. In seven years of conference play, NU won the regular season league title four times and shared the top spot two other years. We also won five of the seven league tournaments.

Even better, we went to the NCAA Division I tournament four of the last five years I was there, and advanced to the second round three times. Not bad for a program that was always overshadowed by the pro teams in New England, not to mention Boston College and Boston University. If you wanted to read stories about NU basketball, it was best to start looking in the back of the local newspaper sports sections. I'm extremely proud of the 135-47 record I posted at NU, and of the five NCAA tournament berths we earned.

Getting It Done

IN 1985 MY NORTHEASTERN team played UConn in Hartford in the Connecticut Mutual Classic, a Christmas tournament hosted by the Huskies. It's weird, but I've never forgotten a little incident in that game. Before a game starts, the officials usually chat for a few seconds with each of the coaches. It's a little basketball ritual, a courtesy.

I remember one of the officials, before the game, talking with Dom Perno, the Connecticut coach. But the official didn't say a word to me—not even the briefest nod of acknowledgement. It didn't mean anything, but it was a slight and it bothered me. More than I realized. My Northeastern team was pretty good that year, better than UConn, and I wanted a little respect for our team. I was proud of how my staff and I had improved the Northeastern program, and I'm sure I was looking for a tiny affirmation of our effort. When I didn't get it in that game, it stung. And I remembered it.

We beat UConn pretty easily that night. I didn't realize it at the time, but that win became a major catalyst for my career. Dom Perno retired after that season, and the University of Connecticut seemed interested in hiring me to replace him. I was one of three people who interviewed for the job.

I was happy at NU, but after fourteen years in Boston, I was also intrigued by the idea of a new challenge. But I worried that Connecticut wasn't quite the bright light I was searching for. I had gotten a few offers from bigger programs in previous years, notably Texas and Northwestern, which I had turned down.

At that time, Connecticut's basketball program was trying to find itself. Much like Northeastern, UConn had recently moved up in competitive class and wanted its little slice of the national spotlight. But it wasn't easy for the Huskies to shoulder their way into the Big East. It was a muscular conference, and UConn got sand kicked in its face. Storrs is an isolated spot—and even now, after a long stretch of exceptional success, the town will never be confused with Westwood, California, home of the UCLA campus, or Lexington, Kentucky, or Chapel Hill, North Carolina.

UConn was founded in 1881 as the Storrs Agricultural School. It was a state land grant university. Twenty years ago, the most exciting thing to do on campus was get ice cream from the creamery. My first year in Storrs, everybody I met on campus asked me the same question: "Have you tried the ice cream? You *gotta* try the ice cream. Best ice cream you'll ever have."

Yes, the ice cream was good—but there wasn't a good hotel, clothing store, or restaurant in town. Competing coaches used to try and scare prospects away from us by telling them they'd have to take a helicopter to the campus from Hartford, the state capital, twenty-four miles away. Hartford is known as the "insurance capital" of America, because a handful of big insurance companies are headquarted in the city. That's *not* a factoid that we use to impress recruits.

John Toner, the athletic director at the time, offered me the UConn job. He's a wonderful friend and outstanding man who's now retired and living in Georgia. He took Connecticut into the Big East Conference, and got Gampel Pavilion, our on-campus basketball arena, built. It opened in 1990.

John liked my intensity, and the fact that I'd built a winner at Northeastern, where I had to juggle a lot of off-court duties. He recognized the similarities between Northeastern's ambitions and Connecticut's. He had a feeling that if I accepted the position, I would be very hands-on and grab the opportunity by the throat. He also liked my life experience—the fact that I'd had to work hard for a long time to turn NU into a good program. Toner and Dee Rowe, a former Huskie coach who was also on the search committee, had talked to various basketball people about the Connecticut job and me. The consensus response was that Calhoun "could get it done."

I wasn't so sure at first, but the university did offer some potential. UConn is a big state university with about 25,000 students, and there are plenty of good basketball players in the state. And because there are no pro teams or other major colleges nearby, I knew if we could build a winner in Storrs it would be noticed and appreciated. In addition, the school administration clearly wanted to improve the basketball program. That was important.

Dee Rowe, who's a good friend, spent days trying to sell me on the job. He did so by doing what I try to do with my players when I want to motivate them: He appealed to my pride. "You're a competitor, Jim," he said. "This will be a challenge and you've got to take it. You'll get to play [then Georgetown coach] John Thompson and [then Villanova coach] Rollie Massimino two times each a year." Dee and I talked twice late into the night.

I then had breakfast with Dr. John Casteen, the president of the university. We talked for a few minutes, and I told Casteen that I had a question for him. "How would you define success and failure for this job?" I asked.

Casteen's response was just what I hoped to hear. He didn't tell me that I should win the Big East title within three or four years, or that I should average twenty-five wins annually, or that he wanted to see sellout crowds. Had he been that specific, I would have turned down the job. He told me that he hoped that the team would be competitive. He said he'd heard that my standards were high, and he assumed that if that were true, the team would reach my goals sooner or later. He wanted the players to take their academic responsibilities seriously and be good representatives of the university.

In May of 1986, I accepted the UConn job.

That was the good news.

The bad news was I truly had a big challenge in front of me. Now I had to figure out how to build the winning culture I've been talking about. Now I had to take a perennial underdog and give it some teeth. Now I had to put my leadership and management philosophies to the test. It was time to raise standards, win games, or shut up.

Just as I did at Northeastern, I set about turning the UConn program upside down. Determined to be successful, I rolled up my sleeves and charged ahead. I knew I'd need to sell myself, and our team, to the public, and waste no time doing it. I had to create some positive vibes at a university that had grown a little apathetic about basketball. I had to change that mindset.

I made myself accessible to the media, and tried to repeat the approach I'd employed successfully at Northeastern—work harder than the other guys, emphasize the fundamentals, and recruit. My players would run faster, jump higher, dive for more loose balls, practice harder—and win more games. Lots of people in the media and even at the university were skeptical, but I was eager and a good quote, so they gave me the benefit of the doubt.

Most new coaches fire all the assistants who worked for their predecessor. I decided to keep one coach from the previous UConn staff—Howie Dickenman. We'd known each other for years. When I was a player at AIC, Howie played at Central Connecticut University. We saw each other on the recruiting trail when I was at Northeastern and Howie was an assistant at UConn, working for Dom Perno. I was comfortable with Howie, and liked his work ethic. He ended up being my top assistant for ten years.

I'm a basketball coach, but Howie has used a football analogy to describe my management style. He says I'm like a fullback who takes the handoff and plows ahead, bowling over defenders who are blocking my path. Well, my first year at UConn, I grabbed the ball, raced ahead—and got slammed to the ground.

The first year was miserable. Assistant coach Dave Leitao and I shared a grim apartment in Storrs. The place was a cockroach motel. I drove a dull-looking, light blue sedan issued by the Connecticut State motor pool, with the state emblem on each door. I called it the Dodge Shitbox. It didn't have a radio. Driving around, I felt like a building inspector.

There were other problems. The school's facilities were antiquated. The basketball offices were on the second floor of the old Guyer Field House, which had been built in the early 1950s. It was dark, dingy, and incredibly hot. In the summer the place was 110 degrees. I would sit at my desk and sweat.

The field house had a funky smell. For weeks I couldn't figure out what it was. Then I learned that it came from the synthetic track that encircled the basketball court on the first floor. Every visitor to the office would scrunch up his face and ask, "What's that smell?" Of course, after spending a few months in the hothouse, I no longer noticed the odor at all. "What smell?" I responded.

The office conditions would have pleased the Spartans. My office was small, twelve feet by twelve feet square. I had a metal desk and a couple of couches that must have been from the Salvation Army. My three assistants—Howie, Dave, and Bill Cardarelli—all shared an office next door that was the same size as mine. Each had a tiny desk and a state-issued black rotary phone.

One day Howie told me with a straight face that the rotary phones were making it harder for the staff to recruit. Recruiting involves making a ton of phone calls, and Howie had calculated that it took him nine seconds to dial up a prospect's home with a rotary phone versus three seconds with a push-button phone. He was lobbying for push-button phones.

During the winter, the basketball team had to share the main floor of the field house with the track team. There was a curtain around the basketball court, which we pulled closed to keep the noise out. Didn't work. We could still hear, for example, the track runners knocking over the hurdles. That wasn't the worst problem. The court only had two baskets—not enough when you're trying to conduct a practice with fifteen or twenty players.

But the worst thing was, we were a bad basketball team that first year. That first year, the team's two best players from the previous year, Clifford Robinson and Phil Gamble, were declared academically ineligible in the middle of the season. Without them, we were toast. In 1986–1987, our record was 9-19. We were 3-13 in the Big East, good enough for last place. That year, we lost to Yale. I wouldn't mind losing a debating contest to Yale—but not a basketball game.

I told my wife that I thought I'd made a huge mistake by taking the UConn job. I said to Pat, "We are out of here. We are *out* of here." I don't think I've ever been that low in my life. I truly came close to quitting. I felt it, but never would have until the job was done.

Pound the Pulpit

AND SO IT BEGAN. The old phones were one small but telling sign of an organization that wasn't ready to be competitive. The program needed an overhaul, and my assistants and I used a mix of guts and gospel to fix it.

Good leaders are a bit like evangelists: You're to get people to believe in your message. In my case, I was preaching the Gospel of Good Hoops: Praise the Lord and Pass the Ball.

One day that first year, as Howie and I were walking down the back steps at Guyer, I stopped suddenly and asked if he could hear anything. Howie said no. "Exactly," I said. "That's the problem. We're in the athletic field house, in the late afternoon, and nobody is playing basketball." No shoe squeaks, no basketballs thudding against the floorboards, no chatter. Nobody was playing the game. The place was too damn quiet.

I made a point to change that, and a few other things. I know that I ruffled a few feathers the first couple of years, but it couldn't be avoided. We got push-button phones for the offices, and suddenly felt like we were part of the real world. We got a couple of extra baskets for the basketball court. I asked the athletic director if the team could start spending the night before home games in a local hotel, rather than in the dorms. I wanted to get the players off campus, so that they could be secluded the night before a game and spend time with their coaches and teammates. There are too many distractions otherwise, especially with family and friends around.

The request raised eyebrows, but it was granted, and every major college basketball and football team in America does this now. I certainly wasn't the first to do it, but my coaches and I saw the benefit of getting the kids settled on the night before a home game and focused on the task at hand.

I also felt like we needed a good academic support service for the athletes. I was upset about the eligibility issue involving Robinson and Gamble. When you invest a lot of time and money recruiting kids to your university, why would you want them to flounder in the classroom or flunk out?

Yes, often the players themselves are to blame. Some skip classes and don't study. I know. But basketball, like other sports, also makes major demands on a student athlete's time—at least three hours of time devoted to practice daily, along with lots of out-of-town travel during the season—which can impede a player's academic performance.

And let's not forget, the players are representing the university. Our goal is for every player to earn his degree. Also, unlike most other major college programs, UConn does not have a "general studies" program with fairly easy majors for athletes who may not be the most dedicated or ambitious students. My basketball players have to major in politics, history, or business, like everybody else, which is fine. But we must give them the proper support, considering the demands placed on them.

Not everyone on the academic and administrative side agreed with the idea of starting what is now called a life skills center for student athletes, but there is hardly a major university in America that doesn't have one these days. UConn started its Counseling Program for Inter-collegiate Athletes (CPIA) in 1988. My first two years were a constant effort to get CPIA. There's no question the service has been invaluable for all the student athletes, not just basketball players.

The CPIA provides supervised study halls, individual tutors, and tutoring centers—such as an English/writing center, a math center, and a reading center—learning skills seminars, and secures other appropriate counseling services, such as anger management, from within the university when needed. Thanks to the academic support program, Connecticut's student athlete "retention rate" over the last four years has been 99 percent.

Each sports program has its own academic counselor. We've been extremely lucky to have professor Ted Taigen as the basketball team counselor for the last fourteen years. We call Ted "Doc" because he has a Ph.D. from Cornell. An associate professor of biology, Doc teaches one full-time class and spends half a semester counseling Huskie basketball players. He monitors all aspects of their academic life. He helps set up their class schedules and arranges for tutors when necessary. More generally, he ensures that all the players are making progress toward their degrees. Ted has a wonderful sense of humor, cares deeply about the kids, has a great deal of integrity, and he's been an invaluable asset to the program.

Prepare to Win

BUILDING A WINNING BASKETBALL program is not simply about getting good players, although that certainly is important. It's not terribly hard to put together a single good team—a one-year wonder. That happens a lot.

What is difficult is *winning consistently* over time, year after year after year.

To do that, you've got to build and maintain a culture of winning. That means establishing high standards, making everybody aware of them, and exhorting everybody—in ways both polite and not-so-polite—to reach for those standards every day.

At UConn, I expect my players to practice hard, take care of themselves, learn proper basketball techniques, and to respect their colleagues, teammates, and fellow students. I set equally high goals for my assistant coaches, medical trainers, managers, and administrative personnel.

If an assistant coach fails to make a call to a prospect, and we lose that prospect to another school, he has arguably hurt the program and our chances of winning. If a trainer fails to make himself or herself available to the players, he can hurt our chances of winning. If a player fails to work out on his own—doesn't run, lift weights, or practice his jump shot when he's got a couple of free hours—he's not with the program. He's not engaged with the idea of helping the team and himself to get better. (And then he and I will "engage" in my office.) If I miss a media interview because somebody forgot to tell me about it, we've missed a little opportunity to spread the word about Connecticut basketball. I need and expect everybody to work hard and work together for us to win.

Everybody likes the *idea* of winning, or being successful, but a lot of people don't like the sacrifice and hard work that are usually required to get ahead. Why do people buy lottery tickets? Because the lottery offers a chance to get rich without doing any work. You give the clerk a couple of bucks, grab a ticket, and cross your fingers.

But the odds are very much against winning the lottery. Get-rich-quick schemes don't work very often in real life. What does is the old mix of inspiration and perspiration—talent, hard work, and great ideas. Talent is important, but you'd better bring a lot of desire and enthusiasm to your job, and a ferocious work ethic, or you will underachieve. Others with equal talent will worker harder and pass you on the road to the top.

It may sound odd, but as a coach I never preach to my teams about the importance of winning games. What I preach is *the importance of preparation*—of getting yourself ready to play well, to excel, and winning will follow.

If you practice hard and prepare properly, chances are you'll perform well, whether you're an accountant, violinist, or architect. And if you perform well, chances are your organization will succeed as well. Any team can play mediocre basketball and still win games occasionally. The same with business people. A medical equipment salesman can make the big sale once in a while, and everything seems okay. Maybe a project manager can wing his way through a meeting without really doing the research and having his ducks in order.

But lack of preparation will catch up with you. It always does. And before long, you're embarrassing yourself: A client asks you a question and you don't have the answer, because you haven't done the research.

Create Some Discomfort

WHEN WE LOSE, I'M not a happy man. It may sound backwards, but one way to create a culture of winning is to make everybody in your organization fearful of, or uncomfortable with, the thought of losing. In my early years at UConn, none of my assistant coaches wanted to sit next to me on the trip home if we lost an away game. They knew I'd be in a nasty mood. I might not say a lot, but I'd be surly—and not just for a couple of hours. More like a couple of days—on the practice court and in the office, until I felt we as a team had corrected our mistakes or weakness and done the things necessary to get better.

Michael Jordan was revered for his tremendous athletic ability along with his six NBA titles, but what sometimes gets overlooked when evaluating him is how fiercely competitive he was. I know Michael pretty well, and he hates to lose—at anything, including golf and poker.

He's a Hall of Fame player, but it takes more than just individual greatness for a team to win six NBA championships. Jordan was a leader, too, and he didn't like losing. His Chicago Bulls teammates picked up on that and played better than they might have otherwise.

Larry Bird, the great Celtics player, often spoke about how nervous he got before games. He was one of the game's premier players, but he was always jittery before games—he got butterflies!

Why? He said more than once that he *feared* playing poorly. Even though he was a gifted basketball player, he was unnerved by the idea that he might go out, on any night, and stink up the joint. It seems ludicrous, but fear of failure motivated him to play well. He never assumed that he could just stroll out on the court and excel. Every game for him was an opportunity to validate not just his skills—which were many—but also his work ethic, his competitive fire, and his mental toughness. Like any top performer, he was driven daily to succeed.

Both Jordan and Bird set very high standards for themselves and those they played with. Jordan used to glare at teammates if they screwed up. What basketball player wants to be glared at by Michael Jordan? What teammate of Larry Bird wants to screw up when he's busting his tail and making good decisions? Nobody.

Focus on Your Strengths

A LOT OF COACHES will fixate on their team's weaknesses and spend a lot of practice time trying to make them disappear. I don't do that. In 2005–2006, we had some weaknesses, for sure. The main one was that we couldn't dribble the basketball very well. We had some shooters and some shot blockers. But we had only one guy, point guard Marcus Williams, who could beat his man off the dribble.

We lacked players who could create on their own and just go by people, which is to me the essence of the game—one guy's ability to beat the guy guarding him. Caron Butler, Chris Smith, Ray Allen, Richard Hamilton, Ben Gordon: They could put the ball on the floor and beat their defenders. On the 2005–2006 team, Marcus was really the only guy who could do that. Rudy Gay was a tremendous athlete, but he wasn't an exceptional ball handler. In addition, we were a little suspect defensively on the perimeter. We were not the most ferocious defenders at the guard and wing positions.

We work on our weaknesses and try to disguise them. But our emphasis is mostly placed on trying to enhance our strengths. Last year, our rebounding and shot blocking were strengths, and we played to them. Our fast-break offense was a strength—and so we made a point of playing up-tempo basketball, of getting out and running with the ball, every chance we could.

The No-Joke Zone

WINNING, TO ME, IS also about setting boundaries. It's knowing when to be serious and when to lighten up. Good managers sense the mood of their organizations and manage accordingly. Sports has become a pretty serious business in America, even at the college level, but it's still important to have fun.

Like all teams, my guys like to horse around. We do so on off days, when we're on the road, or maybe after a practice while we're on a bus or plane. Rashad Anderson, who graduated after the 2006 season, was a funny guy, and he'd occasionally imitate my intense coaching style. He's stomp around, yell, get all worked up. But never in front of me! When we are on the practice court, I might tease a kid who trips over his own feet, pointing out how tough it can be sometimes to cross those lines. If we are watching a tape of one of our games and one of the kids makes an especially awful play—misses the basket altogether with a shot or throws the ball into the stands—there will be more than a little good-natured teasing.

But we also know when it's time to focus and get down to business. I have one unspoken rule: In the hours before a game, I want everybody in a no-nonsense frame of mind. I want jaws tightened and minds focused. Doc Taigen and others call it our "no-joke zone."

It's true. I am focusing on what we need to do to win the game—play our best, whether it's rebound, reduce our turnovers, play better defense—and I fully expect everybody else to be single-minded as well.

I NEVER ENTERTAIN THE idea of losing a basketball game. I don't believe in moral victories. I am not encouraged by exciting, close games that end in defeat—unless we're really young, or have been playing poorly, and we play well enough that I can see the team making progress, like last year. Every good manager wants to see his group making progress, taking steps in the right direction. Last year was unusual in that we had five new starters. I think that was a first for me. As young as we were, I knew we might struggle early in the Big East.

But I did expect to see steady progress from game to game, but even that didn't happen until late in the year. As every season unfolds, I want to get a sense that the kids understand their roles, that they are developing some confidence in themselves, and that they are starting to understand what it takes to win basketball games at the top collegiate level. If that is happening, I might be encouraged in defeat.

But I don't much believe in moral victories. It's not my nature. I'm all about the bottom line, and that is winning. I never want my players feeling good after a loss. If they do, I'll kick their ass. Nobody should ever be proud of losing. You should be proud that you gave your best effort in a game, but as I said last year, it's no fun walking into a locker room after a loss. We're not used to it and we don't want to get used to it.

Excellence by Design

WHEN PLAYERS WALK OUT on the floor in the NCAA title game—or the World Series or the Super Bowl or for any crucial showdown—they aren't simply showing up with their skill set. They're bringing a bit of their athletic and personal history onto the court with them—their attitude, their work ethic, their competitive instincts, and mental toughness honed by time spent on the practice court and by tough games and situations. Their performance will be a function of how they've prepared to perform in previous days and weeks.

As I often tell the kids: *Excellence is not by accident but by design.*

You'd be surprised, but teaching young people to work hard is, well, hard work. Most kids don't have a strong work ethic when they get to college. That's because, often, they weren't pushed much in high school. As basketball players, they were just better than other people. Bigger, taller, stronger. Playing well was easy.

But in college playing well is not easy. Nobody gets by on talent alone. That's because everybody is talented, so the competitive bar is raised. There are lots of highly skilled players around, on my team and almost every other team in America. We see that in the NCAA tournament every year. My coaches and I don't just tell the kids to work hard. We've got to get them to understand *why* working hard is important.

Hard work is not an end itself. It's a key part of the process of preparing to win.

Hard work leads to increased productivity. We have players who may not get a lot of playing time, but when they are on the court they're productive. They put up numbers, as we say. Postive numbers. A kid who plays ten minutes a game, but is getting six points and four rebounds during that time, is a very productive player—and surely a very hardworking player. That's what you want from everybody in the organization—productivity as a byproduct of hard work.

An Independent Contractor

I'M NOT A BUSINESSMAN. But I've always considered myself much like an independent contractor or small businessman, and the basketball program at UConn is, in some sense, a business unit. We generate $5 million in ticket sales, $3 million in corporate partnerships, and $7 million in fund-raising.

I am the equivalent of CEO of the Connecticut basketball team. I run the program—but just like a CEO reports to a chairman and board of directors, I must report to the president of the University of Connecticut, Philip E. Austin, and also to our athletic director, Jeff Hathaway. They can fire me if my performance is unsatisfactory—if the basketball team performs below expectations, or if the student athletes on our team fail to live up to the university's academic and behavioral standards. For all the attention the athletes garner as basketball players, they are in school first and foremost to get a good education.

The assistant coaches, administrative personnel, and players might be considered the basketball program's senior management, middle management, and student workers, if you will. I manage them and—in the case of the coaches, trainers, managers, and administrative personnel—they work to fulfill the goals of the program.

My team has customers—the students, alumni, and fans of the University of Connecticut. I've got to get them excited about our "product"—the team. If I can do that by putting together a dynamic group, they will buy tickets, put their fannies in the seats, and ultimately help spread the word about Huskies basketball. Any young or rebuilding organization needs to perform well and then use that improved performance to generate positive buzz.

Public relations—good word of mouth—can help build organizational momentum. That's an important point: Don't underestimate the power of good publicity. It can help hasten your success, once you've got the wagon train moving forward.

The basketball program also has investors—the many people around the state and the country who make contributions to the UConn athletic department. Some of those contributions are invested in my unit—to pay assistant coaches, to pay expenses incurred for recruiting, to buy uniforms and basketballs. Just as Carl Ichan, a major investor in Time Warner, can and does complain about that company's lackluster stock price, athletic department contributors at all schools have been known to vent when athletic programs underachieve. Fortunately, that hasn't happened too often with the basketball program over the last twenty years.

Dealing with the Horde

LIKE MANY BUSINESS LEADERS, I have to deal with the press. There are scores of newspapers, radio, and TV stations in Connecticut, and they've all got reporters covering Connecticut basketball. During the season, a few of them are around almost every day. I answer their questions about the team, about player performance and personnel decisions, and about our opponents. I try to create a positive image of the team and the university, which is an easy thing to do.

Dealing with "the horde," as I sometimes call the press, is not always an easy thing. I've generally had a good relationship with reporters and broadcasters, though tensions sometimes flair. In 2006, Jeff Jacobs, the chief sports columnist for the *Hartford Courant* newspaper, the biggest newspaper in Connecticut, criticized me in a somewhat bizarre column the day before our home game against Pittsburgh.

Jacobs accused me of using harsh language and trying to intimidate him and other members of the media. He declared, melodramatically, that he was breaking off relations with me. It was an odd piece, mostly because Jacobs had spent very little time talking to me in recent years—he was very rarely in my office.

I wasn't happy about the column—nobody likes being criticized in public—but I shrugged it off. Jacobs and I have since ironed things out. We aren't the best of friends by any stretch, but we aren't supposed to be. By the way, he is a talented writer, but our positions will create conflict.

When you run a big program, or a big organization, you are going to be scrutinized pretty thoroughly. And the more successful you are, the more you and your team will be watched.

That's the nature of the media beast—and it's especially true at UConn. The state of Connecticut has no pro sports teams, and no other big colleges to speak of. Athletically, we are the only game in town, and so everything we do gets magnified. That's more good than bad: When I walk into a store, or pull up to a restaurant drive-in window, fans and students are always stopping me, saying hello, wishing me and the team the best. When things are going well, UConn is "basketball heaven," as our top recruit, Stanley Robinson, said recently.

But I also spent months in 2005 explaining how two of my players, Marcus Williams and A. J. Price, came into possession of laptop computers stolen from a dorm room—an incident that got one of them suspended from the basketball program for a year, and the other for six months. That was a tough period for the players, for me, for the basketball program, and for the university.

I was disappointed in the players—they acted foolishly—and the incident cast a bad light on the program. The negative stories dragged on for about a year. I was criticized, unfairly, by some in the media for supposedly influencing the outcome of the university judicial process. Some pundits suggested that because Marcus, our starting point guard at that time, had been suspended for only the first part of the season, that somehow I'd swayed the university to go soft on him.

That was preposterous. I had nothing to do with the punishment handed down to the players, which incidentally was fair and consistent with punishments meted out by UConn and other universities for similar misdemeanor student offenses. The players were punished by the university and by the community, and they each had to perform hundreds of hours of community service to make amends.

Needless to say, I was happy to get that incident behind us, and it was gratifying to see A.J. finally start his Connecticut career last year and begin to fulfill his promise. He was our top recruit in 2004, and we'd been waiting on him. I expect he'll be a better person and a better player because of all he's been through.

The First Sweet Taste

MY SECOND YEAR AT UConn was much better than the first. Dom Perno had recruited some talented players—particularly Cliff Robinson and Phil Gamble—and after getting back in the school's good graces academically, they got back on the court and helped us turn things around in the 1987–1988 season. Robinson, a power forward, averaged almost eighteen points a game, and Gamble, a swing man, averaged fifteen. Tate George, a sophomore point guard, ran the team beautifully—he was one of the best point guards I've ever had at Connecticut.

We were 20-14 for the year, winning eleven more games than we had the previous year. Our conference record was again terrible—we finished ninth in the Big East—but we qualified for the National Invitation Tournament and came into our own in the postseason. We beat West Virginia on the road in overtime in the first game of the NIT. After that we went on a roll, won our next four games, and surprisingly won the NIT title. At Madison Square Garden, we beat Boston College in the semifinals, and then topped Ohio State in the championship game.

The NIT is a far cry from the NCAA tourney, but it was a championship nonetheless and I was happy to earn it. It just the impetus we needed to get the program off and running. There is a historic picture of Gamble and Jeff King, a player who has since passed away, sitting on the top of the backboard with their feet on the rim at the Garden after that 1988 championship game, their smiles a mile wide. As the authors of a book titled *Hoop Tales: UConn Huskies Men's Basketball*, wrote, that victory was "the first sweet taste" of major success for UConn basketball.

Two years later, I was the consensus national coach of the year. That was a big honor. Suddenly, what had started as a mule train was turning into a hot rod. Everybody associated with UConn basketball was feeling good. We were walking with our heads higher. There was more bounce in our steps. We were turning the corner, building momentum.

My staff and I could feel it. We were beginning to establish a winning culture at UConn, though there was still much work to do. We'd set high standards, knowing that if we could approach them, the victories would come. And they were.

Our best days were ahead of us. And that can be true of almost any organization if its leaders are strong and uncompromising. Set high targets, establish a dynamic, ambitious culture—and then focus your efforts like a laser on reaching your goals.

3

MIND GAMES, OR HOW TO BE A
TOTAL MOTIVATOR

ALL GOOD LEADERS HAVE two key responsibilities which are vital to organizational success. First, you have to surround yourself with good talent to achieve goals. Second, you've got to be a hellacious motivator to develop your talent every day so that it performs at a peak level. Not a decent motivator or even a good motivator, but a *hellacious* motivator—somebody who's working 24/7 to get his people in a winning frame of mind.

What's the single biggest distinction between an exceptional leader and a mediocre one? In my opinion, it's pretty basic: An exceptional leader maximizes the productivity of his people, while a mediocre leader does not.

In the sports world, look at college basketball coach Bobby Knight. Bob, whom I've known for years, had some great Indiana teams, and won three NCAA titles between the mid-1970s and mid-1980s. He had a ton of great talent when his Hoosier program was going strong.

But what really makes Bob a great coach, in my mind, is that he wins with teams that aren't full of All-Americans. It's called overachieving, and he's been doing that the last few years with Texas Tech—getting better performances from his team than might be expected. And he does it by being hardnosed about fundamentals, and by motivating his kids with a preacher's fervor. Bob may have his detractors but he's brilliant, a great coach and a great friend, especially to coaches.

Dean Smith, the great North Carolina coach, was the same way. Dean coached a lot of super players at Chapel Hill over the years, but what really accounted for his success was his system, and in particular his genius for getting star players like Charlie Scott and James Worthy and many others to buy into the team concept—to put the team's goals ahead of individual stats. It takes a special leader and motivator to pull that off.

In the National Football League, New England Patriots head coach Bill Belichick is much the same. He's proven himself to be a tremendous coach, arguably one of the best ever in pro football. Why? Not just because he won three Super Bowls in five years, but rather because he's won three Super Bowls with teams that weren't overloaded with superstars.

Belichick has certainly had a few great players at key positions—quarterback Tom Brady and former kicker Adam Vinatieri will be Hall of Famers—but the Pats, in my opinion, have never had the type of dominant team that we saw in the Pittsburgh Steelers in the 1970s, or the San Francisco 49ers under Bill Walsh, or others. Belichick has lost a lot of players to free agency or injury in recent years. And yet because of his attention to detail, because of his intelligent game plans and emphasis on fundamentals, and because of his competitive fire, the Pats are a formidable threat year after year. The team's personnel changes, but the Pats keep winning.

WE ALL KNOW ABOUT Google, the Internet search company that's become a phenomenal success story. The company likes to hire the best and brightest young tech talent in the world. Hey, that's a great thing. But most organizations aren't like Google. They don't have Stanford Ph.D.s and MIT grads sitting behind every desk. They have a mix of hard chargers and laggards. (I couldn't get hired by Google unless they were looking for a company basketball coach. That's one job I *could* perform for the Web giant. Maybe we wouldn't win many games, but we'd sure have the smartest and coolest team in the corporate league.) Most leaders want All-American–type talent at every spot in their company or organization—whether it's a sales position, in marketing, or a center on a basketball team. But it seldom works out that way in real life.

One reason is that few executives, coaches, or CEOs have a hand in *every* hiring decision, especially in big companies. Former General Electric CEO Jack Welsh was a legendary corporate leader. He was smart enough to surround himself with excellent managers, whom he put in charge of GE's most important business units—such as plastics—and many of them have gone on to lead big companies themselves. Welsh picked a smart group of lieutenants and then entrusted them, in turn, to make good hiring and management decisions. Welsh's job, in a nutshell, was to motivate top GE executives—and as has been well documented, he was pretty damn good at lighting fires under people.

No leader operates in a vacuum. Whether it's a blue-chip corporation, a local mom-and-pop store, a nonprofit organization, or a sports franchise, the man or woman running a team must surround himself or herself with people—technicians, planners, accountants, or in my business, assistant coaches, players, academic advisors, and administrators—who are both skilled and dedicated. You'd like staffers to be both, but having at least one of those qualities is a necessity. Kick-ass talent can help you whip the competition, and a reliable support staff can keep your organization on top.

Talent is a variable thing, however, and not as easy to recognize as one might think. Michael Jordan, perhaps the greatest basketball player ever, was cut from his high school team. Larry Bird was slow and not recruited by all the college basketball programs. He started out at Indiana University, coached by Bob Knight. Then he transferred to play at Indiana State University. Reggie Lewis, God rest his soul, died of a heart attack at age twenty-eight. He was one of the three best players I've ever coached, did not start on his high school team and, like Bird, was not recruited by top college programs such as Duke, Kentucky, or

North Carolina. I persuaded him to play for me at Northeastern, knowing only that he was an athletic kid and seemed coachable. I was fortunate that he loved the game, loved to work, and was very talented, which allowed him to develop into an NBA All-Star.

But even if someone's skills are obvious, talent alone never guarantees success. Personal habits play a big role in life. A brilliant golfer or a musician who's temperamental or irresponsible or lacks discipline will not realize his or her potential. Like all coaches, I've seen a few kids with amazing basketball talent squander their athletic careers because of poor personal behavior. One prerequisite for success is having your head screwed on straight.

Pulling Potential out of People

IN SPORTS, YOU HEAR this word a lot—*potential.* Lots of people have it, and lots of people also fail to fulfill it in their lives. My job, boiled down, is to pull the potential out of each of my players. The more I can do that, the better my team will be and the better the players' lives will be.

But motivating people and unleashing potential are not easy things to accomplish. It's not like pulling a rabbit out of a hat. It's not giving some employee, or group of employees, a single pep talk and then hoping for the best. Motivating people is an ongoing process. It's a daily challenge. In my opinion, good managers are good communicators. Good communication is the way that you build bonds with people, and when bonds are established, motivating people is a lot easier. That's the way that I work.

I'm lucky, to an extent: I can and do make the final decision about all Connecticut scholarship offers, which high school prospects get them and which don't. I get a lot of recruiting advice from my assistant coaches, and I rely on it heavily, but I ultimately decide who wears the Huskie uniform every year. And the two things that I always look for in a prospective player are *drive*—the desire to improve—and ears.

Ears? By that I mean the willingness to listen. If a kid listens, and wants to improve, I'm ahead of the game. I know I'll be able to motivate him—develop him. And that is hugely important in college athletics.

Here Come the Diaper Dandies

EVERY SUMMER, WE BRING a handful of new student athletes into my basketball program. Each is eighteen years old and straight out of high school. Each new athlete is young, naïve, impressionable, maybe even a little scared. Some might even be new to the United States. My assistants and I have to grab them, once they've set foot on campus, and teach them the concepts of personal responsibility and personal accountability as quickly as possible. All kids, regardless of social or economic background, will have from some to a lot of bad habits. They can be a little lazy or lackadaisical, and often don't realize it. That's because my assistants and I demand a lot more of them than anybody did in high school.

More than anything, we've got to teach the new student athletes how to motivate themselves *every day*, so that each can become a productive student and basketball player in the shortest time possible. Even self-motivated kids tend to take days off mentally, especially as freshmen. The college pace sometimes gets the best of them. College, really, is a crash course in maturity.

Crash is certainly a word I became familiar with last year, when my assistants and I faced arguably our biggest teaching and motivational challenge. After losing only four games the year before, we fell in fourteen games.

Here's why: Our thirteen-man UConn team had no upperclassmen at all, no seniors and no juniors. That was a first for us. We lost the top six players on the previous year's Huskie team (2005–2006) to either the NBA or graduation, or both. Three of those who left were underclassmen. We had a record five players taken in the 2006 NBA draft. Four Huskies were picked in the first round—another first. It was a proud day for the program. Of the six players who left, the only one who didn't get chosen in the NBA draft but should have, Rashad Anderson, is playing professionally in Europe. Not bad.

To fill the massive talent hole, we signed eight—count 'em, eight—freshman players. That was yet another first for us. We'd never signed such a large group of freshmen, but we had no choice. The small army of first-year kids joined with four returning sophomores and, presto, that was the 2006–2007 UConn team.

It's not unusual for college teams to be young these days—it's common, in fact—but I think we took the term Diaper Dandies (a favorite expression of ESPN college basketball analyst Dick Vitale) to a whole new level.

And not always a good level either, as anyone who followed us last year would acknowledge. Young teams make a lot of mistakes, and we made enough for two seasons. I could feel my hair getting grayer on the sidelines. One of the sophomores, guard A. J. Price, hadn't played a minute of basketball during his first two years on campus. He had a brain hemmorage that kept him off the court his freshman year, and then last year Price was suspended because of a legal problem. (Student athletes are given five years to use their four years of college eligibility. Price was "redshirted" as a freshman, which is why this year he'll only be a junior in terms of his athletic eligibility, even though it will be his fourth year in college.) So he went through a long adjustment period. And then freshmen, as a rule, tend to play helter-skelter.

Our strength last year was our quickness. We were athletic on the perimeter with our guards, and in Hasheem Thabeet we had an imposing seven-foot three-inch shot blocker in the middle. Both made us a good team defensively. We held our opponents to an average shooting percentage of .371–the best in the country. We led the country in shot blocks for the sixth straight year.

But what we gained on defense, we lost on offense. We really struggled to score points for most of last year. We had long scoring droughts in most of our Big East games, and we lost because of them. Hell, we couldn't throw the ball in the ocean some nights. But we improved late in the season. Guard Jerome Dyson became the go-to scorer we desperately needed. Jerome is a slasher, but it was his three-point shooting that really helped us win five of our last eight Big East games and develop some offensive confidence going into this year. And Jeff Adrien, our power forward, became more active and effective in "the paint" (the area in front of the basket), which we also badly needed.

Late in the year, we lost to a good, young Louisville team in Hartford. Louisville was on a roll at the time—playing some of the best basketball in the country. The Cardinals, coached by Rick Pitino, had a good defense team. They were long and athletic. And yet we played our best offensive game of the season. We shot nearly fifty percent for the game, and I thought our guards, who were erratic all year, really settled down and played well. We lost, and as I've said before, I'm not a believer in moral victories. But it was a game that showed we were learning how to play on both ends of the court.

For only the seventh time in my twenty-one years at UConn, we failed to make the NCAA tournament last year. (And three of those down years were my first three years as coach of the Huskies.) No question, 2006–2007 was a tough year for everybody associated with the program—me, my assistants, the players, and the administrative staff. I think even the bugs in Gampel Pavilion, where we work, were depressed. It was our tenth straight winning season, but we were and are not used to losing at UConn. We don't expect it. No organization should.

Young teams are exasperating. But they're also fun to coach in a lot of ways. For one thing, unlike some veteran squads, the players are enthusiastic and don't need a lot of motivation to play hard. The problem was really the opposite: My coaches and I had to teach them to play under control. They were like new colts, ready to bolt out of the barn door and run off in every direction. Getting them to play cohesively was by far the biggest challenge. Still, it was a very coachable group, and they gave great effort all year. I was proud of them for that.

I was reminded of a few coaching truths last year. One of them was that no matter how hard you practice and play, no matter how much raw talent a squad might have—and we had some talent—there is no substitute for experience.

We had almost none last season. We had only two players, Jeff Adrien and Craig Austrie, who'd played significant minutes the previous year, and they were both subs. It's one thing to try and integrate two or three new players into a team with several returning players, whom we coaches count on to be role models. But when almost everybody on the team is brand-new, you've got lots of questions and almost no answers. When it's crunch time in a game, every team hopes to lean on veteran talent. We didn't have much. I'm not sure my coaches and I realized how tough it would be until we got into the heart of the Big East schedule and started taking our lumps.

SOME FRESHMAN STUDENT ATHLETES are smarter and more mature than others, but the one thing they all share, as I've mentioned, is athletic *potential*. That's the reason we recruited them in the first place, and gave them scholarships. They demonstrated in high school and in Amateur Athletic Union (AAU) tournaments their potential to be good college basketball players—and also their potential to be good students, loyal teammates, and responsible people. My staff and I spend thousands of man-hours evaluating high school prospects, and only hand out a few scholarships every year. Yet we're never quite sure what we've got—whether our freshman signees are *truly* talented— until we've seen them on the court for at least a few weeks.

Potential is a funny thing: It's easy to see it in people, but it can be hard to develop. For one thing, the leap from high school to major college basketball is a long one—even for "can't miss" prospects. I've learned a lot of things over the years, and one of them is that there's no such thing as a "can't miss" prospect. Every year there are, maybe, fifteen five-star, blue-chip prospects who—if you believe the recruiting "experts" and other pundits—are destined for instant college stardom as the first step toward a glittering career in professional basketball.

But guess what? A lot of them don't make it. A lot of high school stars don't pan out in college, for a variety of reasons. That's why recruiting is always a bit of an educated crapshoot. Some kids just aren't as good as you projected them to be. They were stars in high school, just physically better or bigger than the kids they played against. But their skills don't quite stand out when the athletic bar is raised and they must perform against tougher, major college competition. At UConn or other top programs such as North Carolina, Duke, Kansas, or Louisville, almost everybody on the team is a heavily recruited top prospect. That means that players must raise their game and steadily get better. If not, they will find themselves either sitting on the bench or getting outplayed by guys on other teams.

In sports, getting better is not just a function of showing your skills. You've got to have a strong base skill level *and* have a desire to get better—every day, every game, every year.

The difference between good players and great players is typically nothing more than desire and work. The great ones have it, the good ones don't. UConn has more players in the NBA than any other college program, and the main reason, I think, is that we're pretty damn good at developing talent. We take players with various skill levels and make nearly all of them better players, and better people.

In my mind, developing talent is mostly a function of instilling people with passion. I have a passion for basketball, and winning games, and working hard, and so do my coaches. We coaches chop a lot of wood—which is the equivalent of taking responsibility for winning. But our goal every year is to give the ax to the incoming freshmen, and teach them how to swing it. Then we can move out of the way and let the players shoulder some of the leadership responsibility that helps to win basketball games. My point is, we train kids to motivate themselves.

Some people are naturally driven to achieve. Emeka Okafor, the center on my 2004 NCAA title team, was a prime example. He was not a blue-chip prospect when we recruited him. He was a Top 100 high school player—considered good but not great. Meka, as we called him, was six feet nine, and athletic. He was mobile. He could run the court. He could rebound. He could block shots.

He was a little thin, and like most freshman, his offensive skills were raw. But it didn't take me and the other coaches long to recognize that Meka—who grew up in Houston, Texas, and is of Nigerian descent—was a special kid. After we saw him for a couple of months, my coaches and I were turning to each other with little smiles on our faces. We knew he was going to be *better* than anticipated.

And why not? Meka's full name is Chukwuemeka Noubuisi Okafor. His first name, in the Nigerian language, means "God has done well."

Meka was amazingly mature for his age. Even as an eighteen-year-old freshman, he acted like a twenty-five-year-old graduate student. He had a high energy level—what sports coaches sometimes call a "big motor." He needed almost no motivation from me or any UConn coaches or teachers to realize his wonderful potential as both a student and a basketball player. He was intelligent and driven to succeed the moment he set foot on campus. Nobody had to tell him to go to class. He majored in finance—the honors program—and in his three years in Storrs he was twice an Academic All-American.

I didn't have to bug him to work on his basketball game either. He was often the first player in the weight room and the last to leave. Meka *wanted* to get better—every day—and the combination of his skills, athletic potential, and desire to improve helped transform him from a promising 200-pound player as a freshman into an imposing 250-pound All-American as a junior. After practice, he would often spend extra time in the gym working on his post moves.

I used to say that Meka operated on cruise control. And certainly all his hard work paid off: He was not only a first-team All-American as a junior, but conational player of the year, along with Jameer Nelson of St. Joe's. He was twice named the national defensive player of the year by the National Association of Basketball Coaches and was twice named Academic All-American of the year. He played on the

USA Olympic team, winning a bronze medal in Athens, Greece. And of course, he helped us win a national title in 2004, and was honored as the "most outstanding player" at the Final Four. Meka was the number-two pick in the 2004 NBA draft—and not surprisingly, was named the NBA Rookie of the Year.

Meka was a bit reclusive as a freshman, but only because he had so many things to do every day. He proved what those with discipline and good time management skills can accomplish: a lot. He set such high standards for himself, my biggest worry was that he was going to burn himself out. But he quickly grew as a person, and was a willing student of the game of basketball. Though he's in the NBA now, Meka would be a success in any profession.

Frankly, I treated Meka differently than other players. I gave him some leeway that others players didn't necessarily receive, because there was never a doubt that he would do the work and get himself ready to play. If he needed to miss a practice to attend a lab class, then he did. I was happy to grant such requests, and I made sure to tell the team why he was missing practice: because he cared about his academics and felt it was important to attend every class.

I rarely screamed at Meka. If I wanted to get a basketball idea through to him, I'd sometimes try an indirect route. I'd holler at one of our *other* big men, Hilton Armstrong or Josh Boone, knowing that Meka would be listening and absorb the thought. It's odd, I know, but I felt Hilton and Josh were pretty good at accepting criticism—and frankly, they needed more of it. I knew that if I made a point to and through them, I could avoid messing with the head of my best player.

Unfortunately, self-motivated guys like Okafor don't come along very often. I bring new kids into the program every year, and many have natural athletic abilities equivalent to his. What they lack, however, is Meka's maturity, which is needed to raise their games. My job is to help these kids to grow up as quickly as possible. My coaches and I take those who might be a bit lackadaisical, or cowed by their new environment, and instill in them a mix of passion and fear. And yes, it sometimes involves some screaming on the basketball court.

But I do more than yell at them to work hard. I show each player how he and the team can benefit from a rugged work ethic. Sometimes, frankly, it's just a matter of mentioning that Meka is making $5 million a year playing for the Charlotte Bobcats, or that Ben Gordon, a shooting guard on the 2004 title team, is making $3 million annually playing for the Chicago Bulls.

At major college basketball programs, there is no denying it: Kids want to parlay their talent into fat contracts with NBA teams. Money *is* a motivator. It's why we get prospects like Curtis Kelly, a six foot nine inch forward from Rice High School in Queens, New York. He was certainly one of the two or three best basketball players in New York City as a high school senior in 2005–2006, and that is saying something. Two newspapers, the *New York Daily News* and the *New York Post*, named him the city's player of the year. Curtis has talent, and he wants to play in the NBA. And he's certainly got a chance to.

Rudy Gay, a phenom out of Baltimore, was the same way. Rudy came to UConn in 2004 partly because he and his family knew we'd put more players in the pros than any other college program. He wanted us to groom him for the NBA, and we did. He's now playing for the Memphis Grizzlies, who drafted him eighth in the first round in 2006.

Tricks of the Trade

LEARNING HOW TO MOTIVATE is probably the biggest challenge facing any leader. Some are better at it than others. There are tricks to the motivational trade—methods to the madness—which I'll explain. But I also have a pretty hard and fast rule that makes my job easier. I don't tolerate players who aren't interested in becoming self-starters. As anybody who knows me will acknowledge, I am not a patient man.

When a player comes to UConn as a freshman, he doesn't really know what he's got himself into. He doesn't know how hard we work, how demanding we can be, how much we will expect of him as a player and a person. For that reason, I may cut a new kid some slack early on, for the first week or two of his UConn career. During that time it's my responsibility to show him the lay of the land. I call it laying a motivational foundation.

In fact, that's one of my motivational principles. Every day at UConn, we try to make and lay a few motivational bricks. The bricks can be defined as the incremental progress that individual players and the team are making day after day after day. Pretty soon, if we're working hard, we've made, say, 500 bricks and built a $500 wall. And we keep adding on. Eventually the goal is to build not a wall but the most beautiful cathedral in the world.

Rashad Anderson, who graduated last year and is now playing in Greece, had an outstanding career at UConn. But it wasn't an easy four years for him. Most freshmen struggle to adjust to college basketball, and Rashad was no different. Rashad was a great kid with a sparkling personality. He was always making jokes, always wearing a smile when he came into the basketball office. He was especially good at imitating people, including me.

Rashad loves basketball. Let me amend that: He loves shooting the basketball, and is very good at it. He's got the confidence of a cat burglar; he can miss ten straight shots, but will not hesitate to take shot eleven because he's certain *that* one's going in. Somebody asked me recently how Rashad was doing in Greece. My response was, "Still shooting." Rashad released the basketball in an odd way—it came out of his hand with very little rotation, like a knuckleball—but it went through the hoop consistently, which is all I cared about.

I wasn't sure for a while if Rashad would develop into a good, productive player. His game was a little slow to come around. He had some great games, but he was not consistent. We had to push him to get in shape and to play defense. Late in 2004, near the end of his sophomore year, all the preaching and the practice seemed to come together for him—and for us. His game started to click. Down the stretch of the 2004 season, when we won the national championship, I started him fourteen games, and we won thirteen of them. He averaged eighteen points in those games, and he went on to make the All-Final-Four team. We wouldn't have won the title without him.

Last year, when he was a senior, I opted to bring Rashad off the bench as our so-called sixth man rather than start him. It was a good role for him. He was an instant spark plug, and usually gave us both high-energy play and a few baskets. We relied heavily on his three-point shooting last year. His three-pointer at the buzzer saved us in the wild NCAA tournament game against the University of Washington. The shot tied the game, and we went on to win that rock fight in overtime.

Some kids take longer to adjust to college life than others. It's a completely new and different environment—new surroundings, new friends, many more responsibilities—and their heads spin for a year or two. They are away from home and on their own for the first time. A big-city kid—and we had two players on last year's team from inner-city Los Angeles—might face a little culture shock when he arrives in quiet Storrs, Connecticut. You can't get lost in the crowd in Storrs. You stand out.

Other kids adjust to college life without much difficulty, but not to the new level of basketball they're playing. Some, competing against really good players for the first time, lose confidence. A star high school player might find himself on the second team in college—coming off the bench, or not playing much at all. For kids who've been pampered for years, and who are accustomed to being told by friends and family how great they are, it can be a shock to realize that you may not be as good as you thought you were.

In college, kids can't just roll out of bed, stroll out on the court, and wow everybody like they did in high school. They've got to do something that may be a little alien to them—in other words, bust their tails every day—to even have a chance of playing.

Athletes have fragile psyches, probably more so than most people, and confronting the realities of life in college—the classes, the meetings, the tough practices—can be jarring. Some freshman players retreat psychologically or emotionally. Even veteran players can be fragile, because they are constantly dealing with both success and failure.

A player can excel for a short stretch—make a couple of shots, play good defense—and suddenly feel really good about himself. Then, just as quickly, the positive mojo can disappear. He misses his next few shots, turns the ball over, makes a mistake on defense. The next thing he knows, he's walking off the court with the sound of my voice ringing in his ears. Then he's sitting on the bench.

Basketball is an up-and-down game. Every game, every minute, is full of highs and lows. As a leader and coach, I've got to teach my players how to be emotionally tough enough to deal with little failures. You can't lose your confidence as a person, or a player, if you have a bad moment or two, or a bad day. Look at a lot of the people who succeed in life: They're resilient. They understand that life can kick you in the ass sometimes, and have the personal grit to come charging back.

We can't afford for my guys to lose their confidence or their toughness when things go poorly in a game—and yet, frankly, that is precisely what happened to us many times last year, because we had no upper-class leadership. We had a team full of first-year players, and we had to play some of them more than they should have played. Without any veteran leadership to speak of, my young guys would let three or four minutes of poor play affect their poise, and the next thing I knew, the game was spinning out of reach. A four-point deficit would turn into twelve. Game over.

Whether a kid is mature or immature, almost ready for the NBA, or sitting on the end of my bench, we've got to teach him how to *prepare* to play well. I have to teach players how to work hard and play smart, so that the Connecticut Huskies as a squad can reach its potential. That's the biggest task most organizational leaders must face—improving individual talents, and then melding the parts to build a cohesive and powerful whole.

Good Leaders Sell Change

THAT'S AN IMPORTANT POINT, I think. Organizational leaders spend a great deal of time trying to promote individual and group change. Small changes and large changes. You might want to bring a salesman in from the field and make him a manager, or move a store manager from, say, Los Angeles to Minneapolis. You might decide to change the culture of your organization fundamentally

People often resist change, so you've got to convince them that they will benefit from the change you have in mind—that it will be good for them and, hence, good for the group. That's not easy to do, if the change doesn't offer obvious benefits to the person who's being affected. I could have easily started Rashad Anderson last year, and he certainly expected to start for a while. But my staff and I decided that he might help us more coming into games fairly early as a substitute.

It made sense to the coaches. But we had to make sure that the move didn't alienate or discourage Rashad. That meant assuring him that his playing time wasn't going to go down because he was on the bench at the start of games. He'd get the same number of minutes on the court, maybe even more. More important, we had to convince him that he'd be more valuable to the team as a key substitute rather than as a starter, because he could give us some scoring punch at points in the game when our opponent might be playing subs, too, but of a lesser quality than Rashad. He accepted the idea, and in fact the move did strengthen the team.

The well-known corporate consulting firm, McKinsey & Company, recently published a study on the psychology of change management. In it, McKinsey analysts Emily Lawson and Colin Price reinforce my point. They write: "Employees will alter their mind-set only if they see the point of the change and agree with it—at least enough to give it a try."

They add: "If people believe in the overall purpose [of organizational changes], they will be happy to change their individual behavior to serve that purpose; indeed, they will suffer from cognitive dissonance if they don't. But to feel comfortable about change and to carry it out with enthusiasm, people must understand the role of their actions in the unfolding drama of the company's fortunes and believe that it's worthwhile for them to play a part. It isn't enough to tell employees that they must do something differently. Anyone leading a major change program must take the time to think through its story— what makes it worth undertaking—and to explain that story to all of the people involved, so that their contributions make sense to them as individuals." I couldn't agree more.

Motivational skills are *crucial* to good leadership. And the opposite is equally true: Weak leaders tend to have mediocre motivational skills. Pick a great organization and you can bet that its leaders are passionate and effective at nudging employees or, if more is needed, giving them a swift kick in the butt.

In business, frankly, the job of developing talent is easier than it is in college sports. Even the youngest employees in business are in their midtwenties, at least, and most have graduated from college. They've spent some time out in the real world, on their own. In a word, they've matured.

Coaches are in a different position. Our charges are still kids. They're *in* college, starting the transition from adolescence to adulthood. They're starting to mature, but in many cases haven't gotten there yet. That means, simply, that it's not easy to yank potential out of them.

Some executives don't believe much in the need to motivate their people. Maybe it's just the fact that doing so can be a full-time job. Some leaders have a distinctly hands-off management style. They delegate to the managers below them—give them their marching orders, and then assume that they'll follow through.

I'm like this with my assistant coaches. But I'm much different with my players. With them I'm absolutely a hands-on guy. I feel like I have to be, because the buck ultimately stops with me. I respect former President Theodore Roosevelt because he was a fairly wise but tough-minded leader. He didn't shrink from making difficult decisions, even when he knew that he'd be criticized. When the American people had concerns about companies with monopolistic powers, he sat down with corporate chiefs to talk and listen. He was a hands-on guy.

Dr. Freud, I Presume?

MOTIVATIONAL SKILLS ARE ESSENTIALLY psychological methods for improving performance and productivity, for transforming average employees into better ones. Motivational methods vary greatly. Some leaders work mostly through positive reinforcement. Others prefer to induce fear—"Make that sales number, Griswald, or you're fired!"

Whatever the method—and I try to mix fear with favor—you want to get people fired up, light a charge under them, so that they're not just willing to ride into battle with you but are *eager* to do so. The thing that separates a good, competent soldier from a warrior is motivation; the warrior is completely, totally invested in the task at hand, and will sacrifice to achieve goals. The Marines have a saying: "The shield or on the shield." It means, essentially, I'll fight and, if necessary, die for the cause.

Business people, students, and athletes aren't soldiers. But it helps sometimes if employees think like them. Highly motivated individuals can focus and excel in highly competitive, high-pressure environments. The world is competitive, so motivated people are very important to the success of an enterprise. Motivated individuals and units tend to be very goal-oriented.

In sports, as in business, success is often measured by numbers—

whether it's shooting percentage, rebound and steal totals, or most important, your win-loss record. Those who fail to reach their targets consistently may lack skills, or may be unmotivated. An unmotivated employee is often indifferent, bored, unhappy, for whatever reason, and therefore not very productive. If you have too many unmotivated employees, your organization's morale is going to suffer and you'll get beat by the competition. Even one malcontent can ruin the cohesiveness of a group.

Tough Love

MY MOTIVATIONAL PHILOSOPHY, GENERALLY, can be summed up in two words: *tough love.*

I'm a big believer in the tough-love school of coaching. It's the way I was coached when I was a player, and I think it's a very effective way to motivate people. Simply put, I'm a demanding coach. No question about it. I push my kids, and often pretty hard. I yell at them sometimes, especially during games. I'm emotional and not easy to please, and I won't apologize for it.

I demand that my kids and my assistants work hard at all times, and have a winning attitude at all times, because I do. I do not tolerate people who don't give good effort, or don't have positive attitudes, or don't have a strong will to improve and to win. Those are all qualities that I strongly value, and I want everybody associated with Connecticut basketball to have them, as well.

Managers or leaders who don't push might be popular with their employees or players. That's why certain men and women are called "players' coaches." But in my mind, people who aren't pushed don't tend to improve much. I want my kids to improve—a lot. My job is to push them 365 days a year.

But pushing is only half of the equation. At the same time that I'm pushing, I'm also letting each of my players know regularly that I care about him as a person. That's the crucial second part of the tough-love philosophy. I make sure every player knows that if he works hard, is a good team player, I will be there for him when he needs me.

When Marcus Williams and A. J. Price got arrested for possessing stolen merchandise last year, I was extremely upset and disappointed with them. I fully supported the legal process—both at the university and in the city—that played out and resulted in their punishments, which were suspensions from the team, and lots of community service.

But I also stood by the players because I knew they were good kids, from good families, and I don't believe in abandoning good people because they make one stupid mistake. My players all know that I will push them relentlessly to be better basketball players. They also know that I care about them as human beings, because I make a point to praise them whenever possible. Doing both creates trust and solidifies the bond between my players and me.

My point is simply that people need both positive and negative reinforcement. But balancing the criticisms and the compliments can be tricky. All good managers break down people, but you can't ever leave them broken, psychologically, or you've lost them.

Which raises my second key point about managing and motivating people: *Individuals perform best when they feel good about themselves.*

Billy Packer, the basketball analyst for CBS Sports, came to one of my UConn practices during the NCAA tournament a few years ago. After watching us work out, he said to me: "You should play well tomorrow, because your kids seem to feel good about themselves." And he was right. We won the game.

One way to make people feel good about themselves, of course, is to acknowledge their performance. Last year, a few times after a game or a practice, I would stop Rudy Gay in a hallway, on his way to class or a meal, and say, "Hey, you were great today." Nothing more, nothing less. I would do the same with others. If Marcus Williams, our point guard, had a particularly good practice, I might tell him, "Hey, it's too bad we weren't playing a game today; you were sharp."

I'm not somebody who throws out a lot of cheap praise. So when I say something like that to a kid, it's meaningful to him. We have anywhere from twelve to fourteen players on the team most years, and they all get positive private feedback from me at different times during the season—and often fairly regularly.

The essence of tough love is essentially demanding that your people perform at their highest potential level. Over time, I see what my players are capable of. I see them at their best and at their worst.

Tough love is simply asking them to play their best consistently. When they don't, when a twenty-point-a-game scorer has been scoring fourteen in recent games, or a ten-rebound-a-night center falls off to seven, it's time to push some buttons.

More often than not, I frame criticism in a constructive way. Last year, there were a few times when I went to our center, Hilton Armstrong, and asked, "Hilton, explain to me how one of the best rebounders in the country only got six boards [rebounds] in each of the last two games? You're too good to get fewer than ten rebounds a game."

Or, as I said to Marcus Williams last year: "You're the best passer in the country, Marcus. So why are you making bad decisions on the [fast] break and throwing the ball away?" In both instances, I'm criticizing the players, letting them know that I'm dissatisfied with their performance, but very subtly—within the context of telling them that they're too good to play mediocre basketball.

Appeals to personal pride can be a terrific spur, too.

If a kid is shooting the basketball poorly, missing a lot of shots, I might say to him: "Joe, I can only think of two reasons why you're missing shots. The first reason is that you're simply a bad shooter. The second reason is that you're a good shooter, but you're taking a lot of bad shots." (In other words, the player is taking shots when he's not really open or not in a good spot from which to shoot.) The player will of course accept the second reason, and start working on making better decisions about when to shoot.

HERE'S ANOTHER MOTIVATIONAL PRINCIPLE of mine: *It's good to be unpredictable.*

I make a point of being unpredictable with my players and with my teams. Unpredictability, as a motivational method, can be effective. The players aren't sure, day to day, what they'll get from me—what my mood will be, or what my reaction will be to a performance. It's part of my management style.

People want to pigeonhole other people. They come to certain conclusions about specific people and their personalities—he's quiet, she's loud—and anything that contradicts their assumptions definitely grabs their attention. In my business, that's a good thing. Being unpredictable keeps my players on their toes.

Some days at practice, I can be low-key and in a good mood. Other days I might be a little animated and abrasive. I can be calm after a defeat—sometimes—and difficult after a win, pointing out individual and team deficiencies, especially if we win a game despite lapses in effort or judgment.

But let me add: While my mood can be variable, my core values and standards—the basic qualities I expect from the players—always remain the same.

Often, you can motivate people by saying nothing. If somebody is playing below his potential, I might not say anything to him for a few days. To a player or employee who likes and expects feedback, especially positive feedback, the silence can be deafening. Inevitably, the lack of comment will eat at the player for a couple of days, and he'll come to me and ask: "Coach, is there anything wrong?" That's a good sign: It shows not only that he cares about his performance, but that he cares about how I perceive his play.

The individual is looking for a little stroking; I've withheld it, and now I have some leverage with which to motivate him. I might say, "Yeah, I'm glad you came by. You've been playing well on offense, but your defense has been crap. You're not fighting through picks like you can. If you don't start working harder at it, I'm going to sit you."

Tough love can work quite well with your most talented people. Ben Gordon was one of the top shooting guards in college in 2004, when he was a junior and playing for me. He was big, strong, and an excellent shooter, and he could put the ball on the floor. But it took a while for Ben to get just how good a player he was. At times, he was like a virtuoso pianist who seemed content playing in hotel lounges. I used to tell Ben: "Everybody wants to be you but you."

Typically, Ben would play well, but he wouldn't dominate games as the coaches thought he could. He was low-key, and didn't seem too comfortable with the idea of dominating a game. The other coaches and I knew he could do more.

I used to tell Gordon occasionally, after a game or practice, "You were okay today." After a pause, I'd add, "Yeah, I thought your performance was okay—ordinary. You were an ordinary player."

He absolutely *hated* hearing that—as any player would. I was needling him in a subtle way, of course, letting him know that he was capable of playing better. He'd usually get the message.

I took the same approach with other great players we've had at UConn—Ray Allen and Richard Hamilton. Nothing bothers talented people more than hearing that they're ordinary. You might as well tell them that they're bad.

Saying "No" Can Be a Good Thing

MOTIVATION IS SUCH AN integral part of my job that it's pretty much my default operating mode. When I'm at the office or on the court, interacting with my players, I'm in a motivational frame of mind almost all the time. It's second nature to me, so much so that I seldom actually make conscious decisions to motivate players. Whereas older corporate workers might be set in their ways and resistant to change, young workers have more respect for authority. They aren't jaded.

If a kid is missing classes, then I obviously know that strong motivational—in this case, meaning disciplinary—action must be taken, and quickly. But otherwise, when I'm around one player or the entire group, I'm trying to engage them, activate them, get their heads focused on things that will benefit the team. Like a lap swimmer turning his head out of the water to take a breath, I don't consciously think about motivating kids all the time. I just do it. The vast majority of them are coachable—meaning they want to get better—and they want feedback from the coaches. So they listen, for the most part, to what my assistants and I say.

No question, college coaches have to be more aggressive motivators than managers in the business world. Frankly, I almost consider myself a professional psychologist. I have to be.

Kids *are* harder to motivate these days than, say twenty years go. For one thing, there are more distractions. A lot of student athletes these days have been coddled in the past, by their parents, by friends, and by various hangers-on. The player is accustomed to being showered with compliments and advice from his fan club. Prominent players can sometimes have an entourage—a posse. After a game, he isn't just met by a parent or a girlfriend. He might have ten or fifteen people ready to hang out with him—aunts and uncles, stepbrothers, old friends, supposed friends who just want to be his agent.

Students today aren't quite as communicative. How can they be when they're wearing iPod earphones fifteen hours a day, watching movies on their laptops, or yapping on their cell phones? It's not easy getting kids to tune in when they're part of Generation Tune Out.

As a result, it takes more commitment from the coaches to reach them—and sometimes to discipline them. I believe that the word "no" has virtually disappeared in America. Somehow, it got removed from the dictionary.

People rarely say to young people: "No, you can't do that." Parents want to express their love for their kids, and they do so by saying "yes" all the time. "Yes, you can do that; yes, you can have that." I'm not that way. I say no to my players. I punish them when they screw up—when they miss class or are late for a meeting. Saying no can be a good thing, so long as you explain your decision.

I'll go home after practices occasionally feeling bad because I rode one of my players pretty hard. But I realize it's probably okay, because I almost never criticize a player without putting my criticism in context. If I express displeasure with a player, I almost always make clear what he's doing wrong. And I try to remind him that he's too good, or talented, or special to be screwing up. "You have so much to offer," I'll tell him. "If I continued to allow you to shortchange yourself, to not give your best effort or be the best person you can be, then I wouldn't really care about you. And I do."

So tough love really means wearing a black hat some moments and a white hat other times—and often both at the same time. I have standards and values, and if I wasn't true to them, if I held back from criticizing a guy because I didn't want to hurt his feelings, I'd be a phony. And that's not me.

MANY PLAYERS, PARTICULARLY YOUNGER ones, tend to believe that talent alone will carry them along. It's not their fault: That's the way it was for them in high school. They were naturally better than their peers, often without really having to work very hard. That doesn't cut it in college. They've got to marry their talent with a strong work ethic to succeed, and it's my job to help them do that.

Top college athletes also assume that they'll soon be playing professional basketball, driving an Escalade, and buying a beach house with their multimillion-dollar contracts. I recruit a lot of kids with pro basketball potential—and I like ambition, don't get me wrong. I've had eleven players leave early for the NBA in the last ten years, including three last year.

But the allure of the NBA can make my job more difficult. In 2005–2006, we had a few players who may have felt some pressure to play well to enhance their NBA draft status. Denham Brown and Rashad Anderson, who were seniors and perhaps borderline NBA players, may have felt they needed to have big years. Rudy Gay, the best pro prospect on the team, got a lot of press attention and was definitely feeling some pressure to live up to his star billing and show that he was worthy of being a top-ten NBA draft pick. Marcus Williams, our point guard, at times felt pressure to spread the ball around evenly to everybody, so that everybody could show off their skills. He told us that.

And I know that some parents were worried about how much playing time their sons were getting. Same reason: They were thinking about the NBA. I wouldn't want to be a young coach today, partly because the best prospects these days—and their parents—are so focused on getting that professional contract.

It can be a challenge and a distraction for a coach if you don't stay ahead of the situation. I do. During the season, I don't talk to any player about his professional potential. That comes after the season, and the players all understand that.

Don't get me wrong: My players on the 2005–2006 team were a terrific group of kids. In fact, it was the only year I can remember when nobody on the team came to me and complained about his playing time. Not one player. They were great to be with, and made most of my days enjoyable, and they were very good at competing on the basketball court. We had a very good season.

I don't worry at all about how much playing time my guys are getting. They play for as long as they deserve to play based on their performance at practice and during games. They either earn the right to stay in the games by playing well, or they don't. I respect my players' professional ambitions, I talk to them about what they've got to do to get to the next level, and I will help them get there. But the professional aspirations of my players have no effect on my decision-making as the

Huskie coach. My approach is to sell them on the idea of winning—and if we do that, everybody will benefit.

It's also important to keep this in mind: For all the talk about the NBA potential of certain players, the vast majority of student athletes do not get drafted or play in the NBA. TV has given many kids in our society a warped impression of life: All they see are those few pro athletes who've reached the top and the bling-bling that goes with it.

Money is a great motivator, and it can be a strong incentive for players with pro potential. But it's not the way I want to motivate my players. I try not to sweat the little things, like playing time. I worry about the big picture—how we are playing as a team. That's the only thing that matters.

I tell my kids all the time: "Be the most successful player and student you can possibly be. If you do that, even if you fall short of your goals, you'll still be in a terrific place."

Connect with Your Talent

THERE IS NO ONE way to motivate people. Every individual is different. Everybody thinks differently. Everybody reacts differently to adversity. Some people are naturally more talented than others. Some people are talented but don't work very hard. Some people work very hard but aren't very talented. Some people accept criticism more easily than others.

All of which is to say that good leaders tend to tailor their motivational techniques to the psyches of each of the people working—or playing—for them. Jimmy Johnson, the former Dallas Cowboys and Miami Dolphins football coach, was once asked if he treated his players equally, and he replied: "Hell, no! I have fifty players, and I treat them fifty different ways. If a rookie falls asleep during a team meeting, I'm liable to scream at him, 'Pack your bags and get out!' If the player snoozing is Troy Aikman, I'll walk up to him and gently whisper: 'Troy, wake up, we're having a meeting.' "

I'm the same way. I manage everybody who plays or works for me a little differently. I think I learned it from Red Auerbach, the legendary Boston Celtics coach. I attended Red's basketball camp when I was a kid. I was a counselor at his camps when I was playing ball in college. And I played for him briefly after college, when I hoped—futilely—to get into the NBA.

I watched how Red handled his Celtics players. He was a genius at scanning his roster and knowing which players would need a lot of his attention, and which players he could leave alone. He would heap praise on some players and heap scorn on others. He left Bill Russell alone, because the great center was self-motivated. But he was hard on Tommy Heinson, and especially Sam Jones. Sam Jones was an excellent guard who would become a Hall of Fame player. But Red intimidated Sam. So Sam tried to limit his contact with Red. It didn't always work, but the two got along well enough to win ten NBA titles.

Whether you take a hands-off or hands-on approach to managing people, I think one thing is crucial: *You've got to connect with your top talent.* Good things emerge from strong relationships.

It's imperative that you have a strong relationship with the people who can best help you reach your organizational goals. I really believe in building my teams around two or three great players, and then having a bunch of good role players to round out the team. I want to have a tight relationship with my top players, because, frankly, they can make or break the team. I need to know what makes them tick.

Ben Gordon, when he played for me between 2002 and 2004, was a gifted shooting guard. He was the first or second best player on our 2004 NCAA national title team. He was the third player taken in the 2004 NBA draft.

While Emeka Okafor was bright and outgoing, Ben was the opposite. He was not easy to get to know. He was introverted, shy, and a bit regal. On the court, he could be explosive, but he also seemed indifferent at times. That's not what you want from your best scorer. I made a point of trying to connect with Ben, because we weren't going to be a great basketball team with him playing at three quarters of his potential.

Make Them Selfish

I TOLD BEN I needed him to be more *selfish* on the court. That's a contradictory idea in a team game. Basketball *teams* are supposed to be unselfish. We coaches preach to our players all the time—share the basketball.

But great basketball players should be a little selfish. You've heard the old expression, "If you've got it, flaunt it?" The same applies to talented athletes. If I've got a guy who's capable of scoring twenty-two points a night without shooting excessively, I want him to score twenty-two points a night. Not sixteen points, but twenty-two. If that same guy can beat his defender off the dribble and take a key shot for us at crunch time, I want him doing that—not passing the ball to a teammate with less offensive skill as the shot clock is ticking down to zero. That doesn't help the team.

Talent is supposed to be utilized, and that's what I wanted Ben to do—play aggressively. Big East games are rock fights. To win them, I need my best players to be great. Great players are not afraid to dominate a game. They know instinctively when to give the ball up and pass it to an open man, and when to keep it and score. In the NBA, Tim Duncan understands that, while Stephon Marbury has not mastered the concept. Bill Russell and Jerry West understood it. Wilt Chamberlain did not.

Larry Bird and Michael Jordan may have been the best examples ever of guys who knew when to be selfish, and when not to be. Bird was a brilliant passer, but he was always ready to take—and make—a big shot, and he'd keep shooting the ball if he was in a groove, which was most of the time. (Bird once told his teammates: "Just give me the ball and get out of the way.") Jordan made too many game-winning shots to count, but he was happy to have his Chicago Bulls teammates John Paxson and Steve Kerr take and make crucial late-game shots in

NBA championship series. Paxson clinched Chicago's third straight NBA title in 1993 when he sank a three-pointer in the closing seconds of game six against the Phoenix Suns. And Kerr did the same in game six against the Utah Jazz in 1997. Jordan could have taken those shots, but Paxson and Kerr were open, and the Bulls were confident they would make the shots.

Ben Gordon and I did bond over time. But it wasn't easy. About halfway through his junior year, which would be his final year at UConn, I asked Ben about his grades, knowing that he was a good student. He said they were okay. I replied: "Okay? Umm, I hope they're better than okay, because you've got to be eligible to play for us next year if the scouts say you're not quite ready to be a first-round draft pick for the NBA." That was probably the worst thing I could have said to Ben, and I knew it. The comment hit him like a hammer. And guess what: Ben the Indifferent started playing like Ben the Conquerer. And we were a much better basketball team. To win, when you need a basket your players should have the ball. Ben became as good in the clutch as anyone we ever had.

My philosophy is this: If I go to the office, run into one of my key players, and have an opportunity to spend twenty minutes talking with him, man to man, then I've had a very good day. That twenty-minute talk will strengthen my relationship with one of my best players, and that's always going to benefit the team. Even if it's a three-minute talk, it's a good thing. To motivate people effectively, it helps to have some sort of bond with them, and you establish bonds by talking with people.

Let the Thoroughbreds Run

I DON'T ALTER MY playing style too much nowadays—we like to run the basketball up the court on offense and play tough man-to-man defense. That was how Auerbach and his great Celtics teams used to play, and Red was my coaching role model. But I am open-minded enough to alter my schemes to fit the players' talents.

In the late 1980s and early 1990s, we weren't blessed with a lot of offensive talent. We rebounded well and played good defense, but didn't have a lot of great shooters. As a result, our half-court offense wasn't very good. So we pressed a lot—we liked to run a three-quarters 2-2-1 press—partly as a way to try to generate some offense.

In the mid-1990s, we got better players. Ray Allen, Doran Scheffer, and Donyell Marshall were all athletic and could shoot. They liked to play the style of up-tempo basketball that I loved. They weren't methodical, half-court players. So we pressed less defensively, but employed a running, fast-break offensive style to fit their talents. We've stuck with it ever since.

I remember saying to my assistants: "We've got some thoroughbreds now, so let's let them run and not turn them into plough horses." It was a matter of matching our system to our talent, which any smart coach will do. We still pressed, but not as much, because we didn't have to. We could score without pressing, and therefore could save some of our energy.

The players liked the change. I want to keep all my players in a positive frame of mine, but especially my best players, because their performance and productivity levels are vital to the team's success.

In fact, I'm always telling my top players how important they are to the team. I'm always giving them little "reminders" of how special they are, how much potential they have. I want to keep their engines running and keep them focused on improving their games.

Connecticut senator Chris Dodd, a friend of mine, once told me that everybody's two favorite words are their first and last names. It's true: We all have an inflated opinion of ourselves at times, especially those of us in the sports world. And that's especially true if we are performing at a fairly high level. Players and coaches, too, can get big heads. We assume we know everything. We've done it all, we've won titles. There is nothing new to learn.

Wrong. Life is about getting better all the time. It's about moving forward constantly. You take a step, you progress, and then you work on taking the next step. And then the *next*. My kids used to read the Dr. Seuss book *Oh! The Places You'll Go!* It's a wonderful tale, with a wonderful message about life: Persevere. You don't quit while you're ahead. You don't take anything for granted. You don't give up when things don't go your way. If one path to success and achievement is blocked, you try another. If you believe in yourself, you can move mountains—"99 and 3⁄4 percent guaranteed."

My job, every day, is to show my student athletes the places they can go.

Why shortchange yourself? How many owners of a horse that wins the Kentucky Derby decide, after the victory, to sell the horse or put him out to stud pasture? None. They saddle him back up and run him in the Preakness, and if he wins again, the Belmont Stakes. They go for the Triple Crown.

I try to impress that idea on my players—keep running. Nobody at age twenty has reached their potential. Nobody at age twenty has scratched their potential. Keep going. I'm sixty-three, and I don't think I've reached my potential. Don't ever assume you've accomplished all you can in life. That's a recipe for staleness and mediocrity.

In 2004, right after Emeka Okafor and Ben Gordon were picked second and third in the NBA draft, I called Charlie Villanueva, a power forward on the team, and left him a voice message. At that time, Charlie was a player with loads of potential—there's that word again. He was tall, agile, and he could shoot. For a big man, his footwork was excellent. He could score inside or outside.

I said to Charlie in my phone message, "Did you see the draft? Isn't it great that Ben and Meka went so high? I'm just calling to say that you've got the same potential, and I'm curious to know what you're doing today. I hope you're working to get better every day, like they did."

A couple of months earlier, just after the 2004 season ended, I'd sent Charlie a brief handwritten letter. Like the phone call, it was a little motivational booster shot. I told Charlie I thought that he'd had a very good first year, that there were great things ahead for him and the team if he worked hard. I was trying to light a fire under Charlie. I wanted him to know that he was a good player, that I appreciated him, and that we'd be counting on him to play well the following year. He did, and now he's in the NBA, too.

Tweaking Personalities

DAVE LEITAO, WHO WAS a top assistant for me at UConn for a long time before going on to be the head coach at DePaul and now the University of Virginia, once paid me a complement by saying, "The psychology of motivation is critical to Jim. He can prod, push, give a guy confidence, break down the confidence of another guy. He works on it twenty-four hours a day. He's always thinking how can I get through to this kid."

That's true. Every player can contribute something positive to a team. The challenge is getting each player to understand and accept his role, and that means pushing certain emotional or intellectual buttons. When Richard "Rip" Hamilton played at UConn in the 1990s, he was a lanky guard—all arms and legs. He could handle the ball and had good court vision. Rip fancied himself another Magic Johnson—a sort of combination point guard/scorer.

But we had a natural point guard on the team, Khalid el-Amin. The other coaches and I saw pretty early on that Khalid could lead the team and run the offense. What we needed from Richard was points. We wanted him to play off the ball, as a so-called two guard, use his quickness to get open, and shoot the ball more often. Richard had natural scoring ability, so our job became to convince Richard to concentrate on that aspect of his game. I had to sell him on a new role.

He fought the change at first, for about a year and a half. But then he and I reached a mutual understanding, and Richard adapted to his new scoring role. He stopped trying to dribble the ball so much. Instead, he used his incredible fitness to get free, knowing Khalid and others would get him the ball when and where he wanted it.

They did, and the rest is history. In three years, Rip scored 2,036 points—the second most in UConn history. And he did it in only three years. By the end of his college career, he was one of the best pure scorers in the country—just incredible coming off screens and shooting the basketball. And he helped lead us to the national championship. He's now the top scorer for the Detroit Pistons.

When Dave Leitao played for me at Northeastern, I persuaded him that he could best help the team by rebounding and playing defense. That's what he did, and he helped lead us to two straight NCAA tournament berths when he was a junior and senior. The art of persuasion often starts with a private meeting in my office. When a kid comes into my office for a talk and I ask him to close the door, it's time for brass tacks. That's when I hope to work some motivational magic on a player one way or another. Whether he likes it or not!

Sometimes, motivating a person means tweaking his personality. Needless to say, that can take time. I've talked a lot in this chapter about Emeka Okafor. In the early part of his UConn career, the only thing he lacked was swagger. He didn't have that cocksure attitude that most great players have. He was, in a way, too disciplined and too humble. But over time, as he became more comfortable with his game and his talent, Meka acquired some brashness—and that made him an even better player.

Caron Butler, on the other hand, who played for me between 2000 and 2002, was a little too cocky when he arrived. Caron is special to me because he fought through a lot of adversity in his life. At age fourteen, he was arrested in his hometown of Racine, Wisconsin, for possession of a gun and narcotics. He spent nine months in a juvenile detention facility, then six months in jail. He got into a fight in jail and spent ten days in solitary confinement.

There, he had an epiphany of some sort, for he vowed to change his life. And he did. He worked for a while, until he and his mother and grandmother could find another school for him. They did, in Maine. He attended the Maine Central Institute, where he matured and demonstrated his formidable basketball skills. As a senior, he averaged twenty-six points and thirteen rebounds a game. He was one of the top prep players in the nation.

And not long after he got to Storrs, he became one of the best players in college basketball. Caron was a skilled, six-foot seven-inch forward—athletic, and an excellent ball handler. He could beat you off the dribble.

But he wasn't fit when he got to UConn. We got him into shape, and he led the Huskies in scoring as a freshman. As a sophomore, I sat him down and told him he needed to do more, that it was time to push his game to the next level. He told me later that the talk boosted his confidence.

It must have, because in 2002 he was co-player of the year in the Big East. He also carried us to the conference tournament title, where he was the MVP. And he led us to the Final Eight in the NCAA tournament. (We lost to the eventual national champion, Maryland.)

Caron only stayed at UConn for two years. He was drafted tenth in 2003 and now plays for the Washington Wizards. While Okafor acquired some needed swagger in college, Caron lost a little of his brashness. He matured, developed a touch of humility. We smoothed out some of his rough edges.

Caron and I are still close. We talk on the phone a lot, and he calls me "Pops." He was on the *Tonight Show* with Jay Leno a couple of years ago, and at one point he proudly told Leno that he'd attended the University of Connecticut. That was a nice thing to hear.

The Power of Trust

CARON BUTLER'S REDEMPTION BRINGS me to another of my motivational principles: *Make sure your people trust you.*

Trust is crucial if you want people to bust their butts so that your organization can achieve its goals. Trust essentially means doing what you say you're going to do, whether it's positive or negative.

This is an important point. Leaders lose respect when they say things and then don't follow through on them. No false words. My young players, in particular, need to know that when I say, "Enough," I mean it. "Not one more inch." They are around a lot of people who blather about various things, say things they don't mean. Leaders can't be that way. If you say you're going to do something, follow through and do it.

Rudy Gay was an outstanding player for us as for two years. He was a highly recruited player out of Baltimore: a six foot nine inch winger who could jump through the roof and had a soft, high-arching jump shot. He can do some incredible things on the basketball court. It was fairly clear when I signed Rudy that he would leave for the pros early. The only question was, when?

Rudy grew up in a rough part of Baltimore, but attended Archbishop Gibbons, a Catholic high school. He was a quiet kid when he got to Storrs, easygoing, with a captivating smile. He was coachable because he wanted to be good. And when I got on him, he accepted the criticism because he understood its purpose. He had a good but not great freshman year—he wowed people with his athleticism and potential—and afterwards mulled the idea of turning pro.

We sat down and talked about it after the 2005 season. I told him that he'd played well, made a huge amount of progress, and that he'd be a pro soon. I'd help him get there. But I also told him he wasn't ready yet for the NBA. He needed more time to improve his game.

He needed another year to get stronger and work on his ball handling. I told him to come back, play even better as a sophomore, and then we'd sit down and reassess the situation.

I told Rudy that if he turned pro prematurely, he wouldn't be a lottery draft pick, wouldn't get a great contract, and he'd end up sitting on the bench for a year or two. And then, because of his lack of playing time, he might have to sign a modest second professional contract. That wasn't in his long-term best interest. Better to stay another year, get better, be a high draft pick with the potential to be an impact NBA player—and get a bigger rookie contract.

Rudy and his family understood. He believed what I told him, because he trusted me. He knew that I would tell him to turn pro when I thought the time was right. Rudy played for us another year and, as I predicted, was a top-ten pick in the draft.

I did the same thing with Richard Hamilton. He thought seriously about turning pro after his second season at UConn. I told him that if he did, he'd probably be about the twentieth player picked in the pro draft. If he stayed in college another year, he'd be a top-ten pick and make a lot more money. He stayed, got drafted the following year in the top ten, and as a result got a much more lucrative NBA contract than he would have gotten a year earlier.

Establishing trust is all about doing what you say you're going to do. If you're honest with the people you manage at all times, you will build trust with them and strengthen the bond of manager and employee, or coach and player. Your unit, company, or team will benefit. Trust is a powerful force.

Life Lessons

I DO A LOT of coaching and teaching during games. I think it's the perfect time to get through to kids, really. You can instruct players at practice, and that's fine—they will absorb a lot. I don't say much to my players after games. I've found that it's a tough time for people to absorb information—they're too caught up in the emotion of the game. It's human nature. I don't tend to point out mistakes right after a game, because if we've lost, the player might think I'm blaming him.

My high school coach told me a long time ago that games were excellent teaching opportunities. I didn't believe him then, but now I very much believe it's true. There is tension, noise, physical exertion. The players are focused, and that's the best time to give them not just basketball lessons, but life lessons. That's why people see me getting intense, and sometimes in the face of my players, in games. I usually do it after I've pulled a kid out of a game and sat him down on the bench.

Some coaches say that they don't like to criticize their players during games, for fear it will ruin their confidence. I disagree. In games, players are exposed; they're emotionally naked, and so what they hear tends to sink in. If I pull a guy and scream at him—"Marcus, you're playing so lousy you're not going to play another minute in this game!"—I will get his attention. He will listen, closely, when I tell him *why* he's playing lousy. And, of course, I don't always mean what I say. Two minutes later, I might yell at him again: "Marcus, get back in the game!"

My kids are used to my passion and intensity. If I stopped being emotional in games, the players would wonder why. In fact, three or four times in years past, I tried to tweak my own personality. I purposely decided not to go ballistic during games. I would be a model of politeness, a paragon of decorum. I was curious to see what effect it would have on the team. The idea backfired: The players didn't like the new me. They didn't like my subdued behavior on the bench. They came up to me after the games and said, "Coach, what gives? Why don't you believe in us anymore?" That was tough to hear. I went back to the old, natural me. I started yelling again in games. I felt much better. So did the kids.

One last thing about motivation: Don't give up on people unless you're ready to fire them. In my business, I don't have any choice. I can't get rid of players and don't want to, although some do transfer. It's my job to help my guys get better, year after year, so that they can contribute to the team.

Hilton Armstrong, a center, mostly sat on the bench for three years. He was playing behind Meka, and he never played well when he got minutes. Bad things would happen. But by 2005, Hilton was ready to break out. He'd paid his dues. He'd developed, physically and mentally, and was ready to show his stuff. He not only became our starting center, but a very productive player who was the eleventh player taken in the NBA draft. Hilton was like a volcano that lay dormant for three years and then, *boom*, he suddenly exploded. It was very gratifying to see because Hilton never gave up on himself. He'd come to believe what we'd been preaching the prior years.

After three or four years in the program, if a player hasn't improved his game significantly, then there are only two reasons why: Either he simply isn't very talented or I didn't do a good enough job of motivating him to improve.

Ninety-five percent of the time, I reach and motivate my players. I come back to Ben Gordon: He was a terrific talent and scorer naturally, but the other coaches and I pushed him to improve. He took our advice to heart. For two years, Ben spent a few nights a week in the gym, on his own, practicing his jump shots. During the season, he'd practice with the team in the afternoon till about 4:00 P.M., go back to his room and study for a couple of hours, go to dinner, then come back to the gym and, with the help of one of our student trainers who retrieved basketballs, take about five hundred jump shots. He'd move around to half a dozen spots on the court, and shoot.

Take that many practice shots every other day, and you'll become a very good shooter. That's what happened to Ben. With a little push from me and a little prod from Tom Moore and George Blaney, Ben got religion. He came to realize that some extra work could really pay off for him and the team. It did.

Effective leaders know how to get individuals to cross that long bridge between potential and great performance. You do it by inspiring them, by being tough and demanding and caring at the same time. Tough love? It works.

4

FLEXIBLE THINKING AND
THE POWER OF PLAN B

THREE YEARS AGO, A balky back almost derailed our chance for a second national championship. The back in question belonged to our All-American center, Emeka Okafor. Meka was the most important guy on the team, a tremendous rebounder and shot-blocker, and a big guy who could really run the floor. He suffered periodic back spasms during the 2003–2004 season, which kept him out of several games. The back problem flared up again in the Big East tournament, only days before the start of the all-important NCAA tourney. I was worried.

Meka didn't play the quarterfinals and semifinals of the 2004 Big East tournament, but fortunately he felt well enough to play in the Big East title game against Pittsburgh, which we won. And he stayed healthy throughout the NCAA tournament, enabling us to win all six of our games and, as a result, the national championship. Had Meka's back acted up during the title run, there's no way we'd have cut down the nets in San Antonio.

I sometimes joke that my UConn players are running up and down the court every year with my paycheck in their mouths. What I mean is, no matter how hard my staff and I work and plan, we are sometimes rattled by developments beyond our control. We were lucky that Meka's back held up in our last six games in 2004.

But luck runs both ways in sports and life. Two years ago, before the season started, our highly touted freshman guard, A. J. Price, suffered a brain aneurysm that almost killed him. We were expecting Price to play a significant role on the team that year; he was one of the top guard prospects in the country. Instead, he didn't play at all, and we had to improvise, using a one-guard lineup throughout the season rather than the two-guard lineup we've always played. That was a problem, and so was the fact that we were a young team in 2004–2005, with relatively inexperienced big men. Though we lost in the second round of the NCAA tourney, we still finished the year with a record of 23-8 and a number-seventeen national ranking. Not bad, but a little bit of a disappointment by our standards.

All leaders set goals and then formulate plans for reaching those goals. I've been around a lot of businesspeople, and I know they're always focused on *growing* their numbers—sales, earnings, return on investment, share price. Miss the numbers, and investors and stock market analysts growl. I try to grow our numbers, too. I want our team shooting percentage to go up over the course of a season, along with our assists and steals totals—and, of course, our number of wins. If they don't, some fans grumble.

I've learned over my career that all organizational leaders must be flexible thinkers. The reason is simple: No matter what the business, bad breaks are bound to happen. That's my *polite* way of saying it. Just when you think you've got it all figured out, when your organization seems to be breezing along, life jumps up and knocks you on your ass. That's true no matter if you're the CEO of a Fortune 500 company or the owner of a local coffee shop. Unforeseen circumstances turn your assumptions, your projections, and sometimes your life and career upside down. And then what do you do?

A few months back, I was reading a story about Tyson Foods, one of the world's biggest sellers of beef and chicken. The company was cruising along, and then almost out of the blue, two new and dangerous diseases popped up in the world. One of them was mad cow disease, and the other was avian influenza, better known as bird flu. Neither has proved a serious threat to consumers, but they are scary diseases, and the fear factor for both has dampened demand for meat and chicken in key markets outside the United States, denting Tyson's sales and share price.

The Tyson CEO had to do something. To cut costs, he closed less efficient processing plants. He decided to put more marketing emphasis on products such as pork, which wasn't susceptible to consumer health jitters. And he ordered up a global consumer education program, showing that for all the worry about bird flu, it so far poses very little risk to the health of chicken eaters. The CEO, recognizing potential threats to his company and its goals, had to alter his plans. He had to become more proactive in his thinking.

I realized, reading the Tyson story, that I had more in common with the head of a big company than I had imagined. Sports coaches don't deal with nearly as many variables as business leaders, and thankfully so. But our jobs are a bit more complicated and strategic than they might appear from the outside.

Essentially, I have to find very good basketball players and, with the help of my assistants, push them to improve individually and to play cohesively as a team. If I've been successful at doing those things, I can, in theory, sit back and watch them win basketball games. Mission accomplished!

Sounds simple, but the reality is far different. Even if I've got good players, no season ever goes by smoothly. There are *always* complications—injuries, illness, an occasional player suspension, an especially tough stretch on the schedule. As I said, things happen, and my staff and I have to be ready for them.

Get Ready to Adapt

BASKETBALL TEAMS, LIKE MOST organizations, are always in flux. That means we are never far from Plan B—or Plans C or D, for that matter. Rarely does a week go by when we are not tinkering with our lineup. We've got to improvise, think through problems, adapt.

That's especially true in games. Over the course of a forty-minute basketball game, I will make scores of decisions about personnel and plays and tactical schemes, all oriented toward gaining some advantage over the team we are playing.

In 2006, for example, we played two exciting and important games against Villanova, one of our biggest rivals in the Big East conference. (Syracuse and Pittsburgh are two others.) Villanova had a small but very athletic and aggressive team that year. Jay Wright, the Wildcat coach, started three guards—all of them talented—and often played four guards at the same time. It was unusual, but Villanova's guards were the strength of the team, and Wright was smart to use them. Two of them, Randy Foye and Allan Ray, were First Team All Big East players. The third, Kyle Lowry, was a very good all-around player—quick, feisty, and he could score. The fourth member of the guard quartet, Mike Nardi, was a streaky shooter.

They all made Villanova a formidable opponent—a tough matchup for anybody. The Wildcats came very close to beating eventual national champion North Carolina in the regional final in 2005. Were it not for a questionable traveling call, they might well have won that game.

So it was not surprising that our two games with Villanova in 2006 were brawls. Both teams were ranked in the top five nationally when the games were played. Villanova beat us in Philadelphia— when we were ranked number one in the country and they were ranked number four—and we returned the favor a couple of weeks later in Storrs. Before playing the Wildcats, I had to decide whether we were better off playing a bigger or smaller lineup against them. That year, we started almost every game with two big men—power forward Josh Boone and center Hilton Armstrong. They were good rebounders and shot-blockers. (We've led the country in shot-blocking for five straight years.)

But we were also capable of playing well with a smaller lineup. In games, I would typically pull one of my "bigs" after a few minutes of combat and substitute a wing—usually Denham Brown or Rashad Anderson. Doing that gave us more scoring, more athleticism, and the potential to play more of an up-tempo style.

Rashad and Denham were almost clones. They were about the same size—six feet five inches, and six feet six inches tall—and had similar games. Rashad was a great three-point shooter and scorer, the leading nonstarting scorer in the country, averaging fourteen points a game. Denham was a little better at handling the basketball and could penetrate inside, but he didn't score as much as Rashad. Both of them gave me the luxury of being flexible with my lineups—and because Rashad and Denham were both seniors, they were also good leaders.

Against Villanova, I essentially had to decide whether our bigger players were an asset or a liability against a team with superior quickness. My assistant Tom Moore called us the "anti-Villanova," because of our size. Our bigger lineup gave us a rebounding and defensive advantage inside. But Villanova's three guards "played big," as we coaches sometimes say. They were good rebounders for their size—and they could run circles around guys who were tall but slow. Normally, I almost always play to our strengths and never allow an opponent's style to dictate what we do. But at the same time, it's pretty rare to face a good, three- or four-guard lineup. In the end, I opted to start both games with my regular lineup, meaning two big men, Armstrong and Boone, but I also switched fairly quickly to a smaller lineup in each game, the better to counteract Villanova's strength. And as it happened, Rashad and Denham ended up playing more than my bigs in both games because they were more effective.

The first game was pretty tight throughout. We played well, led in the second half, won the rebounding battle—but Ray got very hot from the outside for Villanova, and the Wildcats rallied in the second half to win 69–64—knocking us out of the top spot in the national rankings. Ray finished with twenty-five points. For us, Rudy Gay had nineteen points, and Anderson and Marcus Williams, our point guards, had twelve points each. The difference, essentially, was that they made nine three-pointers in the game and we made four.

In that game, I ended up giving my backup point guard, Craig Austrie, more playing time—eighteen minutes—than Boone—seventeen minutes. Craig, along with Denham and Rashad, was a key part of Plan B. Craig is a good defender, and while he's not a big scorer, he's steady and makes few mistakes. He had five assists in the game and played well. Most important, along with Denham and Rashad, he gave us added quickness on the court against a quick opponent. I learned as each game unfolded that our B lineup gave us the best chance of beating Villanova.

In the second game, at Connecticut, we were ranked third in the nation and Villanova was ranked second. In that game, I played Denham and Rashad even more than I had in the first game, and Denham essentially made the difference. He was Plan B. He played twenty-nine minutes—the most playing time he would get all year—and scored twenty-three points on eight of thirteen shooting. It was his high point total for the season. Rashad also played well, scoring seventeen points in twenty-four minutes. I again played Craig more than usual, and Josh Boone less than usual. Again, I could see early on that our smaller lineup matched up well with Villanova—a little better than I expected, actually. Craig enabled us to pressure the ball more on defense, which we needed; we got more scoring out of Denham and Rashad, and our rebounding didn't really suffer. Plan B worked.

Basketball is not rocket science. The outcome of most games is determined by which team shoots the basketball better, though there are many factors that affect a team's shooting rate—ball movement and shot selection, to name two. My job as a coach is to quickly figure out which players are feeling strong and confident in a specific game—who seems in a defensive and/or offensive groove—and give those players as much playing time as possible. In the first Villanova game, we shot 46 percent from the field and lost. Normally, a 46 percent team shooting percentage is plenty good enough to win a game. But Villanova made too many three-point shots that day. In the second game we shot even better—55 percent—and won. That's an outstanding number. Denham and Rashad both came into that game and shot well from the get-go, so it was an easy decision to let them play for long stretches of time. Stick with the hot hands: It's a cardinal rule in basketball.

IN SPORTS, IN EVERY game, there are always injuries and other vagaries to deal with. Maybe our center gets into early foul trouble. Maybe our point guard twists his ankle. Maybe the officials are calling the game too tightly, with too many fouls, or not tightly enough, with few fouls. How do we respond?

Basketball is, to some extent, a game of trial and error. Coaches make *many* tactical and personnel moves during games—scores of them. Many of them may seem arbitrary, but they're not. Most are based on research we've done on our opponent prior to the game—and yet we're never sure if the decision is smart or not until we see it played out on the court.

We might decide to play a lot of full-court press against, say, Georgetown, because their guards haven't shown themselves in previous games to be good ball-handlers. If Georgetown loses the ball twenty times because of our pressure defense, my staff and I look like geniuses. If, on the other hand, Georgetown has spent a lot of its recent practice time on ball handling and breaking defensive pressure, and as a result easily beats our press and scores a bunch of easy baskets in the game, then we coaches look like dunderheads. If we think that a streak shooter like Rashad Anderson can take advantage of weak perimeter defense by one of our opponents, and then Rashad goes into the game and clanks his first four or five shots, we don't look so brilliant.

In the course of a game, I will almost certainly make a few decisions that don't work. That's a given. What's important is that I recognize when specific moves aren't working and then rectify them as quickly as possible, before they prove costly. In that sense flexible thinking can be more important than strategic thinking.

For example, there were a few games last year when I wanted to give freshman guard Doug Wiggins some additional playing time. Doug, who grew up in Hartford, close to Storrs, was not a starter last year but he is a dynamic athlete. And like all freshmen, he needed game minutes to speed his development. He wasn't getting much playing time early in the season, but midway through the year, when it became clear that our other young guards were struggling, I decided to play Doug more. My hope was that he could help jump-start our offense, which was like a weak battery most of the season. But Doug didn't really help us as I'd hoped. Like UConn's other freshmen, he was erratic, and the extra minutes didn't really help his game. He shot poorly, and the offense continued to flounder. So I was forced to rethink that idea, reduce his minutes, and essentially go back to square one.

One idea that we tried did work. Last year the other coaches and I were eager for A.J. Price to take over the point guard position, after the departure of Marcus Williams. In 2004, A.J. was our most celebrated recruit. Everybody on the coaching staff agreed that he had immense collegiate potential. At six feet two inches tall, he was quick and had an excellent "handle"—meaning he was a good ball-handler. A.J. could also pass well, break down a defense with flash or precision, and score.

The problem was, A.J. hadn't played in two years due to medical and then legal issues. That's a long layoff. Even so, neither my assistants nor I thought that A.J. would show much rust. He'd been working out a lot, had played in a summer league before the 2006–2007 season began, and everybody on the UConn staff believed in his talent.

We still do, but it became clear halfway through the season that our thinking was wishful. A.J. was struggling with his game, and struggling to run the team. He wasn't playing badly, just not particularly well. He played fairly well to start the season, against some less than stellar competition, but once we got into the meat of our schedule, A.J.'s performance fell off. So did practically everyone else's. His shooting percentage and assist totals tumbled. An offense revolves around the point-guard position, and, quite simply, our offense through the first half of our Big East conference schedule was ugly. As our associate head coach Tom Moore told Mike Anthony of the *Hartford Courant* newspaper, "A.J. was a highly publicized recruit, and we're a high-profile program. The fact that everybody had to wait two years just led to a lot of talk about his potential and his ability. We as a staff were probably a little unrealistic in our expectations early on. And I think he was also. It's taken a little longer [for him to develop] physically than we thought."

A.J.'s difficulties were partly due to the fact that, offensively, almost everybody on the team was young and erratic. Our center, Hasheem Thabeet, who grew up in Tanzania, didn't start playing basketball until he was sixteen. To say he was a work in progress would be an understatement. I don't care how good a point guard you are, if you're passing the ball to inexperienced freshmen at the wing and center positions, the results aren't going to be pretty. And that's the situation we faced. A. J. certainly would have benefited from playing with some proven scorers.

Still, about halfway through the 2006–2007 season, my staff and I decided to make a change at the point guard spot. We started playing Craig Austrie more at the position, and we moved A.J. to the number-two guard position—what we call the off-guard, or scoring guard. After a frustrating stretch during which we lost four straight Big East games, the move seemed to settle the team. Craig doesn't have as much raw talent as some guards, and so is a guy whose skills can sometimes get overlooked. He filled in admirably for Marcus Williams the previous year, starting the first month of the season when Marcus was serving a suspension, and played well. Craig is a solid defender and a guy who can manage a team. He makes very few mistakes, and that is key. Every coach wants to have a great point guard. But at the very least, you'd better have a guy who's not going to cost you games by making a lot of mistakes. Craig settled the offense, A.J. seemed to flourish in his new role, and we played better as a team, winning two straight. It was nothing to shout about, but it was encouraging. Going into the year, I never thought that A.J. wouldn't be our best point guard, but the coaching staff knew we had to stay flexible in our thinking, and it paid off for us.

Meetings of the Minds

ASK MY ASSISTANTS TO name one surprising thing about me as a coach, and they're all apt to say this: *I like meetings.*

When the topic is basketball, I'm a talker. I can chew hoops fat for hours, and often do so with my staff. I don't simply want to talk. I *need* to. It's a key part of my management style and my decision-making process.

We have a lot of meetings in the "bunker"—the Connecticut coaches' meeting room—and they can sometimes run for hours. Back in the mid-1990s, we lost an away game to Providence. We played so poorly that I called a coaches' meeting as soon as we got back to campus from Rhode Island. It was about one in the morning.

I could have waited until the next day to hash out our performance and how it could be improved, but I didn't want to wait. Perhaps that's a window on how intense I can be. We sent the kids back to their dorm rooms and bed, and we coaches gathered for a talk. The session went on until nearly dawn. I wanted some immediate feedback on the game and our personnel, and I obviously felt a sense of urgency about it. The game was fresh in our minds, I figured. What better time for a review?

Not surprisingly, when Tom Moore, George Blaney, Andre LaFleur, Patrick Sellers, and I meet, we mostly talk about our players: Who's playing well? Who's not? If somebody is not playing well, what's going on and how can we fix his game? Who should be playing more, or less? We also talk about our opponents, about Big East games we've seen on TV, about various teams and talent around the country. We talk about schemes. Should we use some full-court press against Louisville? Should we try to pound the ball inside more on offense against Seton Hall?

We spend a lot of time mulling personnel decisions. In the middle of last year, our point guard, Marcus Williams, had a stretch of four or five games when his productivity fell off. He was lackluster. His defense wasn't good, he wasn't making good decisions with the basketball. It was unusual, because Marcus was arguably our steadiest and most important player. It's one thing when, say, the fifth best player on your team goes through a bad patch. But when one of your best players is struggling and seems a bit mentally out of focus, you don't want to wait around and hope he snaps out of it. It's time to be proactive.

As a staff, we had a pretty good sense of what was going on. Because of his suspension, Marcus wasn't allowed to practice with the team or use our facilities for six months. He rejoined the team in December, but physically he wasn't a hundred percent. He wasn't fit, and as a result his game had lost some sharpness. It's the same problem that affected A.J. last year. When you haven't played for a long time, it takes weeks to get back to a peak performance level. I'm sure piano players or golfers would say the same thing. You can go out to the practice range and hit balls, but that's no substitute for actually playing in a PGA tour event.

Marcus is a very talented player. In my opinion, he was the best passer in college basketball last year. A native of Los Angeles, Marcus was one of the funniest guys on the team. Off the court, when the players were hanging out, he was a cutup and a joker. But on the court, his personality was more subdued. He was sort of L.A. cool, laid-back. Marcus could be hard on his teammates at times, when they made mistakes. We tried, with limited success, to enhance his leadership abilities.

In any case, the coaching staff noodled ways that we might get Marcus going again. We decided to take a contrarian approach. We had two freshman guards in 2005–2006—Rob Garrison and Craig Austrie. Craig had started the first eleven games of the season, while Marcus was serving out his suspension, and of course Rob was eager to play. Though we knew that Marcus needed as much playing time as he could stand, we decided to play him a bit less, not more, and give Craig and Rob a few more minutes of game action. Both had been practicing fairly well.

It was a minor personnel adjustment, but it seemed to do the trick: Marcus snapped out of the doldrums, perhaps fearing that he wasn't as valuable to the team as he'd thought. He was, but fear can be a great motivator, and Marcus's game suddenly seemed to snap into focus. He started making smart passes again—he averaged about eight assists a game—and he started scoring more. He played very well in the latter part of the season, and showed a knack for taking over games down the stretch. He played a tremendous game against Notre Dame—tying the game with a basket late in regulation that enabled us to go on and win it in overtime. In that game, he registered season highs in points (eighteen), assists (thirteen) and rebounds (ten). Those are crazy-good numbers for a point guard. And he was our best player in the NCAA tournament. When we needed somebody to step up and take charge in the second half, he was the guy.

Another example of flexible thinking: In 2006 we decided, over the course of the season, to give more playing time to a burly freshman named Jeff Adrien. Why? Though not especially tall at six feet six inches, Adrien weighs about two hundred and thirty pounds and has long arms. He plays strong near the basket. He plays bigger than his height, and he gave us something we lacked at times last year—

some heft and muscle inside. Our two starting bigs, Hilton Armstrong and Josh Boone, were fine, but their play tailed off some as the season progressed. Hilton was turning heads with his play early in the year—blocking shots, running the floor, showing some offensive moves and a scoring touch around the basket that would later help to ensure his place in the first round of the NBA draft. But neither Hilton nor Josh was really a space eater; they relied more on their mobility rather than their muscle.

Mobility is a good thing. But most basketball coaches will tell you, it's good to have a "widebody" inside. Jeff is physical, and so we increased his playing time as the season moved along. That was a smart decision: He's not just a muscular player, he's got good hands and can move, and he helped us in some key spots last year. His best game was our last one, against George Mason, when he gave us a huge lift off the bench, scoring seventeen points and grabbing seven rebounds. (We lost that game, ironically, because George Mason had a space eater inside—a 275-pound bruiser named Jai Lewis—and we had a hard time controlling him.)

Because we got Jeff on the court a lot in 2005–2006, he had some valuable seasoning coming into last year, when he started and was our most dependable player. In fact, he and Craig were the *only* two guys on the team with any real experience. Had we not exposed Jeff to the rigors of Big East competition—getting him accustomed to the pressure of big games, hostile crowds, and banging against quality power forwards in our conference—what was a tough transitional year for us would have been even more frustrating.

My point is simply this: If you think an individual or employee has potential, you are better off giving him *some* responsibilities early on, rather than waiting around for him to polish his skills before pushing him into the arena. That could take time. Give him some quality work, see how he performs, and go from there. If he produces, you give him more responsibility. If not, you back him down a notch. You don't want to give a new kid too much, too soon—say, the task of

making a major client presentation. You might end up watching in
horror as it all goes horribly wrong and the client storms out of the
building. Then you're left trying to save your new employee's confidence level, and perhaps even your own job.

THE NICE THING ABOUT sports is that we can analyze our performances thanks to videotape. We can break down a player's performance if we want to, play-by-play over the course of a game or a
season. And we can do the same with the entire team. In the same
way, we can analyze how our opponents perform—we study tapes of
their games. Corporate or public organizational managers can't do
that.

In fact, we scout every team we play. My assistant George Blaney
was a longtime head coach himself (three years at Dartmouth, twenty-
two at his alma mater, Holy Cross, and three at Seton Hall) who won
almost 500 games. He has seen a lot of basketball in his career. He
spends several hours each week during the season reviewing tapes of
our opponents. Before every game, he writes up an analysis of our opponent, including the team's collective strengths and weaknesses,
along with assessments of its individual players, all supported by sta-
tistics. If, say, Georgetown likes to press their opponents after making a basket, we'll know about that tendency. If West Virginia likes to
"run" with the basketball—meaning fast break—after their opponent
misses, we'll know about it. If the St. John's point guard prefers to
drive to his right, if their small forward is a weak three-point shooter,
if their center likes to pivot and drive along the baseline after getting
the basketball, we'll know. We'll be familiar with all those tendencies
ahead of time, and use them when formulating our game plans. (And,
let's not forget, our opponent will be scouting us in the same way.)

We show taped clips of every one of our opponents to the players
in meetings a day or two before the game. If we're playing Syracuse,
for example, we might show our team a clip of the 2-3 zone defense
that Syracuse coach Jim Boeheim has played almost exclusively for

decades. Our guys can get a sense of what each Syracuse player's defensive responsibility is in the zone defense, and we, the coaches, can point out the best ways to attack it. We'll then go out on the practice court and try to practice what we preached in the meeting.

Last year Pittsburgh had a very good, seven-foot center named Aaron Gray. He wasn't just tall, but big, too, and he moved reasonably well for a guy his size. For a widebody, he had good hands and a decent shooting touch. In 2006 and 2007, he was the only player in the Big East to average a "double double"—meaning he averaged double figures in scoring and rebounding. When Gray got the ball inside, he would often make a strong move toward the baseline and then go up forcefully for his shot. Before our first 2006 game against Pittsburgh, in Storrs, we showed our team a tape of Gray in action, on offense, and decided that our "bigs," Josh Boone and Hilton Armstrong, would have to double-team Gray occasionally after he got the ball.

Later that day, we had Boone and Armstrong, and the rest of our centers and forwards, practice our anti-Gray "double down" defense. It featured our center and a forward quickly double-teaming an opposing center when he gets the ball near the basket, with a wing rotating over to fill the space vacated by the forward. During the actual game, we doubled Gray quite a lot. Despite our efforts, he still had a pretty good game, but we beat Pittsburgh in Storrs in what was a typically close, grueling conference game. We won by two points.

So good planning always helps. But in basketball, as in most sports, games often don't go according to plan. Quite frankly, they almost never do. Basketball games are unpredictable in the extreme—which, incidentally, is one reason why I love the game. Sometimes your best players have poor nights and decent players have great nights. (In the 2005–2006 season, we lost to Marquette when Steve Novak scored forty-one points against us.)

The way a game is officiated will strongly influence the way a game unfolds, and will alter my decision-making during a game. If the officials are calling lots of fouls, then I've got to play my bench more, sending in substitutes early in the game, so that my best players are still on the court at the end of the game—when the outcome is decided. That's why some coaches bench any starter who picks up two fouls in the first half; they don't want the player getting three fouls early, which could then limit his playing time and effectiveness in the more important second half. Fortunately, we had a very deep team last year. We may not have been the most talented team in the country, but we were probably the deepest, and our depth helped us win quite a few games that might otherwise have been lost.

Working the Officials

I'M PRETTY WELL KNOWN for bellowing at officials. All coaches yell at the officials—a lot. It's part of the game. I probably yell more than most coaches, and sometimes I'm a bit more sarcastic. Typically, we yell when we think an official has missed a call, and we think that happens about once every fifteen seconds We question *every* foul call against one of our players, certain that the official has temporarily lost his vision. And we flip our lids if officials fail to call lots of fouls on the other guys. If one of my guys misses a shot or loses the ball, surely it's not his fault. He *must* have been hacked, held, or pushed by a player on the other side—wink.

Sometimes, we genuinely believe an official has erred. But we also chatter with officials in the hope of influencing their calls later in the game. It's called "working the officials" and it's one of the rituals of coaching. Officials are honest, impartial, and hard to influence, but that doesn't stop me and every other coach in America from trying. We carp because we want the next close call to go in our favor, especially during key points in a game. In fact, every coach *has* to work the officials if only to keep the other guy from gaining an advantage. If I sat politely during a game against, say, Louisville and let Rick Pinto work the officials, it's very likely that

Louisville would get more favorable calls and more foul shots than we would. The officials wouldn't intentionally favor Louisville, but it would probably work out that way. Why do companies spend millions of dollars to advertise their products, or hire lobbyists in Washington to promote their interests? Because behavior can be influenced.

Most of the officials in college basketball are veterans. They've been around for years, and I've gotten to know some of them very well. Officiating is not a job I would want, but some college officials make upwards of $150,000 annually, working three or four games a week for five months. That's good money, but it's not an easy job or an easy life!

Anyway, over time I've come to learn just how far I can verbally parry with certain officials before getting them truly mad. Still, I sometimes cross the line. Once, a few years ago, when we were playing St. John's, I was getting genuinely irritated at the officials. We were up by six points with about three and a half minutes to go in the game, but the guards on the other team were holding my players a lot—what we call "hand-checking." I didn't like it, and finally I'd seen enough. I stood up and asked a veteran official named Mickey Crowley a question. "Mickey," I said, "have you ever given me a technical foul for something I've been *thinking?*" He looked at me like I was crazy, and replied, "Of course not, Jim." And then I said, "Well, that's good to know, Mickey, because I'm *thinking* right now that you're calling an absolutely horrible game." Mickey just looked at me and started laughing—a great official and a great guy!

RECRUITING IS REALLY THE lifeblood of any college sports program. You've got to get good players if you hope to compete with the best teams in the country. Good coaching is always vital, but you can't win titles if you don't have the horses. Last year a well-coached Albany team gave us all we could handle for thirty minutes in the first round of the NCAA tournament. But games are forty minutes long, and after struggling for most of the game, our superior talent began to assert itself in the last ten minutes of the game, and we won going away.

Some teams are more talented than their record might indicate, as we found out in the regional title game last year. Lots of college basketball pundits, who don't see enough games to really get a feel for how good some of the smaller schools in America are, complained when George Mason was picked to play in the NCAA tournament. Some felt Mason's record wasn't good enough, and in fact they did lose a few games to some less than stellar opponents. But in the tournament, the Patriots proved that they could play with the big boys.

Did they ever. They beat, in succession, three of the best basketball programs in the country—Michigan State, North Carolina, and then us, all national title winners in recent years. The Patriots were helped by one thing that prominent programs don't see much any more—seniors. Three of George Mason's top four players were seniors, including their starting guards and their center, Jai Lewis, who was big and athletic enough to sign a free-agent contract with an NFL *football* team after the season.

While I don't want to make excuses, three of my best six players in 2006—Marcus Williams, Josh Boone, and Rudy Gay—were underclassman. Marcus and Josh were juniors, and Gay was a sophomore. All left the program after the 2005–2006 season with a year or two of college eligibility left. Rudy was the eighth college player picked in the 2006 NBA draft; Hilton Armstrong, a senior center, was the twelfth pick; Boone was drafted twenty-first, and Marcus, twenty-second. We had four players taken in the first round, tying a record, and five players drafted overall. Days before the NBA draft, Hilton called a friend's dad and said, "I think I'm going to be a millionaire!" He was right.

Three years ago we signed one of the best high school centers in the country, Andrew Bynam. He's seven feet tall, 280 pounds, a smart kid, and he has skills. We were very excited about getting him, and then, out of nowhere, he told me that he wasn't coming to UConn after all; he and his family had decided to jump straight to the NBA. I was shocked—he was the centerpiece, literally and figuratively, of our recruiting class that year—and I didn't agree with his decision. I told him so. With very rare exceptions, high school players who turn pro simply aren't ready for the NBA. They're not strong enough, usually, to compete with older players, and not fit enough mentally to cope with a grueling, eighty-two-game pro schedule and all the travel that goes with it. (And they may not be mature enough to manage their money.)

Even those with loads of potential need a few years to get stronger and learn the pro game. Kobe Bryant and Jermaine O'Neal were two of the best high school players ever to leap to the NBA. But even they took years to develop into good pros. I saw Bryant play during his first couple of years with the L.A. Lakers, and he was raw and unpolished, to say the least. He had phenomenal athleticism, sure, but he tried to do too much. He ran around without much rhyme or reason, and took a lot of crazy shots, few of which went in. The best high school players who opt for the pros will get playing time and take their lumps. But some simply sit on the bench for two or three years—years that might have been better spent in college. By the time a high school draft pick has matured, he's often playing for his second NBA team. That generally means that his original team wasted a high draft pick and a lot of money.

Michael Jordan, when he was the president of the Washington Wizards, picked a high school player named Kwame Brown with the first pick in the 2001 NBA draft. Brown, who is six feet eleven inches and mobile, was the first high school player ever taken with the first pick in the pro draft. But he turned out to be a wasted pick—for the Wizards, anyway—and no team can afford to waste a first-round draft pick, much less the number-one pick in the draft. The number-one pick in the draft should be able to come in and help a team significantly, and right away.

That's not what happened with Brown. He only played fourteen minutes a game as a rookie, and not very well. After six years in the NBA, he's improved, but he's never going to be a great player, worthy of a number-one pick, and he's no longer with the Wizards. After a few lackluster seasons, the Wizards pretty much gave up on Brown and traded him to L.A, where he averaged eight points and six rebounds a game in 2006. A draft should be about getting good value, and an unpolished gem is just that—unpolished. Not a good value. But there was nothing I could do to change Bynam's mind when he opted to try for the NBA.

The NBA has a new rule that players must be nineteen years old to qualify for the pro draft. That means that most kids with professional aspirations will have to go to college for at least one year, or perhaps to a pro development league. Raising the minimum age for the pro draft is a step in the right direction. Had the new rule not been enacted, Greg Oden and Kevin Durant would almost certainly not gone to college. But they each did, for a year. Oden, a muscular center who's got the body of a thirty-year-old, went to Ohio State.

Meanwhile, Durant, a six foot eleven inch forward with phenomenal talent, spent a year at Texas. Both Oden and Durant no doubt benefited from a year of college, where I'm sure they learned some discipline and got to study a bit before starting their pro careers. But I would like the NBA minimum age to be raised again, to twenty. That would give kids a couple of years, at least, to go to college, where they can get some education, improve their basketball skills, and mature physically and emotionally. That could help the players immensely down the road, when they've got to make smart decisions about their careers and their money.

Some people differ, and argue that no one has the right to restrict the freedom of an individual to earn a living. That may be a valid argument, but given the lucrative nature of NBA contracts, the most talented kids will have plenty of time to make plenty of money. College, on the other hand, is an incredibly unique, one-of-a-kind *social experience*. I've been around college kids for thirty-five years, and I can count on one hand the number who didn't value or enjoy the university life-style, including classes. You can join a pro team, make millions, and then go to college, at, say, age twenty-five. Some guys do return to college to get their degrees after turning pro. Hilton Armstrong and Taliek Brown, who was the point guard of our 2004 title team, returned to campus this summer to complete their degree work. It's something we encourage. I want all Huskie players to get their sheepskin at some point in time. Young guys can make a lot of money playing professionally, and I'm all for it, but there is no substitute for a college education.

Top programs such as ours, along with North Carolina, Duke, Michigan State, and a few others, tend to recruit the best high school talent every year. But there are a lot of good high school players out there, and a lot of them end up in smaller conferences like the Mid-American, which includes Bradley, Xavier, and Southern Illinois. I know, having coached at a smaller college for fourteen years. The smaller schools don't get as much publicity or TV broadcast time as the big conferences, and they typically don't get Top 100 high school prospects. But they do get good players, and they generally benefit by keeping their talent for four years, while high-profile schools lose their best players prematurely.

What this means nowadays is that I seldom have a truly experienced team on the floor. My 2005–2006 UConn team was more veteran than most—we had three seniors who played regularly. But we were less experienced, I think, than George Mason. Last year, we could have had a veteran, powerhouse team, had all three of my underclassmen chosen to stay. But they didn't, and instead we were extremely young and inexperienced. And lots of other teams were, too. I'm not complaining—too much. The system is what it is, but so many players leave early for the NBA now that it makes coaching somewhat more difficult. We've got to recruit more players every year now than we used to, because of the early departures for the NBA, and the teaching burden is a little heavier, because we've got more new faces and fewer veterans.

The lure of the NBA is a tough issue affecting all of the major basketball programs in America. It's also an ironic issue: Because Connecticut has sent a lot of players to the NBA, young players with NBA potential increasingly want to play for us. That in theory is a good thing, but because NBA-caliber prospects seldom play for more than two or maybe three years, it's actually hard for us to benefit from the great talent we're bringing in. There is little continuity. By the time a player like Rudy Gay begins to understand the college game, begins to broaden his skill set, he's gone, and then it's back to square one for us. Look at Ohio State and Texas last year. They each had a superstar freshman—Greg Oden at OSU and Kevin Durant at Texas—who was probably capable, over time, of leading those schools to national titles. But they each played a single year and then left for the NBA. And understandably so. They were the first two players taken in the draft. I can't blame them.

I want to think that bringing in great high school players boosts our chances of winning a national title. But you've really got to be lucky. Either your best players have to decide to stay a year or two longer than anticipated, or you've got to have some solid veterans on your teams in those years that you've got some genuine NBA prospects. We could have had an awesome team last year, had Rudy Gay and Marcus Williams and Josh Boone opted to stay one more year at UConn. But they didn't. Two years ago, we did have a nice mix of youth and experience, but we weren't as good as the pundits hyped us to be, and we let distractions get the best of us.

Florida surprised a lot of people and won the 2006 national title, and they did so with a group of good, experienced players. They didn't have any superstars, really, and that worked in coach Billy Donovan's favor, I think. What the Gators did have was a solid, almost proto-typical player at every position—a good ball handler at point guard, a long-armed and athletic defensive winger, a three-point sniper at the shooting guard position, an excellent power forward in Yoakim Noah, who was tall, mobile, and a good passer and rebounder, and finally a bruiser inside. And they played well together. Amazingly, the entire Florida team returned last year and the won the NCAA title again.

Going Against the Grain

WHEN I FIRST GOT to UConn, in 1985, I didn't have the luxury of recruiting the best high school prospects. The Big East, at that time, was full of star coaches and players, but not many of them belonged to the Huskies. We were something of a dim light in a starry league. Top high school recruits were not interested in Connecticut, for the most part because the team hadn't been winning. The greatest salesman in the world was not going to persuade a five-star prospect to turn down scholarship offers from Kentucky or UNC and come to Storrs instead.

That meant that Recruiting Plan A—go out and get the best prospects in the nation—was a nonstarter. I had no choice but to move to Plan B. But we didn't *have* a Plan B! We needed a creative strategy that could attract good, if not great, players to the University of Connecticut, despite our also-ran status.

And we came up with one, which raises a management point I want to make: *Don't be afraid to go against the grain.* Being contrarian can be a very effective operating strategy.

We knew we couldn't appeal to the star high school players in the Northeast. We simply didn't have enough cachet in the mid-1980s to recruit regionally against established programs like Georgetown, Villanova, and St. John's, not to mention some of the powerhouse ACC schools. It was a fool's game. I didn't want to waste a lot of energy chasing blue-chip prospects who simply weren't going to sign with UConn.

So we adopted a contrarian approach. We decided that rather than trying to recruit just in the Northeast, we'd cast a wider net. We opted to pursue a national strategy. It sounds crazy in retrospect: Generally, only the country's top programs have enough sizzle to pull in recruits from distant states. But that's what we set out to do. We decided to pursue not great players from all over the country, but good ones, and we looked especially hard at kids who lived *outside* the Northeast.

And here's the kicker: We felt our Big East rivals could actually help our recruiting effort, with the proper marketing spin. College recruiters often try to raise doubts in the minds of prospects about their conference rivals. The coach at Southern Cal might say to a star high school guard: "You'd better think twice about going to UCLA, because they signed three really good guards last year. If you sign with the Bruins, you might not play." We didn't try to dissuade any of our prospects from attending Georgetown or Syracuse because we generally chased kids who were not being recruited by Big East schools.

What we did, instead, is go around the South, the Midwest, and the West, and *talked up* Big East Conference basketball as opposed to Connecticut basketball. We tried to sell kids not on playing for us, but rather on playing in a high-profile conference that had lots of great players and coaches.

It was a coattail strategy and it worked. The Big East, at that time, was arguably the best league in the country, and anybody with an interest in college basketball knew it. The conference commissioner at the time, Dave Gavitt, had just secured a new TV contract for the league with ESPN. So we started selling kids on the opportunity to play against top-flight competition under the bright lights of Madison Square Garden in New York City, as well as in Philadelphia, Boston, and Washington, D.C. And what of our home in Storrs, Connecticut? "We're only twenty-two miles from Hartford," we used to tell prospects. "It's only a fifteen-minute drive from the capital— you can practically smell the fumes!"

Kids from outside the Northeast were intrigued by the idea of playing in the Big East conference, where they could match their skills against the nation's best in major metropolitan markets. They'd be seen on national TV. They wouldn't be playing for the top programs, but against them. For kids with some talent and moxie, the idea had allure.

And so we landed some good players from Texas, Florida, Georgia, even far-off California. Kevin Ollie, who was an exceptional guard for us in the early 1990s, was from Los Angeles. He started ninety-four games, led the team in assists for three years, and was a member of the first UConn team to be ranked number one. His last two years, we were 57-10. We got Kevin partly by telling his family they could watch our games on ESPN in L.A. right after work, starting at 5:30 P.M. They liked that idea. Kevin had a charity golf tournament last year, and I was happy to take part in it. Brian Fair, another guard who played for us from 1991 to 1995 and who helped us win two Big East championships, came from Phoenix, Arizona.

Ray Allen was something of an exception to our backdoor strategy. Ray, who was from South Carolina, *was* being recruited by some top programs, including Kentucky. All the schools in the South were after him. He made an official visit to the University of Alabama, but complained afterward that all anybody talked about in the state was football. And when he attended the first Midnight Madness practice at Kentucky—most college teams now have a tradition of holding their first workout for students and fans at midnight—he thought all the hullabaloo was pretentious. UConn, in those days, was not too serious about football. "We only talk about basketball around here," I told Ray, but we certainly weren't good enough to be pretentious. He liked that.

I'll never forget when Ray first visited UConn. He was dressed entirely in yellow—yellow pants, yellow shirt, probably yellow socks. He looked like a canary—very dapper—and was a very well-mannered young man. And after he signed with us, we learned pretty quickly that his play was as sharp as his clothes. He could really shoot the basketball, and he has gone on to have a tremendous NBA career with Seattle and now Boston. His mother moved to Connecticut to stay close to Ray while he was at UConn, which really impressed me.

We even ventured to other countries for talent. It's pretty common now for teams to recruit players born in other countries, but we were ahead of the curve. We recruited two terrific players from Israel. The first one essentially fell into my lap. An old New York City basketball guy named Marv Kessler called me out of the blue one day in 1989 and asked me, "Would you be interested in the Larry Bird of Israel? His name is Nadav Henefeld."

Marv coached at various New York City high schools, then at Adelphi College, and was a regular at Howard Garfinkle's five-star basketball camp in Honesdale, Pennsylvania. I said to Marv, "I'd be interested in the Larry Bird of Mars." Marv said that Henefeld was a six foot seven inch forward who was finishing up his three-year stint in the Israeli military, and he wanted to play college basketball in America. He said St. John's was interested in Henefeld, but we might have a chance to nab him if we got on the case. Marv suggested that I call Henefeld's lawyer in Tel Aviv.

I called the attorney, and he confirmed Marv's story. We talked, and I told the attorney that though the signing period had passed, I was interested in Henefeld. But I couldn't make any promises. We both vowed to stay in touch. About a month later, the lawyer called me back and said that Henefeld was in New York, visiting St. John's. He said Nadav liked Lou Carnesecca and the school well enough, but Queens wasn't exactly his idea of a leafy college town. I sent a coach to New York to pick him up, and brought Nadav to Storrs for a two-day visit. He spoke very little English, but he liked the green rolling hills around Storrs, as well as the library, dormitories, and houses of worship. "Zis," he told me, "looks like a college campus."

Henefeld returned to Israel. Luckily, our strength coach at the time, Jay Hoffman, was Jewish and spoke Hebrew. (Jay had married an Israeli woman while he was an extra on the Chuck Norris movie *Delta Force*.) I asked Jay to called Nadav regularly to reinforce our interest in him. He did. Later that summer, Pat and I flew to Tel Aviv so that I could watch Henefeld play for the Israeli national team. We took an hour-and-a-half cab ride outside the capital to watch the game. It was lousy—the team the Israelis played was horrible—but Nadav impressed me. He was a natural passer and defender; he roamed around on defense, making steals. He had a sixth sense about where the basketball was going. We signed him to a scholarship.

A Dream Season

LITTLE DID I KNOW that Nadav would become a key cog in the 1989–1990 season, which was our so-called "dream season." Every organization needs a breakthrough of some kind to become truly successful. Maybe it's a special product, such as TiVo, or a unique service such as Netflix. In sports, it usually means finally putting together a team with the right mix of talent and chemistry to make a name for itself.

We did that during the 1989–1990 season. It was the Connecticut basketball program's breakthrough year. We certainly didn't anticipate it going into the season. Our record the previous year was 18-13, and we had a losing record in the Big East. We lost to Alabama-Birmingham in the quarterfinals of the National Invitation Tournament. No wonder the pundits picked us to finish eighth in the league in 1989–1990.

Instead, we confounded the experts and maybe ourselves. We won the conference title for the first time ever. We were the Big East regular season cochamps, and we won the conference tournament, beating Syracuse in the final by three points. We finished the season 31-6. A last-second defeat by Duke kept us out of the Final Four.

We were led that year by sophomore guard Chris Smith, who would go on to become UConn's career scoring leader. Chris was my first big-time recruit from Connecticut. He played at Kolbe-Cathedral High School in Bridgeport. Chris was the best player in the state, a top-fifty player nationally, and had offers from colleges all over the country. With the help of some faculty and coaches at his high school, we persuaded Chris to stay close to home and start a winning tradition at UConn. We were so desperate to sign him that, just prior to his visit to campus, we rushed out and bought some new furniture for the offices of our assistant coaches. "I didn't know if I was supposed to rent furniture, buy it, or what," coach Howie Dickenman said at the time. "I just knew we needed furniture. I told the salesman, 'I don't care what it looks like, really, just have it here by Thursday.'" Chris still remembers his early days at UConn, "when there weren't many fans," and then the start of what came to be known as Huskies Mania, which really got started after that 1989–1990 season.

That team had several good players. Among them were point guard Tate George, a strong all-around player who was later drafted in the first round by the New Jersey Nets; forward Scott Burrell, who was later picked in the first round of the professional *baseball* draft—and by Charlotte in the first round of the *basketball* draft—and was probably the best pure athlete I've ever had; forwards Rod Sellers and Steve Pikiell; and a couple of relatively slow seven-foot centers, Dan Cyrulik and Marc Suhr, a seven foot one inch kid from cologne, Germany. Nadav Henefeld set an NCAA freshman record that year with 138 steals. That still stands as the most steals in a season by a UConn player.

We also had a good little guard from Maryland named John Gwynn. John stuttered but always had interesting things to say. When he was a freshman, he said to me: "Coach, you're not so tough. You try to act tough, but you're really a good guy." That was before I ripped him a few times at halftime, using some harsh language— f-bombs, as we call them. Later, he came back to me and said: "Coach. I want you to know that I take back what I said. You're tough, all right. Too tough." I laughed.

In 1989–1990, we beat Boston University in the first round of the NCAA tournament, and then whipped California by twenty points in round two. Next up was Clemson in the prestigious Sweet Sixteen. It was a tough, competitive game, and one we seemed destined to lose. With one second to go in the contest, we were down by one point. We had the ball—but under our own basket. Somehow, we'd have to go the length of the floor and score in the wink of an eye.

I realized that there was only one possible miracle play. I put Tate George down somewhat close to the Clemson basket. He was to run his man into a screen and then dart over toward the sideline, about twenty feet or so from the basket. I told Scott Burrell, with his base-ball arm, to throw the ball down the court to the spot where I hoped Tate would be. The whistle blew, Tate made his move, and Burrell threw the ball—perfectly. Tate caught the ball, turned, and shot it in almost in one motion. It was a twenty-two-foot prayer and—swish! When it went through the hoop, giving us a 71–70 victory, I practically jumped through the ceiling at the Meadowlands arena, where the game was played.

It was a miracle win, and put us into the so-called Elite Eight. There, we lost in the same dramatic fashion in which we'd beaten Clemson. This time, playing Duke, *we* had a one-point lead with 2.6 seconds to go in overtime. Duke had the ball on our side of the court. Christian Laettner, Duke's talented forward, passed the ball inbounds, got it right back from a teammate, then jumped and shot the basketball. Swish. Buzzer. End of Huskie season. We lost, 79–78, stopping our bid for a trip to the Final Four. No matter. That year put UConn on the American basketball map in a big way for the first time.

Nadav played only one year for us and then decided to return to Israel to sign a contract with a professional team in Tel Aviv. It was like a day of mourning in Connecticut when word got out that he would not be returning to the Huskies. In 1993 Doran Scheffer, another Israeli, came to play for us. Doran, an excellent guard, was from the same hometown as Nadav, which certainly helped us get him. He played for us for three years. Howie Dickenman, my assistant at that time, made two recruiting trips to Israel, and I went there five times myself.

This year we recruited a seven foot three inch, 265-pound center from Dar es Salaam, Tanzania, by way of Cypress Community School in Houston. His name is Hasheem Thabeet. He rounded out a record size freshman class for us last year. We signed eight players to scholarships.

Hasheem was a later bloomer to say the least. He didn't start playing basketball in Tanzania until he was sixteen. By then he was already seven feet tall. He played soccer but was intrigued by basketball. Watching an outdoor basketball game one day, a coach asked Hasheem why he didn't play. Hasheem was too embarrassed to say that he was intimidated by the strong men on the court. So he fibbed. "I told the coach that I didn't have stuff like shoes for basketball," Hasheem told Marlen Garcia of *USA Today*. The coach got some equipment for him, and Hasheem agreed to try the new game. He sank a free throw and then dunked the ball. "I was like, 'This is easy'," Hasheem told the reporter.

An American businessman approached Hasheem after a tournament in Kenya and suggested that he go to school in the United States, where he could improve his basketball game. With the man's help, Hasheem first enrolled at a prep school in California, which he didn't like, and then he moved to Picayune Memorial High School in Mississippi. That didn't work out either. There were guardianship questions and concerns about his academic background. And so the tall Tanzanian moved again, this time to Cypress Christian School in Houston, where he lived with a family of Christian missionaries. After much work, Cypress Christian obtained a transcript from Hasheem's school in Tanzania, and he was cleared to enroll and play.

Hasheem was a popular guy at Cypress. A former honors student in Africa, his bright smile, intellect, and easy personality won over his classmates. And he was a force on the basketball court, averaging fifteen points and ten rebounds as a high school senior. Andre LaFleur, our recruiting coordinator, got a tip from a Texan about Hasheem, and we were the first major school to recruit him. Our interest in him sparked interest from other programs, including Louisville and Cincinnati, but we got him to our campus first and succeeded in signing him. He liked the fact that Storrs is quiet, and he liked hearing me tell him that defense is very important to Connecticut, and that we've led the nation in shot blocks for five straight years.

Hasheem's strength right now is defense. He needs a lot of work offensively, and we pushed him pretty hard last year to develop some offensive moves. It was an adjustment for him. As I told Marlen Garcia from *USA Today*, "We've had to teach Hasheem that all the great players here . . . all paid special prices. I said to him, 'I know you're upset with us, but we're trying to do extra work with you. You think it's like a punishment. But all we're trying to do, and I know it's selfish, is to help you be good here, so you'll make millions of dollars.' He'll listen and think about [the things I say], and eventually he'll react to it because he's bright and thoughtful."

Like any prospect, it's hard to know quite how he'll develop. We try not to give up on players, and Hasheem has a chance to be great if he keeps working hard. Hasheem was lonely last year—he hadn't seen his mother in more than three years. But he's a strong kid, a mature kid, and I'm excited about him. He's pretty mobile for his size, and he will give us a major presence near the basket.

We recruited a few highly coveted national prospects in my first five years at UConn, but we didn't land too many of them. Ray Allen and Chris Smith were the exceptions. I think it took ten years for us to sign a player from New York City, which is full of talent. These days, we certainly get our share of top prospects, but we've only signed six McDonald's All-American players in twenty-one years. Some schools sign half that many in one year. We signed eight good players last year, but not one of them was a McDonald's AA.

Our biggest success came in 1991, when we got Donyell Marshall, a skinny six-foot eleven-inch center from Reading, Pennsylvania. Donyell was the mid-Atlantic player of the year, and a high school All-American.

Like Henefeld, we were lucky to get Donyell. His first choice was Syracuse, but as any coach would tell you, the kids themselves often do not decide where they're going to college. Parents have a big say in the matter—and especially the mamas. And mamas tend to want their "babies" to stay close to home, even when their babies wear size fourteen basketball shoes. Donyell's mother talked him out of signing with Syracuse because she thought it was too far away. Donyell's next choice was Maryland. But there were some NCAA questions that worried Donyell. After playing in the McDonald's All-American game in Springfield, Massachusetts, Donyell paid us a visit, and we were able to convince him that Connecticut was the best place for him.

But it wasn't long before I was confronting a minicrisis. After his first week of practice, Donyell came up to me, nervously, and said he wanted to talk. We did, and Donyell told me he didn't think he was good enough to play at Connecticut. I told him to put that idea out of his head immediately. "We wouldn't have recruited you if you weren't an outstanding basketball player," I told him. Like most kids, even those with terrific potential, my job was to show Donyell just how good he could be. It didn't take long. He averaged eleven points as a freshman, then two years later set the single-season scoring record at UConn. He played three years, then left school and was the fourth pick in the NBA draft.

Donyell will be entering his thirteenth NBA season this year. He's proud of his four children, and of his years at UConn. He said recently: "When Coach Calhoun came to UConn, he put everything right up front. He told us that if we trust and believe in him, that he would help us become winners on the court and in the classroom. Today, I can still call him and talk to him about anything. I came back for a team barbecue at his house, and he pulled me aside and reminded me that I would always be a part of his family." I'm proud of Donyell, and still watch him play on TV occasionally. And if he makes a mistake, I sometimes call him to say hello and give him a hard time.

RECRUITING TALENT IS ONE thing. Getting talented people to work hard, to believe in themselves, and to dedicate themselves to the game and their team: that's an entirely different can of worms. We've been very good at getting players to reach their potential, and in some cases to overachieve, thanks to our emphasis on hard work. That's why there are fifteen former Huskie players in the pros—more than any other school. Some of them were not considered NBA prospects when they first signed with us. Hilton Armstrong is an example. He didn't even start for us until he was a senior, and he ended up being the twelfth player taken in the NBA draft. It's the hard work that gets them over the top.

My first year in Storrs, we had a burly player from Ontario, Canada, named Gerry Besselink. He was a six foot eight inch wing player who'd been recruited by my predecessor. Gerry, interestingly, served on the university search committee at UConn that eventually decided to hire me. He was the student representative. Gerry knew that the committee liked my credentials and was going to offer me the job.

What he didn't know was how hard I was going to be on him after I took the job. I coached Gerry for one year—he was a senior my first year in Storrs—and he frankly saved the year from being a total disaster. Halfway through the season, we were struggling big-time. Our two best players, Cliff Robinson and Phil Gamble, were declared academically ineligible. That left Gerry, essentially, as the only player standing between us and oblivion. I was pretty tough on him, because I had to be. Though not very tall, Gerry was our center, and he had to compete against some outstanding players—including future Hall of Famer Patrick Ewing, then at Georgetown, and Derrick Coleman at Syracuse. They were two of the best players in college basketball.

I persuaded Gerry to start lifting weights, to improve his strength, and I demanded that he work harder at practice and play harder in games. I chewed him out almost every day at practice. But Gerry was thick-skinned and up to the challenge. He understood what I wanted. I didn't expect him to play better than Coleman or dunk the ball on Ewing. I just needed him to compete. I needed Gerry to rebound and play defense, set screens, do all the little things that help teams win games. By his senior year, Gerry's weight had climbed to 250 pounds and he'd become an effective player—a classic overachiever. In the 1985–1986 season, Gerry had a "double double", averaging ten points and eleven rebounds per game. Patrick Ewing couldn't make the same claim. (He averaged fourteen points as a senior at Georgetown, but only nine rebounds.) Ewing went on to have a brilliant NBA career. Gerry didn't get drafted. But he played at least fifteen years of professional basketball in Europe.

After playing for five months in Holland, he returned to UConn to earn his education degree, then he went back to Europe to resume his basketball career. Gerry now lives in Finland with his wife and three children, where he works with a Christian organization as a mentor to underprivileged kids. Gerry and I remain close—we bonded in that tough first year of mine—and still talk once in a while on the phone. I'm proud of the effort and heart he showed that year, and of the man he has since become.

The Art and Science of Recruiting

NOWADAYS, OUR RECRUITING PHILOSOPHY is much different than it was when I first started at UConn. We have a top national program now, and we go after many of the top high school prospects in the country. Unlike in the past, when we had to be clever to attract talent, many kids nowadays are excited about the opportunity to play for UConn. Most of the kids we sign are ranked among the top hundred players by various recruiting services. Some pundits joke that I don't have to recruit anymore, just "select" the players I want.

That's far from the case. But it is nice to know that we don't have to compete with small or midmajor schools for prospects anymore. That's the upside. The downside is that, by going after the elite prospects, we are competing with the elite in college basketball. When we recruit a top-fifty player, you can bet that North Carolina, Arizona, UCLA, Syracuse, Maryland, Michigan State, and Louisville are recruiting him, too. (North Carolina, like us, tends to throw out a very wide recruiting net. Duke, on the other hand, is very targeted and chases fewer players.)

July is an important recruiting month. The best high school players are competing in various Amateur Athletic Union (AAU) summer tournaments, several of them sponsored by private athletic shoe manufacturers. (Nike started the summer tourney tradition twenty years ago, and Adidas and Reebok soon joined the fray.)

But July is a so-called no-contact period: We coaches cannot talk to the players. So what we do instead is go watch them play in the summer tournaments. Go to one, and you'll see a who's who of college coaches sitting in the stands, all wearing a jacket or sweatshirt or T-shirt on which their school name is boldly emblazoned. I do it to send an indirect message to the prospect: UConn is here to watch you play. I might be sitting close to, if not next to, Lute Olsen of Arizona, Mike Krzyzewski of Duke, Jim Boeheim of Syracuse, Roy Williams of UNC, Tom Izzo of Michigan State, Rick Pitino of Lousiville, or Gary Williams of Maryland, to name a few.

We go to show the prospects that we care, that we are interested in them. It's flattering for the young players, and it gives me and the other coaches a chance to see and evaluate a lot of good players in person. Nothing beats checking out a player firsthand. If Ben Howland of UCLA, Bill Self of Kansas, and I are all hot after the same prospect, and I go to a tourney to see the kid in person, while Ben and Bill send an assistant, then I might gain an advantage, because the word will get to the prospect: "Calhoun came to see you play. UCLA sent an assistant." And the opposite is true, too. That's why I go to most of the tournaments. They're important.

Recruiting is a demanding job—part art, part science. It's a very crazy, intense and unpredictable process, because in many cases you're dealing with teenage kids and their families who are getting sales pitches from a lot of schools. That creates confusion, and kids can often change their minds. For that reason, coaching staffs must stay flexible at all times. Recruiting is a side of college sports that *always* demands that you have a Plan B in your back pocket, and sometimes a Plan C.

Tom Moore, my top assistant, led our recruiting effort for seven years before leaving last year to become the head coach at Quinnipiac University. Tom was my chief talent evaluator and top recruiter. He, along with Andre LaFleur, spent a lot of time on the road in the summer and fall, watching high school players—sophomores, and especially juniors. They watched high school games in the fall, and then watched the best high school prospects compete in the various all-star AAU tourneys during the summer. In between, they worked the phones, calling coaches, scouting services, and the prospects themselves.

We talk recruiting a lot at the meetings we have in the bunker. Every year, we try to figure out what skill sets we are missing on the team, what talent holes we need to fill. Once we've identified a positional need—when we decide, for example, that we've got to sign a good center this year—we next start trying to identify a handful of center prospects from around the country that, at first glance, might fit our needs. After we've settled on a handful of center possibilities, we try to narrow our search further by assessing the specific skills set of every play in the group. The more information we can obtain—about a player's athletic talent and academic and family background—the better recruiting decisions we can make. When evaluating a center, we want to know how mobile the kid is. Can he run the floor fairly well? Can he move his feet? What kind of offensive game does he have? Can he score consistently from down low in the block, meaning close to the basket? Can he make shots from ten feet? Does he like to play close to the basket or eight to ten feet away? Is he a good defender? A good rebounder? A good shot blocker? We discuss his competitive instincts: Does he like physical play? Does he seem tough or soft?

We also evaluate every prospect's academic performance by looking at his high school transcripts, grades, and standardized test scores, if he's taken them. Is he on track to graduate from high school? Has he scored high enough on the SAT or ACT to qualify for admission to college? We don't have easy, so-called general studies majors at UConn that athletes can take as a way to stay academically eligible for years. At other major universities, athletes are often directed toward less than rigorous majors such as general studies to ensure that they avoid academic problems. We don't do that at Connecticut. Guys have to take real majors, and they have to go to class and study. Hilton Armstrong, Rashad Anderson, and Denham Brown, all key players our 2005–2006 team, majored in political science. Josh Boone, a starter, majored in psychology.

And, very important, we scrutinize every kid's character. Has he ever been arrested or had behavioral problems? Does he live with two parents or only one? The best way to determine a kid's character, I've found, is to observe how he interacts with his family—and how he interacts with me when we're talking.

During the recruiting process, I visit prospects at their homes. This so-called "home visit" offers a very revealing window into a kid's character and the environment in which he's been raised. If a young man is not polite to his parents or siblings, then he's got to be considered a character risk. It means that he does not respect authority—a red flag for coaches. Also, if I'm visiting a kid at home and he doesn't pay close attention to what I'm saying, if he's distracted, if the TV is on, or if he gets up and leaves the room frequently, then he's probably not a guy that I want to coach for four years.

I often travel long distances to visit prospects and their parents. Some live in remote corners of the country. They are kids to whom we might offer a four-year scholarship. That's a big deal. There aren't too many high school seniors in America who wouldn't be excited about the prospect of getting a four-year education for free. I therefore expect some respect during my visit. I don't expect the family to roll out a red carpet or treat me like a visiting dignitary. I don't expect a five-course meal—although I often get some very good food in the homes of recruits—but I do want the student athlete and his family to pay attention to what I'm saying for two hours. If a guy doesn't pay attention to me with a possible scholarship on the line, then he's probably not going to pay attention to me or the other coaches with a game on the line.

Last year, we recruited a talented guard out of Detroit. He was a top-fifty high school player, and he committed to play basketball for us. But he had some academic qualifying issues. We helped him gain entrance to a prep school in Connecticut, where, the plan was, he would spend his final year of high school to improve his grades. Then he'd come to UConn. He enrolled at the prep school, spent two days on campus, then quit without notifying me and went home. Apparently, he didn't feel comfortable in the new environment. We stopped recruiting him.

Every bit of information helps us put together the puzzle that is a high school prospect. You don't want to give a scholarship to a kid and then find out later, after he's on campus, that he's a bad apple or a guy who doesn't like going to school. Then you've got a problem.

It's also important to try and project how kids will develop over time. We do that with guys we're recruiting and also with guys who are already on our team. A lot of kids take years to develop—physically and mentally. Hilton Armstrong is one example. He was tall and gangly for years. Didn't have enough size to bang around with Big East centers. Didn't have enough confidence in his offensive game. We were never quite sure if he was going to become a solid player. But finally he gained weight, got stronger, learned some post moves, and by his senior year, Hilton was a changed player. He seemed destined to be a four-year bench player. But he suddenly morphed into a starter—and an NBA prospect. We coaches see the same guys every day, and it's hard to project how much a kid will develop. That's why we seldom give up on kids. And that's why it's doubly gratifying to see somebody like Hilton, who worked hard for four years, blossom into a good player. He was truly a late bloomer. He justified our faith in him—and more important, Hilton justified his faith in himself.

When we were evaluating Hasheem Thabeet, we got a look at him in the Global Games, a six-year-old tournament held annually in Texas that features players of foreign birth. Yao Ming played in the tournament, as did Chris Bosh of the Toronto Raptors. We liked Thabeet's "length." With his height and wingspan, it was obvious he could be a very intimidating defender inside. And we also liked the way he moves his feet. He can run, for a big man. Plus, he's not afraid to mix it up; he's got a competitive streak. All those qualities prompted us to recruit him and he signed in the spring of 2006, even though we'd already put together a large and talented freshman class.

Tom starts every recruiting season with a list of about 200 potential prospects from all over the country. Out of that initial group, we might hope to sign anywhere from three to six high school seniors, typically. As the season progresses, some new kids play themselves onto our recruiting list—these are the late bloomers. And, conversely, after a thorough evaluation we'll decide that some players aren't as good as we thought, or don't fit our system, and we'll drop them from the list.

Some kids drop us. We talk to scores of prospective student athletes and their parents every year, to gauge their interest in UConn, and some simply aren't fascinated with us. One big reason is that kids tend to sign with universities fairly close to their hometowns. We may love a student athlete from Chicago, but he might want to play for a Big Ten school that's closer to home.

That's part of the process. You can't take it personally. It's Tom's job to find the best players in the country who *are* interested in UConn and will qualify academically for college. No coach wants to waste a lot of time recruiting players who, in the end, are not likely to sign with your program. When those criteria are met, Tom and Andre start the hard sell on our program. One big goal: to persuade the players and their families to visit our campus.

I will get involved in the process around this time. I'll call the kids myself and talk to their parents, and I'll go to AAU and other tournaments and watch them play. I don't have to go, but my presence sends a strong signal of our interest in the player. After watching the players in person, the staff and I will have meetings in the bunker and try to hash out who our top targets should be. There are disagreements. Sometimes Tom was very high on a player who didn't impress me. Sometimes the reverse was true. The other coaches, George and Andre, weigh in with their opinions. They've often watched tape of many of the prospects and Andre has talked to many of the kids on the phone.

I want the assistants to be passionate about the kids they like, especially when I have doubts. I want my assistants to feel a certain independence, and to speak their minds. I want them to have their own views, their own opinions, and feel free to disagree with me. I don't want yes men around me, and I'm convinced that those leaders who discourage disagreement or discussion are setting themselves up for a fall.

So we haggle and try to reach a consensus. I listen and, ultimately, make the decisions about who gets a UConn scholarship offer and who does not. Scholarship offers are a big deal, so we are very selective. You don't want to offer kids who you're not absolutely sold on, and then have second thoughts about the decision later—when they're wearing your uniform.

There is risk in the process. We always want to sign the very best prospects, but at the same time, we don't want to lose good players by spending too much time pursuing great players who end up choosing to play for another school. That's why we, as a staff, make a point not just of working hard, but working smart and efficiently.

In recruiting, it's crucial to get a sharp read on your final group of target prospects—the last twenty or so who clearly have *some* interest in UConn. The question is, how much? It's important that we try to find out which of them is extremely interested in us, and which only seem to be moderately interested.

For example, we might be very high on three shooting guards. The best of three might have us among his top-five favorite colleges, but we seem to be near the bottom of that five-college list. Maybe he's from Atlanta, say, and he really likes Georgia Tech and Georgia. In that case, the odds don't look too good. Meantime, the kid who's our second favorite guard prospect might have us near the top of his list, along with one or two other schools. We've got a decent shot at him—if we fight hard. And the third best shooting guard prospect is absolutely sold on UConn. We don't like him as a player quite as much as the other two, but he's ready to commit to play basketball for the Huskies.

This presents a dilemma. We then have to decide whether we take a bird in the hand—accept a commitment from the third-best guard—or hold off on offering him a scholarship until we find out where the first two guards decide to go to college. My inclination is typically to hold off, *if* I think we've got a decent chance to sign a better player.

But the third guard and his family may not want to wait on us indefinitely. He's probably gotten scholarship offers from other schools—say, Seton Hall, N.C. State, Cincinnati, Miami, Xavier, and some SEC schools. When recruiters from those schools find out that we've got the kid on hold, they'll pull out the recruiting knives. They'll tell the prospect that we don't really want him, that we're waiting on better players. This is an effective tactic. We don't use it; we just tell players that if these recruiters talk about UConn they don't have much to say about themselves. Kids want to play, and they want to be wanted. If a prospect and his family don't like the idea of waiting on us to make a decision, then he might sign with one of those other teams, leaving us in jeopardy of getting *none* of the top three guards if we don't play our cards right. For this reason, we have to recruit multiple players at each position every year, to assure that we end up with at least one very good player. It's the way the game is played.

The NCAA allows every Division I school to host twelve prospects and their parents on campus each year. You can fly in a prospect and his parents, put them in a nice hotel, take them out to dinner, show them the campus and your athletic facilities, have them talk to our academic adviser and faculty members if the student knows what he wants to major in. The official visit, as it's called, is our opportunity to showcase UConn as a university and basketball program.

I always bring prospects to my office for a talk. If I can get a prospect in my office, I feel like I've gained an advantage over some schools, because there are a lot of symbols of success inside. There are twenty big action photographs of former Huskies now playing in the NBA. There are two national title trophies, numerous Big East trophies, the John Wooden National Coach of the Year award, a few net cords, and lots of other memorabilia. My point is, the office sends a pretty strong statement to the recruit and his family: We've been very successful, and you can share in our future success if you sign with UConn. I'd prefer a less cluttered office, frankly, but it's too effective as a recruiting tool to change.

A lot of kids and their families are confused or coy about their decisions. No coach likes wasting time, so I make a point of asking kids up front whether they are serious about UConn or not. If they are, I will eventually visit their homes, along with either Tom or Andre. During a so-called in-home visit, I will usually spend about two hours meeting with the prospect and his family. During the first hour, I will show the prospect a highlight tape of UConn basketball.

It is a showcase of the past season, with a special emphasis on what UConn basketball is.

The second hour is the most important. That's when I show the prospect and his family how passionate I am about UConn basketball. It's not too difficult. I talk up the university and the basketball program. I go over our record of success. It's a pretty strong sales pitch. I'll tell the prospect and his parents why I think UConn is the right place for him, and why I think he'd be great asset to the team.

I am pretty straightforward and businesslike, I think. I can cover a lot of topics pretty quickly, perhaps because I've been doing it for twenty years. After my initial talk, the prospect and his parents will have questions. They typically want to know about housing, about academics and academic support services, and about the Big East Conference. Many are fixated on how much playing time their kid might get as a freshman or sophomore. That's of special concern to the top prospects. If the parents fail to ask a question that I think is an important topic, I'll bring it up myself.

Sometimes, my talk is a hard sell. I will definitely be more aggressive when we need to get a pretty firm decision from a prospect, either a thumbs up or a thumbs down. The certainty of knowing where you stand with a kid is much better than prolonged uncertainty, even if it means disappointment. Uncertainty entails risk, as I explained above. If we've given a recruit and his parents time to chew on their decision before my visit, I will press them to give me a commitment. If they can't, and we have other prospects at the same position whom we like, we drop the kid and move on. Plan B. If it's early in the process, I might take a softer approach and give the prospect more time to mull the decision.

Recruiting is relative: How we recruit one kid often depends on our relationship with other prospects who play the same position. It's definitely one aspect of my job where it's crucial to have contingency plans, just like in business. If somebody quits a corporate job, it's nice to have a bank of previously qualified applicants from which to choose potential replacements, rather than starting from scratch. That's not always possible, but it helps.

Lieutenants Help Win Wars by Spreading Your Message

THE ESSENCE OF STRONG leadership is this: *continuity of message.*

No good leader works in a vacuum, especially those heading sizeable organizations. So passing your values and ideas down through the organization is imperative. It's the management version of the economic "trickle-down" theory. That means hiring good, bright, energetic people to work as your top lieutenants—executive vice presidents, senior vice presidents, managing directors, assistant coaches. The titles aren't so important. What is crucial is that they share your passion for the enterprise, that they understand and support your goals, and that they can communicate effectively with you and with everybody else in the organization.

I have been privileged to work with some outstanding assistants over the years. Most have stayed with me for several years before moving out and up in the world. Indeed, my assistants have contributed hugely to the success of Connecticut—and, in turn, have benefited personally from that success.

Some of my key assistants in recent years are now head coaches themselves, and doing very well. In that sense, Connecticut, like Kansas, Duke, and North Carolina before it, is developing a coaching "tree"—meaning, essentially, that other universities have taken note of our success over time, and when they want to rejuvenate their programs, they give my assistants a serious look.

Dave Leitao, forty-five, the current head coach at the University of Virginia, was one of my top assistants at UConn for a total of ten years over two different periods. I've actually known and worked with Dave for about twenty-five years. I recruited him to play for me at Northeastern when he was a skinny, six foot seven inch forward out of New Bedford, Massachusctts. He was my captain for two years and helped us compile a 79-34 record, earning two NCAA tourney bids. After college he joined his family in California, and was working two jobs when I called him and asked if he'd be interested in working on my Northeastern staff. He accepted almost immediately, then later moved to UConn with me. He left in 1995 to take the head coach job at Northeastern.

But Northeastern was not the same place where Dave and I put together a nineteen-win first season, in 1972–1973. After a tough second year there, Dave came back to work with me in Storrs, and helped us win a national championship in 1999. I've known Dave so long that he's almost like a son to me. He's a quality man—smart, a good recruiter, and he understands the different hats that coaches must wear for their players to be successful. You are part father, part brother, part psychologist, part disciplinarian, part friend. Dave shares my passion for fundamentals—for team-building, and especially for tough defense.

DePaul hired Dave as their basketball coach in 2002, and he took the Chicago university to the postseason all three years he was there, with two National Invitation Tournaments and one NCAA appearance. Then, in 2005, the University of Virginia hired Dave away from DePaul. He's already putting his mark on the Cavalier program in the tough ACC conference. In 2005–2006, Virginia was picked to finish last in the twelve-team conference, but Dave led them to seven league wins, three more than the previous year, and a seventh-place finish.

And last year the Cavs were even better. Dave emphasized personal and team discipline, and with the help of great guard play, he led Virginia to a 21 and 11 record and an NCAA appearance. The Cavs ACC record was impressive—11 and 5, good enough to earn a first-place regular season tie with North Carolina. Virginia has a brand new basketball arena, which should help recruiting, and Dave has that program moving again.

As Dave has said, his challenge at UVA is much like mine was when I first took over at UConn: Improve the fortunes of a program that has some pride and tradition and a lot to offer, but has been struggling to be competitive in a powerhouse league. Just as I had to cross swords with some legendary coaches in the Big East in my early years, now Dave has to battle some of the biggest names in college coaching in the ACC. I'm confident he can return Virginia to prominence.

Karl Hobbs, another longtime assistant, is doing equally great work at George Washington University, where he's starting his sixth season as head coach. Like Dave Leitao, Karl was a key assistant for me. He played basketball at Connecticut for my predecessor, Dom Perno, then served as my top recruiter for several years in the 1990s. A high-energy coach, Karl was instrumental in recruiting and developing Ray Allen, along with Richard Hamilton, Khalid el-Amin, and Kevin Freeman, all starters on the 1999 Huskies national championship team.

Karl was a guard as a player, and he understands the perimeter game as well as any coach in the country. George Washington hired him in 2001, and he's already turning the Colonials into a top team in the Atlantic Ten Conference. In 2004–2005 he led George Washington to a 22-8 record, the A-10 West Division championship and the school's first automatic bid to the NCAA tournament. In 2005–2006, GW was even better, with a 27-3 record, including 16-0 in the conference.

I've had several other talented assistants. Howie Dickenman, the only coach I kept on staff when I took the UConn job, is the head coach at Central Connecticut State University. I kept Howie on the Huskies staff partly because he's got an outstanding work ethic, and also because he's loyal, a quality that I value highly. After I was hired by UConn, Howie never said a bad word about the previous coach, Dom Perno. That impressed me. He and I had a ground-floor view of the reconstruction job that was UConn basketball in the late 1980s. He was a major asset in my early years in Storrs.

Howie has coached the Central Connecticut State University (CCSU) Blue Devils for eleven years. During that time, he's been named the Northeast Conference coach of the year three times. Over the last nine years, the Blue Devils have averaged eighteen wins a year. In the 2001–2002 season, CCSU won twenty-seven games, including nineteen wins in a row, and earned a spot in the NCAA tourney, losing to Pittsburgh in the first round. Howie's proved himself to be an outstanding coach.

So has Glen Miller, a Huskies assistant for seven years in the late 1990s. Brown University hired Glen in 1999 to coach its basketball team, which had just concluded a dismal 4-22 season. Over the next seven years, Glen won more games than any coach in Brown's history. In 2003, Brown was the only Ivy League team other than Pennsylvania or Princeton to win twelve league games. This year Penn, long the dominant basketball team in the Ivy League, hired Glen to replace Fran Dunphy. The Quakers made a great choice. I've known Glen since he played for me at Northeastern. He's got a great basketball mind—his knowledge of the game is as good as any coach I've known—and his success at Brown didn't surprise me. I've no doubt he'll enhance Penn's strong basketball tradition.

Steve Pikiell, who played for me at UConn and was an assistant coach with us in 1991–1992, is another coaching comer. Steve played point guard for us between 1987 and 1991, and was the team captain when he was a junior and senior. A Bristol, Connecticut, native, he helped lead us to the Elite Eight and Sweet Sixteen in the NCAA tournament, two seasons which really brought national attention to Connecticut basketball for the first time. Steve played in 106 career games, and averaged eight points as a freshman.

Last year Steve got his first head coaching job, at Stony Brook in New York. Before that, he'd been a top assistant under Karl Hobbs at George Washington for four years. Prior to his stint at GW, Steve served as an assistant at Central Connecticut State University for five years, working with Howie Dickenman. Prior to his arrival, CCSU had never posted a winning season at the Division I level. During his tenure, Steve helped Howie and CCSU post an 81-63 record. Steve is an excellent recruiter himself, and a special individual, and his best coaching years are ahead of him.

Right-Hand Men

At UConn, we certainly don't have many management layers, as you'd find in a big company. I've got four assistant coaches, and they each have different yet important duties. Tom Moore was a valuable assistant for thirteen years. It's hard to overstate how big a role he played in our success. I think he's the best recruiter in the country, and he's widely recognized as an outstanding evaluator of talent. In major college sports, you *have* to have great recruiters and talent evaluators. In Tom, we had both.

But now Tom will be using those skills at another university. Last spring he accepted the head coaching job at Quinnipiac, a Connecticut-based school that is committed to strengthening its basketball program. They've got the right man for the job. I hated to lose Tom, but it was inevitable that he would become a head coach again; the only question was when. With his energy, astute basketball mind, and leadership skills, Tom should do great things at Quinnipiac.

Like me, Tom's a Massachusetts man. He grew up in Shrewsbury and graduated from Boston University. Before joining my staff, Tom was the head basketball coach at Worcester State College for five years, compiling a 76-59 record. It was the best five-year period in the school's history, and included a berth in the Division III national tournament in 1993–1994.

I hired Tom as my number-three assistant just before the 1994–1995 season. We'd lost an assistant a year earlier, and Tom, who was eager to join a Division I program, applied for the job. He'd heard about it from his friend Karl Hobbs, who had been my number-three assistant and was preparing to move up to the number-two spot. I interviewed Tom and was impressed, but I didn't offer him the position. One of my former players needed a job, and I wanted to give him a break. As you've may have noticed, I have a tendency to hire guys whom I know, especially former players. It's not a foolproof philosophy, but it's less risky than hiring a mere acquaintance. I've already got a strong sense of their personality, their work ethic, their character, and the skills they can bring to the job.

In any case, I offered the former player the coaching position, and he accepted. I called Tom and gave him the bad news. Tom understood. But in that instance, my hiring instinct went awry. The guy had some personal issues, and it quickly became apparent that he wasn't going to work out. So two months later I was back on the horn with Tom. I asked him if I made a change, could he take the job right away. He said yes and accepted, even though he was getting married in a few days. Tom got married, as planned, but missed the honeymoon he and his wife, Eileen, had planned.

Tom spent seven years as the number-three assistant, a job that involves a lot of scouting work on our opponents. Tom also helped run our summer camps, which draw about 1,600 kids—and as Tom likes to joke, about 3,200 intense parents. The only thing tougher than coaching kids is trying to keep their doting parents happy.

George Blaney, who's been with me for six years, does most of our scouting work and additionally coaches our big men. As a scouting expert, he's unmatched. He breaks down each of our opponents, reviewing lots of videotape, finding weaknesses, and helping us formulate game plans. He writes up reports on every team we play. At UConn, our first priority is being the best team we can be. But we also want to take away what our opponents do best. We devise strategy based on George's analysis.

George and I have been friends for about thirty-nine years. With nearly thirty years of head coaching experience himself, there is nothing that happens on a basketball court that George hasn't seen before. He's got an astute eye for the game, and a veteran's calm demeanor. It's needed, let me tell you, when I get worked up during games.

George was a star college player himself, at Holy Cross. He led the team to back-to-back, twenty-win seasons, and was drafted and played for the New York Knicks in 1961–1962. He then moved into coaching. He worked three years as the head coach at Dartmouth, then took over the basketball team at his alma mater. He held the job for twenty-two years, winning 357 games and taking the Crusaders to three NCAA tournament berths. In 1994, he joined the Big East as head coach of Seton Hall, a position he held for three years.

George has won numerous honors. He's a member of the New England Basketball Hall of Fame, and spent twelve years on the Board of Directors of the National Association of Basketball Coaches. I value George's easygoing manner, and I rely heavily on his experienced eye, especially in games. While I'm prone to stomp around, George rarely gets rattled. There is a steadiness about him that is invaluable as we hurriedly discuss substitution possibilities in the heat of battle.

Andre LaFleur, my third assistant, has been with me for six years. He was Director of Basketball Operations for three years—an administrative job now held by Patrick Sellers—before getting a promotion. Andre now works closely with Tom Moore on recruiting, and helps coach our perimeter players, guards, and wingmen.

Like others who've coached for me, Andre and I go way back. He played point guard for me at Northeastern for four years, and was an outstanding player. He came in a recruiting class that also included Wes Fuller and Reggie Lewis, who was the best player I ever coached at Northeastern. Andre holds both the single-season and career steals records at Northeastern, was tenth on the school's all-time scoring list when he graduated, and he ranks twelfth in NCAA history for career assists (894). A native of Los Angeles, Andre has helped to bring in some good talent from the West Coast in recent years, including Marcus Williams and Marcus Johnson, a sophomore swing man for us who should become a good player over the next couple of years.

I think Andre is going to be a special coach. He's got a great feel for the game, works hard, and young players relate to him, which is important. He's got a bright future.

Patrick Sellers, who is in his third year at UConn, handles all of our administrative and logistical needs—plane flights, hotels, transportation, a million and one details. The older brother of former Huskies standout Rod Sellers, he was a former assistant coach at the University of Massachusetts and spent four years with Howie Dickenman at Central Connecticut State University, his alma matter. If we need to find a practice facility in Maui, Patrick handles the job. In addition, he spends a lot of time with the players, helping to keep them on an even keel, and he's a liaison with their parents. When a parent has a question or wants to talk about some issues involving his or her son, Patrick is the go-to guy.

With so many potential NBA players on last year's team, we had a lot of anxious parents who were worried about various things, including playing time. Patrick reassured them. I frankly do not like to talk to parents during the season. It's a distraction. I want the parents to be happy, and I will talk to them sometimes if they are really worried about a serious issue. But I can't get too caught up in parental anxieties about playing time. My ultimate responsibility is to the team. I've had very few difficulties with parents over the years—quite the opposite, in fact. Most have been wonderfully supportive of the team, the program, and of course their sons. And we've benefited from it. Marcus Williams's mother moved from L.A. to Connecticut two years ago to help support her son after he got involved in the theft of laptops on campus and was suspended for six months. "I had to get my mom game up," she said. Great line. She's a special person. And we've had many parents like her, who put their kids first. Josh Boone's mother, Rosalie was wonderful when Josh played for us. And Pam Long, Rip Hamilton's mother, was the same way—caring, happy, fun to be around.

I give my assistants a lot of autonomy. Some coaches want their assistants to dress a certain way, want them to be at the office at a certain time, want to keep close tabs on their activities. That's not the way I operate. During recruiting season, I'm often not aware of what exactly Tom Moore is doing on a particular day. But I do know that he's doing his job—working the phones, looking at tape, watching high school games, whatever it takes.

And the same goes for George, Andre, and Patrick. I want my assistants, above all, to share my passion for the program—and of course do their jobs. I think about how we can improve the team virtually 365 days a year, and I want them to do the same. They each have certain responsibilities and tasks, and I trust that they'll get them done. I also trust them to give me their unvarnished opinions about various issues that pop up every day. I am pretty decisive, but I also am consensus-oriented: Before I make a decision about personnel or recruiting, I want to hear what my staff thinks.

A top manager has to trust and respect the opinions of his staff. You can't expect to know everything about your business or your industry. You have to delegate. Ultimately, a manager's direct hires are arguably the most important decisions he or she will make. Nothing will screw up an organization faster than having weak second-tier managers. I have seen head coaches get fired because they had assistants who either weren't good at their jobs—weren't good recruiters, for example—or had personality issues that created communications problems and a dysfunctional environment. Or they simply didn't work hard enough. When there is mutual respect and professionalism in a group, when everyone shares the same goals and work ethic, then an organization can really take off. When there are individual breakdowns, the unit will develop cracks that, over time, can be devastating.

My relationship with my assistants, therefore, is crucial, and I have to be mindful of what's going on with the staff. We're all adults, and I'm not a hand-holder. But at the same time, various issues crop up from time to time, and I have to keep the well-being of my people in mind. Staffers work best when they feel good about themselves. And they feel good about themselves when they know that they're making a valuable contribution to the organization—and they know that their work is appreciated. I make a point of regularly thanking my secretaries and the administrative people around the program for their hard work. That includes the medical trainers, and the strength and conditioning staff, led by Jeff Anderson and Chris West. Everybody. When everybody's good work is acknowledged and appreciated, the group's morale will rise—and that's good for productivity.

Every year, just before the start of practice in the fall, my assistants and I, and our wives, go off on a little weekend retreat. We might go to Cape Cod or Mohegan Sun for three or four days. The idea is to spend some quality time together before the grueling season ahead. We relax, have some fun, talk about the upcoming season in a casual, no-stress environment. The coaches play golf and trade war stories. The women will shop or go to the spa, and then we'll all have dinner in the evening. Out of the stress-free environment will come our practice plans to the minute for the fall and our goals, objectives, style of play, and evaluations. I love putting this together away from the university, in an environment where everyone gets to express themselves. The trips are just a great way to bond and share in one another's lives.

Every season is a long and arduous campaign. There is a lot of pressure. The retreat is our way of symbolically linking arms and reaffirming the idea that we care about each other and Connecticut basketball. I've been extremely fortunate to have had some outstanding assistants over the years, and the lesson is clear: If you want to be a great leader and manager, hire good people to work not just for you but *with you*. A great staff, no matter how small, can move mountains. And given how competitive everything in life is these days, you'll need to do just that. Make sure you've got a group of quality lieutenants who are ready to battle for you and the organization every day. Great leaders have uncompromising standards but are graceful under fire. They're also smart and proactive, so that when circumstances demand, they can shift to Plan B. Good planning, flexible thinking, a staff that shares your passion and your message with the rest of the organization. Do those things and you'll be ahead of the game.

5

TOUGH IN THE CLUTCH

PICTURE THIS: IT'S THE NCAA Men's Basketball Final Four, March of 2004. Location: San Antonio, Texas. Four teams, three games—two national semifinals, followed two days later by the national championship game—to find out who's the best college basketball team in America. In the first semifinal matchup, my Connecticut Huskies are playing the Duke Blue Devils, coached by Mike Krzyzewski. The winner gets to play, two days later, for the big crystal title trophy.

Mike Krzyzewski's teams are always tenacious and talented. In this game, they've got four players who would soon be in the NBA— All American center Sheldon Williams, sharpshooter J. J. Redick, athletic winger Luol Deng, and talented guard Chris Duhon. I have my own stars to match Mike's—notably All-American center Emeka Okafor and the gifted shooting guard Ben Gordon. They'd later be selected second and third respectively in the 2004 NBA draft.

As I've often said, Duke is an easy team to play preparation-wise, but a hard team to beat. That's especially true in this national semifinal. Okafor gets into early foul trouble, plays only two minutes in the first half, and not surprisingly, we fall behind. At the half, we trail by nine points. With Okafor on the court, we close the gap in the second half. Still, late in the game we look beaten. With two minutes and fifty-eight seconds to go, we're losing to Duke by eight points.

I forget a lot of things, but I'll never forget those numbers: eight points down to Duke, 2.58 to go. They are etched in my mind. Why? Because at that point in the contest, we're a millimeter away from getting beat in the Final Four. The proverbial fat lady isn't singing, but she's certainly warming up her vocal chords offstage. The Blue Devils seem to have the game under control. Krzyzewski's teams almost *never* get beat when they've got a comfortable lead.

But *almost never* is not *never*. There's a time-out, and I kneel down on the floor to address the team. My thought is: "We're eight points down, probably cooked, and Duke has the ball." But I also know that we've been in tough spots before, and that we can still win this game. Hell, we'd done just that two weeks earlier in the Big East title game at Madison Square Garden in New York City. We were down and seemingly out against Pittsburgh in the second half but rallied in the closing minutes to win the game, and the tournament championship.

In the Duke game, I notice some of my players glancing at the scoreboard as they settle on the bench. But I get them focused on the task at hand. "Fellas," I say. "We're fine. *We are fine.*" That gets their attention. I go on: "Here's what we need to do. Each team has six, maybe seven possessions left in the game. We need four straight stops, and then we need to score at the other end after each of them." Then I add calmly: "And fellas, there's no way we shouldn't do that. Our matchups look perfect—and they look very tired to me."

Know this about coaches. We are honest men, but if we have to tell a fib or white lie to motivate our players at crunch time and to win a game, we will. At the time I said it, I didn't really think Duke was tired—but it seemed like a thought that might give a psychological boost to my players in the late stages of a huge game. In retrospect, the Blue Devils actually may have been gassed: Final Four games are an emotional roller coaster, and I rested my starters quite a bit longer than Mike was able to rest his. We had more depth, and our subs had kept us in the game, even though we were playing catch-up throughout.

Either way, my message apparently has a positive effect on the team. They go out—under the glare of 47,000 fans and a huge national TV audience—and do exactly what we have to do to give ourselves a chance to win the game. We stop Duke on four straight possessions—and then score three straight times. Rashad Anderson hits a monster three-point shot, and then Gordon makes two free throws. Suddenly, the deficit is three points—anybody's ball game!

It turns out to be our ball game. Okafor scores five of our last seven points, including a layup with twenty-five seconds left, that puts us ahead for good, and we win the game by one point, 79–78. Two nights later, we beat a good Georgia Tech team to win our second national title.

The Duke win, our fourth straight over the Blue Devils, was the most significant comeback any of my teams has ever had. Over the years, my Northeastern and Connecticut teams have overcome bigger deficits to win games. But an eight-point deficit against Duke, late in a game, is the equivalent of, say, a fourteen-point deficit against most other teams. And, of course, the stakes could not have been higher. The pundits didn't think we could beat Duke, but I believed we could win the game. And most important, the players believed. We got eleven more rebounds than Duke, and our bench outscored Duke's bench by 17–8. Those were key factors in our victory.

I was hugely proud of our Final Four effort, of course. But what made the championship special—amazing, really—was that it showed how mentally tough my guys were. When the chips were down, we didn't panic. When one more missed shot or blown defensive assignment might have resulted in defeat, my guys kept their composure and concentration. When the game was on the line, when we absolutely had to play well, we played our best basketball of the night. My players raised their games when they had to. They showed their mettle.

Toughness is ingrained in me. My life has never been a red-carpet ride. Quite the opposite. I've had to work hard and fight for everything I've accomplished. That's the way it is with most people. You can get ahead if you've got some character, some toughness, and some smarts.

Over my thirty-five-year coaching career, I've adjusted to various social changes and the evolution, if you will, of kids. But I'm still an old-school, no-nonsense guy when it comes to certain qualities that people need to win in sports—and life. And toughness is certainly at the very top of that list. For one reason: We all face adversity in our lives regularly. There are small setbacks and large ones. Jobs are lost, knees are blown out, and family members die. We've all heard the expression, "Sh-t happens." To everybody. As older Catholics like to say, everybody has their cross.

The only thing that varies is how people deal with the hardships in their lives. My view is that winners deal with hardships directly— accept the reality of a situation, confront it, adjust to it—and then move on. After my dad died when I was a teenager, I was in emotional pain. But with the help of my family and my high school coach, I pushed on with my life. It wasn't easy—I was depressed, my grades suffered a bit—but I kept going to school, and kept working part-time jobs to make money. I could have dropped out of school, quit working, withdrawn from my family. But I persevered. I toughed it out. I postponed college for a year and went to work to help support my mother. It was something I felt I needed to do it at the time, and I did it. Instead of breaking open textbooks, I found myself breaking up granite. I didn't like it, it was horrible work, but I didn't feel sorry for myself.

There are people who, after getting knocked down, get up off the ground and jump back in the game. Then there are those who don't react well to setbacks. They dwell on the twists of fate, minor and major, and take a long time to recover from them. In one sense we're all like professional boxers: We all get hit with big punches that stagger us. The question is, will we shake it off and start back across the ring, ready to mix it up again? Or will we wave our arms, say "no more," and give up? How quickly you jump back up after taking a blow, and what sort of attitude you have when you do, is a function of mental toughness. I guess you could say that I've never viewed setbacks as obstacles, only as challenges I want to conquer.

I had some tough coaches when I was a player, and I'm a fairly tough man myself. And so I expect my players to be tough, too. What that means, day to day, is that I want my guys to be mentally and emotionally ready to *compete*.

That's a very important word. Sports can help young men and women in several ways. But if I had to name the single biggest benefit of sports participation, it's that it teaches young people how to compete. And dealing with defeat is part of how one competes. Who doesn't remember striking out when you were in Little League? Who doesn't remember missing the rim altogether with a shot when playing youth basketball? It's embarrassing, but hopefully only for a moment, because we learn early that little setbacks are part of life. And if you learn to deal with setbacks and use them as a motivational tool, as an incentive to improve, you stand a good chance of being a better player and person down the road. That's what being a competitor is all about. And it raises a important point: *Never fear failure.*

I tell my players constantly that they'll never become great if they fear failing. I want guys on my team who *want* to take a big shot. Who *want* to play defense on the other team's best player. You can't achieve anything in life if you're worried about screwing up. Edmund Hillary would not have climbed Mt. Everest had he worried excessively about falling off the mountain. Charles Lindburgh would never have flown across the Atlantic. Two years ago, in the NCAA tournament, we needed a three-point shot to tie Washington in the last seconds of the game. Rashad Anderson wanted to take the shot. He was calling for guard Marcus Williams to pass him the ball before he'd even gotten to the right spot to shoot it. Marcus passed the ball to Rashad, and he shot a twenty-two-footer with the utmost confidence. Swish. Rashad did not fear taking or missing that shot.

Dare to Dream, Dare to Achieve

YOU NEVER KNOW WHAT you're capable of in life if you don't try. We all heard that from our parents growing up. It's a cliché, but clichés have lots of truth in them. And, yeah, trying invites failure. It's a possibility. You might fall on your face. Real achievers accept that fact but don't dwell on it, because reaching a certain goal is very important to them. Think of a salesman who, rebuffed once or twice, keeps approaching a potential client until he gets the answer he wants. Think of the student who wants to attend a top business school, to earn an MBA but does poorly on his standardized test. He takes it again, raises his score, and gets into a school of his choice.

Those are determined individuals, mentally tough individuals. On the other hand, a poor salesman lets a rejection affect his attitude, raising the odds that he will lose the next potential sale as well. A good salesman not only shrugs off a rejection but becomes even more focused on making a deal. A mediocre golfer is one who gets bothered by bogeys, loses his focus, and then makes more bogeys. A good golfer keeps his cool and his concentration after a bogey, and then birdies the next hole.

Look at Tiger Woods and Phil Mickelson. I think they're two of the most talented golfers to come along since Jack Nicklaus was in his prime. Both hit it long, both have excellent short games, both are amazing shot-makers. So why has Tiger won twelve major tournaments compared to three for Mickelson? Why did it take Mickelson more than a decade to win his first, despite his enormous skills? Why did he make a mess of the U.S. Open last year at Winged Foot, making a double bogey on the last hole to snatch defeat from the jaws of victory?

In my opinion, the only difference between Woods and Mickelson is mental makeup—mental toughness. Woods is one of the most focused, competitive, and mentally tough athletes in the history of sports. He's got a competitive personality that was forged out of molten lava. When he's on the golf course, in the hunt for a tournament victory—which is just about every week—his demeanor is steely.

Mickelson isn't quite the same. Maybe it's an easy conclusion to make, since he's not won nearly as many majors as Woods, but Mickelson seemed to take a long time to develop the maturity and toughness needed to win the biggest events. Maybe it's the easygoing smile that's usually on his face, even during crunch time. Mickelson's won more than thirty PGA tournaments, but not long ago one of his coaches said that he had too much of a youthful attitude toward the game. Mickelson himself has said that for a long time, he was obsessed with "bombing" the ball. He seemed to relish taking risks. That was part of his charm.

But at the start of this decade, still lacking a major victory, Mickelson decided to change his approach. He became more conservative on the course. He focused on being more accurate off the tee. He resisted the impulse to be a crowd-pleasing daredevil. He managed his game more intelligently—and suddenly he started winning those elusive majors. He won two Master's titles and a PGA in four years.

He was on his way to his fourth major victory at the U.S. Open in 2006, but then in the last round the old Phil seemed to reemerge. He was wild off the tee, and on the last hole, with a precarious one-shot lead, he again pulled out the driver. Mistake. He hit his tee shot in the woods and lost a major he'd all but won. If Woods needs a par on the last hole to win a tournament, you can bet the house that he will make a par. With Mickelson, you can't be too sure, despite the newfound maturity in his game. He still seems a little fragile at times, which may be why he's so popular with the public. He's easy to like.

I think Mickelson will show everybody this year that he's plenty tough. Losing the Open had to have been devastating. But I wouldn't be surprised if he wins another major or two this year. He may not be as steely as Woods, but he's a lot more resilient than he used to be.

And he's charitable with his time. He will sign autographs at a tour event for hours. That says a lot about his character.

Those who are mentally tough understand that setbacks and criticism are temporary things, and show an eagerness to resume the battle. Because that's what it often is, a battle. Learn from your mistakes and come back the next day, to the next game, on *the next play,* ready to compete harder and better than ever.

Impose Your Will

I WILL SAY IT plainly: Kids who are thin-skinned or overly sensitive can't play for me. Nor can guys who show a weakness for competition. We played a game last year against LSU, in Baton Rouge, where some of the locals call the city by its French translation, Red Stick. I knew it would be a tough test for our young team, but it turned out to be disheartening. Entering the game, we were ranked eighteenth in the country and LSU was ranked fourteenth. As we often did last year, we played reasonably well early and only trailed at the half by two points.

But the second half was bad. We were outscored by fifteen points and lost the game by seventeen points. The loss didn't disappoint me as much as the *way* we lost. Our guys didn't compete well in the second half. They did not show either mental or physical toughness. As the game progressed, we let LSU's players impose their will on us. Usually, that's what we do to our opponents. LSU started playing more physically on both ends of the court. They were leaning on us, pushing us around a bit, and we did not push back. On offense, we started to panic. We played soft around the basket, and we lost our nerve at the foul line. We made less than half of our free throws, eleven of twenty-four. I can't remember the last time that happened.

I said after the game, "If I guy doesn't have [toughness] inside of him, you find that out in games like this. The first time you get stood up, knocked out, whatever, might be understandable. But then it makes the next fight pretty important. I'm making these fighting analogies because the game was pretty close to that. I hated the way we gave in and didn't impose our will."

In hindsight, it's obvious that a team full of freshmen was going to have growing pains. We lost five Big East games in a row at one point, and six of eight. As I said to the media at the time, the team had a crisis of confidence. We were giving great effort, the kids were listening and working hard every day, but the team's emotional state was fragile. We always practiced better than we played, which perhaps isn't surprising since game competition is tougher. When we were struggling, I made a point of telling the players over and over that I believed in them. And I did.

I also knew two things that kept me from pulling my hair out. First, mental toughness can be learned, and it emerges from adversity. Given how much adversity we faced, I figured better days were ahead. (I was right). Second, I knew we had some tough kids on the team. Jeff Adrien is tough. Guard Jerome Dyson, one of our best freshman players and one of our best defenders, is tough. He played football in high school. Jerome suffered a serious back bruise early in the season and kept playing. In a midseason game against DePaul, he took a hard fall that cost him some front teeth. He lost one altogether, another broke in half, and a third one was cracked. After two hours of dental work the next day, he was smiling again and didn't miss a game.

I can accept the fact that some people aren't hugely talented. But I don't have a lot of tolerance for people who aren't tough-minded and competitive. That does not sit well with me. About ten years ago, we signed a couple of talented kids who I thought would be solid additions to the program. Before they showed up on campus, a well-known high school talent scout named Tom Konchalski gave me a call. Tom writes a newsletter called the *High School Basketball Insider,* which nearly every Division I coach in America subscribes to. He and Howard Garfinkel, who runs the Five-Star Basketball Camp, started the service a long time ago. Tom is a great evaluator of young talent, and over the course of our conversation, the names of the two players came up. Tom said to me, "Jim, I just don't know if they're your type of players." He was suggesting that they were a little soft. I disagreed with him, but Tom's assessment would prove correct. A year later, neither of those players was on the team. They both transferred after one year.

In this day and age, I can't imagine how anyone can get by in life without some toughness and resiliency. It's a quality that everybody needs to be successful. As I said, talent is a variable quality. Some have it, some don't. But mettle is a quality that everyone needs, and most people can acquire it if they are ambitious.

By toughness, I'm not talking about physical strength, of course. There are a lot of big, strong people around, but muscles don't help you cope with stress when you must push through adversity without wilting. Think about the few people who sail around the world by themselves—spending many weeks alone in a boat circumnavigating the globe, coping with heavy seas, icebergs, variable winds, faulty equipment, as well as grinding fatigue and almost constant tension. How does one survive such a grueling ordeal? You'd have to be fit, for sure. But it's really all about mental toughness—accepting the idea that you're alone, in a harsh environment; that you won't get much sleep, that equipment will break along the way, and you *alone* will have to fix it. That's pressure!

The mentally tough thrive under pressure. They actually enjoy, or seem to, those brief, defining moments when the success or failure of a project, a deal, or in the case of a round-the-world sail, a life, is in the balance. I have run a few marathons over the years, and as any long-distance runner knows, at some point in the race you hit the infamous "wall." It's that moment in the race when your lungs are tight and your legs feel like they're made of iron. The big doubt begins to creep into your head: I may not be able to finish this race.

Many people quit running when they hit the wall, or soon thereafter. They quit because they've got an easy excuse: "I've run twenty miles, farther than most people can run. I can stop and still feel like

I've accomplished something." The runner who presses on, who keeps putting one leg in front of the other, even though he or she feels on the verge of collapse, doesn't think that way. He doesn't quit, because he hasn't finished the race, even if his body is screaming: "Listen up, Jim, I'm in serious pain here. Let's give up this nonsense and take a well-deserved break."

The mentally tough never succumb to the voice of failure, so long as the goal is still in front of them. That's how we beat an excellent Duke team when trailing by eight points with less than three minutes to go in the game—the game wasn't over. Victory was still possible, and our collective team toughness motivated us to keep reaching for it. You've got to *want* to beat whomever you're competing against, and know that other teams, other players or other organizations, are trying hard to beat you. I think the mentally tough have an inherent knowledge that it's hard to be good at something everything day. As the great philosopher Clint Eastwood once said, "Man got to know his limitations." And, I would add, his strengths. You can't always perform at a peak level. But you can always compete, no matter what your job or profession. Toughness counts.

Human Shock Absorbers

IT'S NO COINCIDENCE THAT the point guards on both of UConn's national title teams were tough-minded kids. In basketball, the point guard is, in theory at least, a coach on the court. In an ideal world, he's the leader of the team. He runs the show. If you've got a tough-minded leader at point guard, your chances of having a good team are much improved. If you have talent at the four other positions, but a weak-minded point guard, your team will probably struggle. It's a crucial position.

In 1999, we were led to an NCAA title by point guard Khalid El-Amin. Khalid was a thirty-year-old man in the body of an eighteen-year-old. He was incredibly bright and extremely tough. Nothing

rattled him and he relished a challenge. Short and stocky, he wasn't
the most talented guy on that '99 team—but he knew how to distrib-
ute the basketball, and most important, he was our leader.

What do I mean by that? I mean that Khalid kept everybody on
the team composed and confident at all times. He was steady. Tough-
minded leaders bring a sort of psychological stability to a unit, so that
it doesn't collapse when adversity strikes. They're like human shock
absorbers.

Khalid lived on the edge a little bit. He had to be pushed sometimes to do his class work, but he was a warrior once he stepped on
the basketball court. He could not be backed down, by anybody. He
loved competition: our five against your five. Let the most talented
and toughest team win. That was his mentality, and he seldom lost his
cool. He never worried much if things weren't going our way, because
he was fully confident that, with our talent and tenacity, we'd get the
game turned around. And we usually did. In the three years that
Khalid was the starting point guard, our record was 91-17.

Khalid's running mate at guard, Ricky Moore, was equally tough.
He was my team captain for three years, and our defensive stopper in
the 1999 season—a guy who relished playing the best offensive player
on the other team and shutting him down. Most of the time, he won
these individual matchups. He was Big East Player of the Year for
two years running and was Coaches Association Defensive Player of
the Year his senior year. Like Khalid, Ricky was a fiery competitor.

Khalid left UConn after his junior season and was drafted by the
Chicago Bulls. His NBA career didn't work out, so he played in Tur-
key for three years, winning the league MVP award twice. In 2005–
2006, he made almost $1 million playing in Russia's top basketball
league, and he was again league MVP. Khalid's team also won the
championship that year. As you can see, one can do quite well playing
professional basketball outside of the United States.

In 2004 we again won the national title, and we were again led by
a gritty point guard—Taliek Brown. Like Khalid, Taliek was strong-

willed and liked doing his own thing. I'll never forget recruiting him: Taliek is from Queens, New York, and there were about fifteen people at his home when I got there, most of them extended family. It was one of the most enjoyable and intense in-home recruiting visits I've ever made. Taliek's mother, who's terrific, worked at the Riker's Island prison in New York City.

Taliek was a loveable kid but had some disciplinary issues. As a result, his first two years at UConn were a little shaky. He missed some classes, and I suspended him a couple of times when he was an underclassman. We had more than a few firm chats about his behavior. He liked to hang out a bit too much with the boys back in Queens. But he was a good kid, and very hard to stay mad at. And his mom and other family members did a great job of bringing him around. Whenever I told him that he'd messed up, he acknowledged his mistakes and vowed to do better.

When Taliek was a junior, his third year in the program, he got religion. He finally bought into what the other coaches and I had been preaching for two years. If we were going to be a great team, I told him, he would have to take more personal responsibility, on and off the court, and become more of a leader. I wanted him to stop pushing back against the coaches and start applying his energy and will toward beating our opponents. Take responsibility for the basketball team.

This time, Taliek listened. He was a highly touted high school prospect, and he took a lot of grief at UConn because he wasn't a classic shooter or scorer. But we didn't need him to score much. What we needed from him was to make smart decisions with the basketball, control the tempo of games, and keep his teammates on an even emotional keel. Taliek was very good at motivating the other guys on the team; they listened to him, and it worked out. He led us to four Big East championships and our second national title.

Once, when Taliek was an undergrad, he committed a silly turnover in a game. I jumped up and screamed at him, "Jesus, Mary and . . . Taliek!" What both Khalid and Taliek proved—to me, anyway—is that character and toughness can be cultivated, if you stick with people and care about them.

In the business world, group heads—whether sales chiefs, project managers, or store managers—must be the equivalent of point guards. They must show energy, toughness, and decisiveness. They must be resilient. They must be steady. They must figure out how to solve problems and keep their heads while they do, to keep team morale high. In short, they must be an organization's leader in the trenches.

When We Benefit, I Benefit

AT UCONN, WE WORK diligently every year at building the concept of team. One idea that I constantly emphasize is this: *When we benefit, I benefit.*

In other words, when the team performs well, everyone on the team will share in its success. I want the players, as a group, to take ownership of the team. And one thing I do to promote team "ownership" is to make sure that every player, whether he's an All-American or a benchwarmer, knows that he is making contributions to the team.

Every player has to know where he fits. And I make a point of telling the team regularly how important everybody is to our success—including and especially the kids who don't get much playing time, and little public recognition of their efforts.

Like every team, we have so-called walk-on players who try out in the fall for a chance, essentially, to practice with the scholarship players every day. The walk-ons aren't on scholarship, and they usually don't travel to away games. But I count on them to do the grunt work—practice hard every day, often simulating plays that our opponents like to run. And I count on them to show a lot of spirit from the bench during games. In those ways, the walk-ons contribute a lot to the team's improvement and success over the course of a season.

Like almost every college program, my teams are composed of a diverse group of individuals. We get kids from small towns and kids from big cities. Marcus Williams grew up in a rough neighborhood in South Central L.A. In 2006, we had players from six states, including two players from California and one, Denham Brown, from Canada. We have white players and African-American players. Over the years, we've had players from Australia, Germany, France, Greece, Senegal, Sudan, and four players from Israel. Some kids come from solid, two-parent, middle-income backgrounds. Others come from low-income, one-parent families. And, of course, every student athlete has a different personality. Among the guys on last year's team, Rashad Anderson was an extrovert, while Josh Boone could be quiet and moody.

My job is to take a broad collection of individuals and mold them into a cohesive, unified team. James Banks, a sociologist at the University of Washington, has described America not as a melting pot, as it's often described, but rather as a mixed salad, where each vegetable or ingredient is unique but must integrate with and enhance the whole. I like that concept, and I try daily to tell my guys that they must learn to appreciate, respect, and care for one another. They should grow from one another. Talent is important, but unity is our greatest strength.

That applies to every organization, which is one reason I'm often asked to talk to corporate groups. Individuals who are unhappy, selfish, envious, or arrogant can destroy the morale of a team by creating schisms or factions within the group. That's why it's crucial that everybody has a stake in the team's success, rather than their own individual success.

I tell my players constantly that UConn is not a collection of individuals. We are a team on and off the court. During the fall, we all tailgate together at UConn football games to promote camaraderie. When we were in Hawaii two years ago for the Maui Classic, we all rode Jet Skis together, players and coaches. When we were in London a few years back, we spent nearly all of our time together, visiting Buckingham Palace and Big Ben and many other historic sites. It was a chance to learn about England's history, sure. But more important, it was a chance for the coaches and players to bond in an environment far from a basketball court. I tell the players all the time, "You may not be best friends with everybody on the team, but you're going to get along." I don't give them a choice.

I insist that my athletes respect the history of the UConn program, and our rules. I don't have many, but I don't bend on those I have. If a kid comes into my office wearing a hat, I ask him: "Is it raining in here? Take off your hat and then we'll talk." The same with iPod earphones: I don't talk to people listening to music when they stroll into the office. And I want my teams to look respectable when we are on the road or at our hotel before home games. If we are wearing UConn sweatsuits, then I want everybody wearing them. No T-shirts, hats, or individual fashion statements.

Certain guys are disciplined enough when they get to college to handle all the stuff thrown at them. They can handle the academic and athletic rigors, and they're going to make it with or without my help. Former guard Kevin Ollie was mature beyond his years. But most kids need that push, that direction, that discipline the coaches provide. They need a strong role model in their lives, to take them through what can be some choppy years. They need somebody to mold them, and I take that responsibility very seriously. There aren't many greater thrills than knowing that you've helped somebody to mature and build a strong foundation for his adult life.

Do I succeed all the time? No. Out of some three hundred guys that I've coached over the last thirty-five years, I'd guess that I've failed to reach maybe ten of them. By failure, I mean a kid who, after spending four years with the program, is as scared and unfocused as he was when he first walked through our doors. That, to me, is failure.

And frankly, I've been unable to get through to a few kids. We had a kid from Providence who was at UConn for four years in the 1990s, and he just never grew up while he was on the team. And though long gone, he still hasn't. He's bright, articulate, caring—but going nowhere fast. And if you're going nowhere, in reality you're going backwards in life.

We were playing at the Providence Civic Center last year, and a guy up there told me he'd seen this former player around town. He said that the young man was still doing what he was doing at Connecticut—partying a lot, goofing around. I said to the guy, "You really *do* know him." The former player doesn't have much of a support network, except for me and a few others at UConn. He's been back to Storrs for a couple of player reunion games, but on both occasions he seemed more interested in picking up his hotel stipends than visiting with his former coaches and teammates. And now, a little good news concerning this young man: we're sending him to England to play professional basketball, then hopefully bring him back to complete his degree. As long as he does not give up on himself, I won't give up on him.

Ted Taigen, our academic adviser, worked with me on this guy for years, trying to convince him to stop drifting through life. Ted, better known as Doc, can be more positive about some kids than I am. He'll say, "Don't worry, Jim, he'll turn around." Often, he's right, but there are a lot of distractions in life, and sometimes they are too much for certain kids, despite our best efforts to keep them focused on their education and their team.

But that former player is an exception. I've had a positive impact on the vast majority of the kids I've coached at Northeastern and Connecticut. I know what they were like when they got to college, and I see what they've become after they leave. I've succeeded a lot more than I've failed, and that makes me proud. When I see former players who go on to do good things in life—teach, or start companies, or just put their noses to the career grindstone like everybody else—I say to myself, "That's why I do this." And quite frankly, we coaches have got to remind ourselves of that occasionally.

FOR ME, BUILDING A tough team starts with recruiting. I want kids with impressive basketball skills, sure. But we also demand three other qualities in the players to whom we offer scholarships: a willingness to work hard, unselfishness (a commitment to the concept of "team"), and good character.

I want toughness on the court—not off it. I don't want bad apples on the team—no coach does. I will not recruit a player, no matter how talented he may be, if my coaches and I determine that he has character flaws. If we conclude that a kid will not be coachable, or has behavioral issues that might keep him from being a team player, we will drop him. We sometimes give kids the benefit of the doubt—one of the most talented players ever at UConn, Caron Butler, was a troubled kid and spent time in juvenile detention when he was an early teen. But he and his mother, who raised him, moved to another state, and Caron put his problems behind him. By the time he signed with us, he was a very responsible young man. Caron and I remain close.

Peer Pressure Is Potent

Nobody performs well all the time. We all have bad days—at the office, in the classroom, out in the field, on the basketball court. Maybe a sale falls through, maybe you do poorly on a test. Maybe there are logistics problems with a product delivery, or a cost issue that throws your business plan out of whack. In basketball, maybe your shot isn't falling. I accept that—I have bad days myself. But as a coach and a leader, I never accept a bad effort day, or a bad attitude day, by a player. I'll tolerate poor play but not a lackadaisical or indifferent attitude. No manager should.

What happens to those who aren't showing good attitude or effort? It doesn't happen much at UConn, but when it does I can be unpleasant. If it's a game, I will yank the player off the court. I sometimes will toss a kid out of practice, if he seems only to be going through the motions. The next day, he may find himself wearing a jersey signifying that he's on the second team instead of the first.

If a player has issues, if he's missed classes or has gotten into minor altercations, then I often try to use peer pressure to straighten him out. How so? By running him—and the rest of the team—at six in the morning. A long run in the dawn chill is a very effective way to focus the mind, I've found. It's a very effective way to build character and toughness, and put an end to bad habits.

The best thing is, by punishing the *team* for one player's mess-up, I give the team the opportunity to set things right and put the offender on the straight and narrow. Believe me, young men don't like being rousted out of bed to run at dawn—and when they learn they're running because one of their friends has messed up and let the team down, they will express their displeasure with him directly. There isn't much kidding around when everybody is sucking wind before breakfast. It's called peer pressure, and it's a force a lot more potent than me at keeping players focused on their group responsibilities.

And that's a good thing: Every organization needs surrogate leaders, people in the trenches. The players hear me yelling and yakking every day, and I get on them all the time. But they can sometimes tune me or the other coaches out. But they don't tune out their friends. When a junior or senior starter on the team gets in the face of a younger player who's struggling, the underclassman will usually listen. Nobody wants to disappoint or upset their teammates—that's the power of groups.

Suicide Runs and Cemetery Hill

ONE WAY WE BUILD toughness is to make sure our players are in great shape. Being physically fit is a prerequisite to good performance in sports, of course. Conditioning is especially important in basketball, because the players run almost constantly. So I put a great deal of emphasis on running and weight training all year.

The college basketball season is long. It lasts about six months; you've got to be physically and mentally strong to get through not just individual games but also a thirty-five-game season, including the year-end tournaments.

We play "up-tempo" basketball every game, and that can take a toll on your team if it is not absolutely fit. I want my kids to have more stamina and energy at the end of the game, and the end of the season, than our opponents. We tend to wear down most of our opponents over the course of a game. In the late stages, we try to crank up our tempo and break our opponent's will to win.

I am a major believer in running, weight lifting, and fitness in general. I try to work out almost every day myself. We have a stationary bike and a treadmill in the coaches' meeting and locker room at UConn, and I use them regularly.

When I was the coach at Northeastern, I ran the team just about every way possible. We ran road races and timed miles. We ran before practice and after practice, indoors and outdoors, in the coldest weather and the hottest.

I've brought that same philosophy to UConn. On the Wednesday before the first official practice, we take part in what we call the Huskie Run. It's a 4.5-mile race around a campus course. All the players participate, and we encourage everyone in the Storrs community to take part as well—students, residents, anybody. We usually get a couple of hundred people. We give out UConn basketball T-shirts and everybody has a good time.

The players don't have quite so much fun in the late summer and early fall. That's when we do a lot of hill running before practice officially starts on October 15. Hill running builds stamina and toughness, because it's hard. There is a hump on campus we call Cemetery Hill. It's seven-tenths of a mile high, and pretty steep. The kids run it on their own on the five Saturdays preceding the first official practice.

The NCAA forbids formal workouts, led by coaches, in the offseason. So our Cemetery Hill runs in August and September are voluntary and led by the team captains. Everybody participates. On the first Saturday, the team runs up Cemetery Hill twice. After that, the players increase the distance by two trips each week. That means on the last Saturday before practice starts every player has to run up and down the hill ten times. We call it the Cemetery Hill test, and every player must pass. It's a rite of passage for all Huskies basketball players. You've got to be in excellent shape to do it, and the players know that if any one of them fails the test, I'll hear about it and the team will run even more after official practice begins.

The Cemetery Hill runs are only part of the volutary workouts. After the hill runs on Saturday, the players lift weights and do calisthenics and other conditioning drills. They play pickup basketball games almost every day during the week in late summer at Gampel Pavilion or the Hugh S. Greer Field House. Those who are truly motivated also run up stadium steps, sometimes wearing thirty-pound vests, and run on various tracks.

But however much the players run in the summer, they will run even more when practice officially starts. As Tom Moore said of the freshmen last year, "The volume of running is going to be hard for them to take."

Both in preseason practices and during the season, we run a lot of so-called "suicides." It's really a four-stage fitness drill: The players dash from the end line to the nearest foul line and then back to the end line; from the end line to half court and then back; from the end line to the foul line at the other end of the court and then back; and then finally from the near end line to the far end line and back. Do that a few times and you'll know why it's called a "suicide."

We generally demand that every player on the team complete the drill in twenty-seven seconds or less. That includes the big men. You've got to run briskly to make that time, and really, anybody who aims to play Division I basketball should make that time. If a player fails to beat the time limit, the whole team runs the drill again until everybody makes the time. Peer pressure! Most high school and college players run the same drill, but many don't push their players quite so hard, especially the big men. We push, and that breeds toughness.

DURING THE FALL, WE also do a lot of weight lifting to build strength and burn fat. Under the supervision of our trainers and strength-and-conditioning coach, the players will lift for forty minutes to an hour every day, working muscles in their legs, arms, chest, and back. We encourage the kids to lift together, and to help each other out. It's good for morale. We'll lift about five days a week from the middle of October until Thanksgiving.

During the season, we cut back on the lifting a little. We'll lift only four or five days a week, for a half hour or so. It's mostly to maintain strength rather than to build muscle. Basketball players can't get too muscular. Basketball is a fluid game; players require ease of motion to shoot a basketball, and jump and run. If you've ever watched a body builder try to play basketball, you'll understand why basketball players are lean.

Obviously, regular folks, who are older and have jobs and families, aren't in a position to work out to the extent that twenty-year-old college athletes do. It's not practical. And you can certainly be successful without being in good physical shape. A lot of people are.

But taking care of yourself is very important, no matter how old or busy you are. Fitness is a reflection of self-esteem, I think, and health experts frequently note the mental benefits of exercise—the release of endorphins, a hormone that stimulates blood flow and promotes alertness. Who doesn't feel stronger, physically and mentally, after they've worked up a sweat? Conversely, if you don't work out, or if you smoke or eat poorly, or drink excessively, those poor health habits eventually will catch up to you. Your work will suffer. I'm surprised by the large number of Americans who eat poorly and are overweight, and don't recognize the importance of exercise. There is nothing more important to quality of life than eating a healthy diet and getting regular exercise.

Never Take a Play Off

WE HAVE A SAYING at UConn: *Never take a play off.*

It's our credo, and we take pride in the work ethic we build in our players. In fact, NBA coaches often praise Connecticut players for their commitment to excellence after they become pro players.

Most kids, even the most diligent, have to be taught to play hard *on every play*. There is a tendency, sometimes, for athletes to take plays off, or to stand around and watch the action if they aren't directly involved. If the basketball is inside the paint, a player on the wing might not move in to get a rebound or a loose ball, or might not hustle back on defense if we miss a shot.

Basketball is a game of almost constant movement, on offense and defense. When players get lazy or tired, they're pretty easy to spot. Their defensive intensity will fade. They stop fighting through screens. Or they don't block out their man before going for a rebound. Or they don't hustle back down the court on defense, after the other team has gotten a rebound or stolen the ball. Lackadaisical defense usually results in the other team scoring points—and *always* results in my pulling the player out of the game.

Somebody asked Andre LaFleur to explain our success at Northeastern. He replied, "We worked. And we worked on the right things. Coach Calhoun's teams were tough to play against, because he emphasized the basics, especially rebounding and defense. And we were tough. All of his teams are tough. We led the country in rebounding one year at Northeastern, and at UConn we've led the nation in shot blocks for five straight years."

Ray Allen has been a star player in the NBA for eleven years, first with the Milwaukee Bucks and mostly recently with the Seattle Supersonics. He's had a great pro career, averaging twenty-one points a game. Last summer he told my assistant, George Blaney, that the key to his success in the NBA was that we taught him how to work at UConn. He said that making the transition from college basketball to the NBA was relatively easy because he worked harder than most other pro players, and still does. In fact, though he's a thirty-two-year-old NBA veteran, Allen's last four years have been his best as a professional.

Richard "Rip" Hamilton, who was one of the stars of our 1999 national title team, is now the leading scorer for the Detroit Pistons in the NBA. He won an NBA championship with the Pistons in 2004, making him one of the very few players to win national titles in both college and the pros. That's pretty special.

Rip is a lanky player who doesn't look the part of a top player. But he's an excellent scorer, mostly because he gives great effort on every play. He's a good shooter, but the key to his game is simple: He works tremendously hard to get open on every play. Watch him play for the Pistons: He's always in motion. He's this generation's version of the Boston Celtics great John Havlicek—which makes him very hard to guard. He's dangerous coming off screens: He'll use a pick to lose his man, get the ball, turn and shoot, all in about a second and a half. Give him a slight opening and he'll put the ball in the basket.

Cliff Robinson, who played for me between 1986 and 1989, was really my first true star at Connecticut. Today, he's one of the three oldest players in the NBA. Last year was his eighteenth season in the pros, an amazing accomplishment. There is only one way to do that, which is working your butt off every year to stay in shape. He's done that. Cliff is a very smart and dedicated guy, and I think we helped him a bit, too, by teaching him how to work and how to prepare for the demanding eighty-two-game NBA season.

There aren't many similarities between basketball games and office work, I realize. Nobody has to fight through screens to get to the water cooler. You don't need to lift weights to get your coffee mug to your mouth. Still, as in sports, there are some company employees who work full speed all the time, and some who don't. A lot of people work at half or three-quarter speed. They have a habit of wasting time. It's human nature, and it's a tendency that workers have to fight and managers have to resist. As Jerry West, the great star of the Los Angeles Lakers, once said, "You can't get much done in life if you only work on the days when you feel good."

Which raises a lifestyle point: *Successful people are busy people.*

They get up earlier, put in more hours, make more calls, do more research, talk to more associates, spend more time strategizing than the other guys. They never get outworked. In their personal lives, instead of wasting a lot of time watching TV, say, they exercise or do things with their families. You'll never hear me tease a Connecticut fan who's missed a game because he or she was at the park with the family, or taking a class, or spending extra time on their career. There *are* more important things in life than sports.

No Hiding—and the Scoreboard Is Always On

ANOTHER WAY THAT WE build toughness in our kids is to promote competition at practice. We break up into groups and compete in various ways. The guys shoot free throws against one another, practice our fast break offense against one another, practice our team defense against one another. And we keep score.

At my practices, the scoreboard is always on. Everything is competitive. There is no hiding on my teams. We want to know which guys, and which units, are winning and losing on every play. After we finish a drill, the winners go to one end of the court and the losers, after running a few laps around the court, go to the other end. You don't want to be seen with the losing group every day. I'll notice.

I have a couple of favorite drills, each of which is effective at building toughness in individuals and the team as a whole. The first is a fairly grueling one-on-one rebounding drill. It's a staple of our practices. It pits one player against another, mano a mano. One guy plays offense, the other defense. There aren't many rules, and we mix up the players, so a six-foot guard might be playing against a seven-foot center.

Here's how it goes: The player with the ball makes a move and takes a shot. If he makes the shot, he keeps the ball. If he misses, he's supposed to go hard after the rebound. The object of the drill is simple: the defender must stop the offensive player from scoring three straight times. But that's not all. He's got to get the rebound after each of the three misses. Let's say the offensive player misses three straight shots. The defender gets the rebound after the first two misses—but after the third, he allows the offensive guy to get the rebound. Too bad. The players must restart the drill.

As you might realize, winning the drill can be difficult. The defender has to play hard-nosed defense—and then when the shot goes up, he's got to "block out" the offensive player. That means keeping his body between the offensive player and the loose ball. Once the shot is taken, the defender turns his body into the body of the offensive player, blocking him out with his back and his butt. Once that is accomplished, the defensive player is in the best position to get the rebound.

Blocking out is a fundamental rebounding technique in basketball. It's also an important part of team defense—it's what sound teams do to maximize their ball possessions and minimize the other team's ball possessions.

Lots of guys will block out occasionally, but it takes commitment and toughness to do it consistently throughout a game. (One of the first signs that a guy is tired is that he'll stop blocking out.) The drill will quickly expose those who are tough enough and dedicated enough to do it and those who aren't. It teaches players to compete. Those who don't will be stuck doing the drill longer than they want. It's a drill we do almost every day during the season, and sometimes it can run for forty minutes, until everyone gets it right.

The second drill is what we call our "shell defense." It's essentially a quick game of four-on-four basketball. Normally, basketball is a five-against-five game, of course. You might not think that removing one player from each side would change the dynamics of the game much, but it does. With only eight players on the court instead of ten, every player has more space in which to operate on offense—and more important, more space to cover defensively. To be successful in the shell drill, every player on defense has to work harder than he does in a five on-five game, because there is one fewer player on your side to cover up a teammate who gets caught out of position or loses his man. Big men have to guard outside, and guards have to play inside and get rebounds. It's a drill that, like one-on-one rebounding, isolates everybody, and it exposes lax play. You either play hard or lose the drill. Losers run—even a UConn practice is based on competition.

Both of these drills are a very effective way of ratcheting up the competitive spirit of our players and the team as a whole—and in doing so, building toughness. They essentially condition players to keep giving effort when they're tired, which is typically when games are won or lost. Down the stretch in close games, good teams are often able to impose their will on the other team, because they're a little stronger, or a little tougher, or a little better conditioned.

We like to impose our will on our opponents down the stretch, and we know we have to be mentally tough to do it. We like to quiet crowds when we play on the road. That is a special feeling, because it means you've played tough and well in a hostile environment.

How do you build mental toughness in group of corporate or public sector employees? It's done all the time, really. Many companies have sales contests; advertising agencies often break up their creative staffs into little groups and ask them all to develop competing advertising or marketing campaigns. Winners get promoted, losers buy beers—and then cry in them. The best company executives often drive their workers, and their operating units, to performance and productivity levels that employees didn't think could be achieved. Improving performance, then, is all about pushing boundaries.

I'm a great believer in the idea that teams are a reflection of their coaches. And I think it applies to any organization. The qualities of the man who's running an enterprise will filter down through the ranks—subtly—for better or worse. A soft, emotional manager is not likely to have tough people directly below him. The opposite is also true. Really tough, flinty leaders aren't likely to have milquetoasts reporting to them. They're bad matches, and will result in chemistry problems.

We typically have steely teams because that's the type of team I want to have. In 1998, we played St. John's on a Monday night and lost. During the game, our starting power forward, Kevin Freeman, broke a bone in his wrist. He was out of action for two weeks. That created an opening for Kevin's backup, Antric Klaiber, to step up and help the team. Antric was a senior, and wanted badly to play. But he wasn't the most talented kid in the world. Worse, he was often in the doghouse.

Almost inexplicably, Antric got into hot water again the night after Kevin's injury. With his opportunity to play at hand, he got into a car accident. The circumstances dictated that we suspend him for a week or two. That left us two players down one day before we were scheduled to play Syracuse on national TV, at Syracuse.

I was furious. Here we were, getting ready to play a big game, and missing both of our power forwards. We had a coaches' meeting, and we kicked around some ideas that might help us compete with Syracuse. We decided to shift a small forward, Rashamel Jones, to the other power forward position. Rashamel was only six feet three inches, but he was tough and strong. We also decided to play a zone defense that night, something we hadn't done all year. I was frankly worried at the meeting, but I had a far different demeanor when I talked to the team in the afternoon before the game. I was brimming with confidence.

Why? Because though we'd been weakened by the Freeman and Klaiber injuries, I knew we had a gritty team and we still had good players. I truly felt we could win the game, and I wanted to make sure the team shared my confidence and resolve. I told the team in no uncertain terms that Rashamel was going to play well, and so was the team. There would be no excuses for losing—because we weren't going to lose.

There are no circumstances, however bad, that would cause me to display a defeatist attitude. In fact, I enjoy adversity precisely because it tests our collective mettle. I spent a good part of my coaching career leading underdogs. As I may have mentioned, I have long considered myself a Don Quixote type.

The upshot: My pep talk struck an emotional nerve with the players. They were fired up, on pins and needles, ready to play. And then they went out and beat Syracuse. Rashamel got twelve rebounds and played very well, as I thought he might.

My big point here is simply this: Life, like sports, must be played. Don't underestimate your power to succeed, no matter the circumstances. Don't underestimate your determination, work ethic, and will to win. People need those qualities, and so do organizations. Don't underestimate your group's ability to achieve goals. Don't assume that you can't do something because you haven't done it yet, or because you've failed to do it in the past, or because somebody else says that you can't do it, that you can't succeed. What do outsiders know about your character?

The most important thing is that, whatever the goal is, you have to *want* to achieve it. Really want it. That's the "natural" quality that leaders have: They've got a passion for reaching goals, for getting things done, whether it's navigating white-water rapids or getting a new retail store opened on schedule. Let's face it: There are a lot of dreamers in the world. People who want to get ahead without working for it. My players and teams always work, and we like challenges.

The pundits didn't expect my Northeastern teams to go to four NCAA tournaments. Nobody expected UConn to win the NIT two years after I took over the program. We certainly were never expected to win two NCAA titles. Those were all entirely new, first-of-their-kind achievements.

Nobody expected us to beat Syracuse that 1998 night, either. But what was I supposed to do? Call the Big East commissioner and tell him we were forfeiting the game because we'd lost two players? That's not the way sports works. It's not the way life works. It's certainly not my nature. It doesn't happen much anymore, but I still like being underestimated. I like proving the skeptics wrong.

You should, too. Maybe you won't ace that accounting test, but maybe you will. Maybe you won't make that big sale, but maybe you will. Maybe you can't make your little business venture work, but maybe you can. Maybe you can't become the top lawyer or engineer or financial adviser you always wanted to be. But maybe you can—*if* you have the mental toughness to push past the doubt and build the same resilience in your staffers.

In the hours or days before a big game, I will have worries or doubts about how we will perform. As a coach, I have to be prepared for the possibility that we won't play well, and have some tactical ideas that can help us win even when our performance is lacking. That's when we coaches earn our money.

My assistants and I spend a lot of time in the bunker, hashing out various scenarios that we might have to confront in upcoming games. In 2005–2006, in our first game against Syracuse at the Carrier Dome, we played so well in the first half I could have gone out for a cup of coffee and the team wouldn't have missed a beat—that's how well the kids played that night. But games like that are an exception. Most teams struggle at different points in a game, and that's when coaches have to be prepared to adapt and make changes. The difference between good teams and mediocre teams is that the good ones win when perhaps they shouldn't, when they don't play so well. I call such games "grinders," because we have to grind out a victory any way we can. If we're not shooting well, then we have to crank up our defense and rebounding and try to make scoring difficult for our opponent. Whatever it takes to win.

Whatever pregame worries I have, they dissipate as we get closer to game time. And by the opening whistle, they've vanished. When the game starts, I never have any doubts—at all. I know that we will win. Even last year, when we struggled more than we had in ten years, I went into every game expecting to win. I didn't know how we'd win, precisely, but I fully expected us to win.

I believe in my team's mental toughness and *will to win*. And if you have the same qualities, you're well on your way to achieving your goals or those you've set for your organization.

6

MOUNTAINTOP MANAGEMENT

I'M VERY FORTUNATE TO have had a successful coaching career. I feel privileged to be leading a premier college basketball program. But I wasn't exactly an overnight sensation. It took me a *long* time to reach the upper tier of college basketball, and I've had a lot of great help along the way.

When Connecticut won its first national title in 1999, I'd been coaching college basketball for twenty-seven years. So while I've climbed the career ladder, I also spent a large portion of my life on the lower and middle rungs, paying dues. I coached high school teams for three years before getting hired at the college level. After that, I spent thirty-five years building two underdog collegiate programs into national contenders.

Like almost every college coach in America, at one time in my career I tried to assure my wife that the stress and strain of the business wouldn't last forever. "Don't worry," I told Pat. "Things will get easier in a few years." There wouldn't be as much pressure. The hours wouldn't be quite as long.

Yeah, right. Like other coaches, I was deluding myself. I thought that if I could make the transition from Division I coach to *successful* Division I coach, maybe win a few Big East titles, the job might become a little easier. If my staff and I could jump-start UConn basketball, then perhaps "big mo," or momentum, would take over and sweep us along to the promised land.

We got to the promised land. But we learned after getting there that, if anything, success brings more demands. And that raises a management point of mine: *If you're willing to pay the price to be successful, then you must also pay the price to maintain your success.*

There are more than a few coaches in college basketball, not to mention top managers in just about any business, who know what I'm talking about. Many individuals and organizations spend years, decades, clawing their way to the top. And when they claim a cherished prize—an industry-leading market share, record earnings, a hit movie, or a national championship—the feeling is sweet. Very sweet.

But it's also fleeting. The good times don't last very long. You slap backs for a few days, get invited to a few celebrity functions, eat a few more "chicken surprise" dinners—and then reality sets in.

And the reality is: "We have to keep it going!" We have to keep doing what we've been doing—winning, essentially—because that's what people now expect us to do. Win! That's what people depend on you to do. Win!

You can't just stop winning because you've reached the top of the mountain. No organizational leader gives that fact much thought during the long climb to the top. He or she is too focused on the damn climb. I've used a mountaineering analogy, but it's really not quite accurate. When a mountaineer gets to a summit, he or she *has* done it. There is a brief period of euphoria, and then the climber starts *down the hill*. That's the only way to go. Real mountaineers know that going down a mountain is time-consuming and often deceptively difficult, but it's generally easier than going up.

In the business or athletic world, there is no leisurely descent after you're reached a peak. You are standing on the top of a mountain, feeling good about yourself and your organization and the great trek you've all made. Then, suddenly, the clouds part and you hear a grave, thunderous voice echo among the mountaintops. It says: "Keep walking, pal!" You look up and realize you haven't reached the summit at all. There is more mountain to climb. You've got to keep going—up.

You've got to keep winning. Why? Because your fans expect you to. Because your shareholders expect you to find new sources of profit. Because your employees expect you to keep making gobs of money. Because your clients expect you to keep up the good work. And truthfully, you want and expect to keep doing great things, too.

It's partly because you're proud, and you realize you've got a reputation to uphold. But there's more to it than that. People who succeed in life tend to be driven individuals, and there aren't many leaders who just flip off the drive switch when they've reached a few goals, no matter how lofty they may be. Simply put, slacking off is not an option.

So I came clean with Pat not long ago. "I lied to you," I said. "I promised you the job would be easier after several years, and that hasn't happened—at all."

She just smiled. I was stating the obvious. I still get home very late most nights during the season. I still fly from Connecticut to California just to see a prospect, and after taking a red-eye back to Hartford, still drive to the office to get a few hours of work in rather than go home and hit the sack.

Early in my career, I sometimes thought of myself as a Don Quixote type—riding a donkey, my trusty assistant alongside, trying to slay windmills. I was the classic underdog, facing great obstacles and fierce opponents, and forced to prove my valor—or win games—with moxie and character. It's always satisfying to beat the odds, to show that you can perform well when you don't have superior talent or resources, by relying on hard work, clever strategizing, flexible thinking, and a focus on fundamentals.

At Northeastern, we led the nation in rebounding one year. It was a nice accomplishment. Rebounding doesn't get a lot of headlines—it's the equivalent of offensive line play in football—but it's crucial if you want to win basketball games. At Connecticut, we've led the nation in shot-blocking six years in a row. Like rebounding, it's a lunch-bucket stat, and one I'm extremely proud of. It shows that we do more than just run up and down the court and take three-point shots. We place a great deal of importance on defense and making it tough for our opponents to score.

David and Goliath

PEOPLE OFTEN ASK ME: "What's it like to be ranked number one in the polls, or in the top five? Do you enjoy it?"

My answer is, "Yes, I do."

I've never been bothered by the pressure that comes with being good. Quite the opposite—it's an honor, a compliment. It means that people—sports writers, my coaching peers, and fans across the country—respect the Connecticut program, respect my players and coaches.

I spent a lot of years coaching underdog teams, and I used the role to my advantage. It's a motivational tool. But I also realize that I've outgrown the role. I can't pretend to be the overachieving little guy anymore. In last year's NCAA tournament, *we* were the goliath that got felled by plucky David—in the form of George Mason, a team some pundits didn't think belonged in the tournament at all. That shows you how little pundits really know. George Mason was good. They beat Michigan State and North Carolina in the tournament, in addition to us, and the team was a deserving participant in the Final Four.

In the past, my teams thrived playing the role of hunter. Now, we are the hunted. Nowadays, the pundits want to make us the favorite in almost every game we play. That's what happens, I guess, after you win two national titles in seven years—as we did—and win either the Big East regular season or tournament titles regularly.

Our competitors circle the Connecticut game on their schedule, because it will be an opportunity to play, and beat, a premier program.

Opposing coaches preach the same message of toughness and tenacity that we emphasized when we were playing more talented teams. (I still emphasize those team values, by the way.)

There is a particular advantage to being an underdog: You're not expected to win. You're playing with house money, so to speak. Everything to gain, nothing to lose.

But nobody wants to be an underdog regularly. It means your program, or your team, hasn't quite arrived. And if you're an underdog consistently, it's a ticket to the unemployment line.

There are lots of good coaches who are content working at smaller schools, with smaller budgets and more modest facilities, and they stay with those schools for most of their careers. But they win games, sometimes lots of them. Pete Carril, who coached at Princeton for almost thirty years, from 1967 to 1996, might be the most prominent example. He won 514 games for the Tigers and lost only 261. Not bad for a program that doesn't offer athletic scholarships!

Coaches, generally, are an ambitious breed. We want to win. We all want to coach the favorite. That's certainly true of me. And if you win enough, there are benefits. Whereas in the past I had to recruit kids by hook or by crook, top prospects now perk up when they realize that UConn is interested in them. A lot of big-time high school players want to play for us because they assume we'll have a very good team, and get lots of media exposure, almost every year.

Fans and the media tend to focus on the big-name teams from the big-name conferences: the SEC, the PAC 10, the Big 12, the Big 10, in addition to the Big East. The word "big" in all those conference names almost demands that the public respect them! But there are good teams in smaller, middle-tier conferences such as the Atlantic 10, Colonial, or Mid-America. Those conferences are generally referred to as "midmajors." George Mason, a Colonial Conference member, made the Final Four in 2006. The Mid-American conference, which includes Bradley and Southern Illinois, might be the most underrated conference in America. Southern Illinois was ranked in the top ten for a long time last year.

Those teams don't get as much national recognition as they deserve because they're seldom seen on TV. And that distorts public perception. How can Southern Illinois, or Bradley, or George Mason be any good if we haven't seen them on TV? In the NCAA tournament, the midmajors are usually a middle seed, and they'll play a big-name, higher seed in the second round. That's why they're considered underdogs. That's the way it was for me at Northeastern.

For the coaches at midmajors conferences, getting to the NCAA tournament is a big deal. First, your team and program get a lot of publicity, which is unusual. And second, if you can make some noise in the tournament—win two or three games, knock off a big conference favorite—you will enhance your status as a coach. That can mean more money or perhaps a job offer from a big-conference team. Bruce Pearl recently jumped from the University of Wisconsin-Milwaukee to the University of Tennessee. I jumped from Northeastern to UConn. It's exciting to step up in class, but also daunting. The opportunities are bigger and the competition is more fierce. You have to be ready for it. I couldn't wait.

The Expectations Beast

THE DOWNSIDE TO BEING a big dog is pretty obvious. You aren't just trying to win games anymore. You also have to *beat expectations*.

And that's hard to do, because after you've won a lot, the expectations spiral up and out of control like a runaway kite. After you reach a certain status as a program and a coach, the fans and the media expect you to win and win big. Every year. You've stepped into The Land Where Few Are Satisfied.

Somebody once asked Bill Parcells, the longtime NFL coach and two-time Super Bowl winner, to explain the difference between being an accomplished coach and being a younger coach who's just trying to make his mark on the league. Parcells said that once you've reached a certain stature as a coach, you don't enjoy winning in the same way that you did when you were younger and the expectations were lower. Winning becomes more of a sigh of relief than a triumph— you've avoided the misery of losing and the avalanche of questions that come when you get beat.

There's a lot of truth to that. Despite the fact that we had no returning starters last year, and a team full of untested freshmen and sophomores, some analysts still pegged us to be a good team. The media picked us to finish fifth in the Big East. I wish we'd gotten that high. We were ranked in the top twenty after twelve or fifteen games, even though we had not yet beaten a top-ranked team.

Some failed to notice that my freshman center, Hasheem Thabeet, had played organized basketball for all of three years before the start of last season. We had only two experienced returning players, and they'd both been reserves the year before. Our only experienced big man, Jeff Adrien, was undersized—six feet seven inches tall. He was our leading scorer last year, almost by default.

Then, when we got into the meat of our schedule and got beat in conference games, the predictable question arose: "What's wrong with UConn?"

Maybe it was partly my fault. I expected us to play better than we did, and the media takes its cues from the coaches. We were very young, and I knew we would have difficulties. But I also knew we had some good young players, and they didn't play quite as well as I thought they would. For one of the first times in my career, we didn't really have a point guard who could consistently ignite our offense. We didn't have a small forward or anybody who could step up and make big plays on offense when we needed them, though guard Jerome Dyson was starting to become a go-to player.

We thought that A. J. Price would play better at point guard than he did, because he's extremely talented. But what we failed to fully realize was that A.J., despite starting his third year in school in

Storrs, was playing his first year of college basketball. He'd had a great high school career, and while he was away from our team, his legend grew. Fans expected him to come in last year and be the next great UConn player. A.J. himself called the expectations "outrageous." I don't know yet how good A.J. will be. He might turn out to be a better shooting guard than a point guard, we'll see. But I do know this, he will get better.

Expectations *can* be a burden—for players and teams.

Connecticut fans are still pleased when we win the Big East title, but they don't get quite as amped about it as they did ten years ago. Why? Because it's not a new experience anymore. Been there, done that. They now think more about *national* titles. Perform well, and the achievement and expectation bars get raised. Fans get spoiled—it's human nature.

Last year we didn't really face a lot of pressure until late in the season, when there was a risk we wouldn't make the Big East tournament. But we won four of our last seven conference games, and made the annual trip to Madison Square Garden.

Even when we were struggling, I was confident that we'd make the conference tourney. The kids worked hard all year; there was never a problem with their effort or their attitude. And knowing my program and the dedication of my coaches and players, I sensed that we'd find a way to win enough league games down the stretch to make the twelve-team field. And we did.

The previous year, the 2005–2006 season, the situation was totally different. That year, the expectations were large. We had a good team, sometimes a very good team. We'd been ranked number one for part of the year. We beat some good teams, won some tough games. We would go on to win the Big East regular season championship. We were a number-one seed in the NCAA tournament.

Late in the season, the media horde suddenly seemed to decide that we should win the national championship. I didn't necessarily agree. I told people all year that we had weaknesses. We couldn't put the ball on the floor—meaning we didn't have many guys who could take the ball to the basket and score—and we clearly weren't as good as the 2004 title team. We just didn't have the star power. Still, I was okay with the idea of being a championship favorite. I knew we had a *chance*.

But somewhat mysteriously, we lost our focus the last five games of the year, starting with the Big East tournament quarterfinal game, when we tried to sleepwalk Syracuse, a team we'd beaten twice during the year. We fell way behind early. We missed our first eight shots, and at one point in, went seven minutes without a basket. We trailed by seventeen points in the first half.

Then, after I barked at them a while, the guys came to realize they were playing a Big East tournament game. We asserted ourselves and in the second half became more aggressive, and came charging back. We started playing our game. And with eleven seconds to go in the game, we had a three-point lead.

To win the game, Syracuse needed to score three points in eleven seconds. We knew they'd try to get Gerry McNamara, their talented guard, open for a tying three-point shot. And we knew we had to stop that from happening. McNamara was a sniper, one of the best outside shooters in college basketball.

During a time-out, my coaches and I told the players emphatically: Try to keep McNamara from getting the ball. We wanted their other guard to bring the ball up the court, and we wanted any Syracuse player *not* named McNamara to take their last shot. We told the players that if McNamara did get the ball, to double-team him. Don't let him get an open shot beyond the three-point line. Force him to dribble the ball past us and toward the basket; let him make a two-point basket if necessary. Or foul him. *Just don't let him get open for a three.*

So what happens? The Syracuse point guard takes the in-bounds pass and starts up the court with the basketball. Okay so far. Then he quickly passes the ball to McNamara. Not okay. That's what we wanted to avoid, but our man failed to guard him closely enough. Then the guy who was supposed to double-team McNamara forgot to do so, because he was worried about his man getting a meaningless layup. Uh-oh. McNamara made a move with the ball, got free for the long shot we wanted desperately to avoid—and drained it. Game tied. We lost the game in overtime.

That was a hint that the NCAA tournament was going to be a challenge for us—a four-game high-wire act.

And it was. For the first time all year, we played a little nervously, I thought. And we played behind a lot. It's tough to win games in which you're in a catch-up mode for long stretches. It takes a lot of physical and emotional energy.

For the first time all year, our team weaknesses became as noticeable as our strengths. In the first game, we had to rally in the last ten minutes to beat the University of Albany. In the second round, we played well against a good Kentucky team and won a very competitive game by four points.

In the Sweet 16, we trailed the University of Washington for most of the game. Rashad Anderson made a three-point shot at the buzzer to send the game into overtime, and we showed some real toughness in pulling out a very-hard-fought victory against a good basketball team. Then, in the Elite Eight, we could not shake a resilient George Mason squad, played another overtime game, and lost. In the end, we had a champion's talent, but not a champion's will.

Numbers tell part of the story. In our last five games of 2006, our performance in key areas fell off. During the regular season we blocked an average of ten shots a game—best in the nation. But in the Big East final and our four NCAA games, we averaged only three. During the season we outrebounded our opponents by an average of nine a game. In the last five games, that margin dropped to four. Perhaps most telling, we held our opponents during the season to a 37 percent shooting percentage. That was outstanding—second best in the country. But our defense wasn't as good in the tournaments. Our opponents shot 47 percent against us in the last five games. And in the NCAA tournament, we got outscored in the paint by all four of our opponents.

Of course, the competition is always tougher in the NCAA tournament. That was one reason why our positive stat margins shrank. But I also think a few of our players started thinking too much in the tournament. Some were contemplating the end of their college careers, while others were mulling the start of their pro careers. Everybody was preoccupied with the possibility of a national championship—too much so, in hindsight. The guys had too much on their minds.

I think our center, Hilton Armstrong, played nervous in the tournament. Hilton was going to be a first-round NBA draft pick, but he also loved college life and was very comfortable at UConn. It was his home, and I think the idea of a life change got in his head a little bit.

I'm not sure our talented swing man, Rudy Gay, really wanted to leave college, either. It's tough to leave college after two years. It takes about a year to adjust to college, and by year two you've settled in and are having the time of your life. So just as Rudy was settling in, having fun, he had to face the reality that he was leaving. It was sort of preordained that he'd leave, whether he wanted to or not, because he was going to be a top-ten NBA draft pick. There was an onus on him to leave.

Power forward Josh Boone, a junior, wasn't sure what to do. He wrestled with the decision to turn pro or not, and that weighed on him. Meanwhile, our other two senior regulars, Rashad Anderson and Denham Brown, were facing the unknown. And that's never a good thing. They were surrounded by guys destined for the NBA, wanted to play in the NBA themselves, of course, but neither of them knew if that was going to happen. Rashad and Denham were good college players. They were tough, resilient, my kind of guys. But neither had quite enough athleticism or ball-handling skills to wow pro scouts.

It's not an easy thing to be a senior with more than a little talent, and know that you might not move on to pro basketball with your teammates. As it turned out, Denham was drafted in the second round by Seattle. Rashad did not get drafted but was signed to play professionally in Greece, and he's doing well.

Interestingly, the guy who played best for us in the 2006 NCAA tournament was Marcus Williams, and looking back I am not surprised. Of all our guys, he was the steadiest emotionally. Marcus, a junior, wanted to turn pro after the season, intended to do that, and was completely at ease with the decision. He had no second thoughts. The comforts of college life didn't tug at him as it did some of the other guys. And perhaps for that reason, Marcus played extremely well in the tournament.

We did great things in 2006. We won thirty games and lost four. But George Mason got a great run going in the tournament and beat us in overtime. One missed last-second shot by Denham Brown kept us from going to our third Final Four. Things happen.

Two years ago I watched an underdog Oregon State football team beat Southern Cal. Eight or nine times out of ten, that USC team would have beat Oregon State, but on that day most everything the Trojans tried to do failed, and almost everything Oregon State did worked. USC trailed 30–10 before making a great comeback. In the closing seconds, they scored to make the score 30–28, but they failed to make the two-point conversion and lost the game. Sometimes the other team just plays well, and sometimes you have a bad night. Your performance fails to match your expectations.

Were there questions after the loss to George Mason? Yeah, and I asked lots of them of myself. I was disappointed, and so were our fans, who hoped we'd win a third national title in seven years. As I told the press later, "We were thirty and four, and they wanted more. There's poetry for you."

People don't realize how hard it is to win a national championship. There are 112 Division IA schools in America, and most are burning with the same desire to win the big trophy as we are. To win the national title once is a huge accomplishment—like winning the lottery. To do it twice is like sailing a Sunfish across the Pacific Ocean. Look out for the squalls and fifty-foot waves. We've won it twice.

Here's how many undefeated college basketball teams there were in America in 2007: zero. Here's how many undefeated teams there were in 2006: zero. The national champion in 2005–2006, Florida, lost *six* games—two more than we did. Even the best teams get beat—that's just the way it is. Same thing last year.

The bottom line is, our 2006 team didn't handle the demands of winning a national title. But I certainly don't worry about facing the same pressure again. In fact, I'm looking forward to it. As the leader of the Connecticut program, I'll be very happy if and when we're again the favorite to win a national title. I *want* more pressure of that kind. It means we've got a good basketball team. You'll never hear me complain about the difficulty of meeting high expectations. My attitude is, "Bring 'em on." High expectations are exciting, and much better than low ones.

And frankly, any coach, manager, or individual who can't handle pressure is not likely to prosper. Life is full of pressures. They start when you get up in the morning. In my business, there is pressure to win every game, every season. Hell, I felt pressure to win when I was coaching high school basketball. Handling pressure is a *requirement* for getting ahead.

Nobody who runs a top organization or company can relax, because somebody always wants what you have. Coca-Cola has been the biggest and most profitable soft drink company in the world for decades, but PepsiCo is always stalking it. Intel has been the world's leading semiconductor company for a long time. It's a great company. But it's been fighting like mad in recent years to fend off a major challenge from another chip maker named Advanced Micro Devices. AMD was a smallish underdog company for decades, working in Intel's shadow, but these days it makes computer chips that are as good as Intel's.

Microsoft has $40 billion in annual sales, but Bill Gates and CEO Steve Ballmer can't be happy watching Google try to take over the Internet world. Xerox was a powerhouse in the photocopying industry for decades, then along came Asian competitors, digital photography, and the industry was turned on its head. So was Xerox.

Name a market leader—Starbucks, Toyota—and you can bet their leaders lose sleep at night worrying about the competition. I do. If we don't stay on top of our game, there are a bunch of other Big East schools ready to take our place. What have you done for me lately?

To keep an organization on top over the long haul, its leaders must excel at what I call *mountaintop management*. What does that mean? Well, for one thing, it means keeping a business or team focused, committed, and competitive *every day.*

It also means working to slay that little devil known as complacency, which sits outside everyone's door. Were we to take our foot off the gas pedal, there are fifteen other Big East teams that would roar past us with grins on their faces. Almost every conference game we play is a rock fight, a playground brawl.

College basketball is ferociously competitive. Nobody cares much about our reputation or anybody else's. You blow the whistle, start the game, and see who wants the victory more. The Big East now has sixteen teams, and nearly every one of them is talented—Syracuse, Villanova, Notre Dame, Pittsburgh, Louisville, West Virginia, Georgetown, Marquette, to name a few. They've all got good players, and they all play hard. We've got to get great players, and play even harder, to win.

I'm not crazy about the super-sized new league, by the way. One big problem with such a large league is that the schedules are unbalanced. As it now stands, we don't play every team in the conference every year—nobody does. And in 2005–2006, we played more games against the better teams in the league than the weaker ones. That makes the road to the conference title a little longer, and a little tougher.

Stick with What Got You There

HERE ARE A FEW of the principles that I think can help enterprises stay on top of the heap, in the short and long term. The first is: *Stick with your standards.*

I talked a lot in earlier chapters about establishing a culture of winning in your business or your life. That culture always starts at the top, and then should permeate an organization. Have you ever walked into a company and "felt" the core of its traditions and its standards? If you've ever walked into Yankee Stadium, or the old Boston Garden, or the UCLA basketball facility, you can feel their winning culture and the standards that helped to establish it.

I came across a quote from Aristotle that was in our Thought of the Day collection. The philosopher supposedly said: "Excellence is an art won by training and habituation. We do not act rightly because we have virtue or excellence, but rather we have those [qualities] because we've acted rightly. *We are what we repeatedly do. Excellence, then, is not an art but a habit.*" The emphasis is mine.

I like that quote because it dovetails with some of my ideas, especially the concept of "winning every day," which means forming strong personal and organizational habits that help you achieve little victories every day, which in turn lead to bigger triumphs.

I use the analogy of building a wall every day, stone by stone. Stick with the job and pretty soon you've built a cathedral. It's having passion for your job and your business; it's learning how to work hard; it's being accountable for your actions; it's motivating the people you work with; it's believing in yourself and wanting to be special individually and collectively, not ordinary. It is daring to dream.

I've succeeded partly because I'm a taskmaster. And I still am. Winning more than 750 games has not softened me up. I'm as tough,

demanding, and intense as I ever was. I still expect my players to practice and play hard every day. I still expect them to make smart decisions
on the court. I still spend a lot of time cultivating good relations with
my players, because it's the best way to motivate them. I still bench guys
for poor play just as quickly as I ever did.

I still upset people sometimes, because I insist that we keep getting better. I still push my staff to excel on the recruiting front, because I recognize how crucial talent is to success in this game. I still
expect my players to go to class—every day—and to behave responsibly on and off the basketball court. Success hasn't changed our
standards.

If one of my players has violated a team rule, I still ask him to pay
a visit to my office. Once inside, he'll wish he was someplace else. If
the violation is minor—a missed class or two—I'll warn the student
athlete to straighten out or risk being suspended. If I were to start
getting soft on disciplinary issues out of apathy or indifference or fa-
voritism toward a good player, I'd be inviting trouble. The other kids
would sense that I don't mean business, and pretty soon team morale
and cohesiveness would start to break down. We've had a lot of great
players come through UConn, and they didn't have any problems
with acting responsibly. So we're not going to change our standards
for anybody.

Passing Down the Gospel

STANDARDS ARE MOST EFFECTIVE when everybody in an organization believes in them. It doesn't do me any good to stand up and
preach about the type of organization and team I want us to be. If my
staff and my players don't have an instinctual sense of UConn basketball standards, if they don't take responsibility for doing the things
necessary for the team to improve, my little pep talks won't mean
much.

Look at any great business or organization in America—General

Electric, IBM, Johns Hopkins Hospital, McKinsey & Company, the American Heart Association, Goldman Sachs, even Wal-Mart despite all the criticism that company gets. They all have one thing in common: a singular culture, their own way of doing things, which gets passed down from leader to leader, from employee to employee, year after year after year.

The leaders of those organizations change, but the culture endures. Wal-Mart is famous not just for its low prices but also for its Saturday employee sessions, where company "associates," as employees are called, gather and listen to company executives give pep talks. It's part of Wal-Mart's internal culture.

One of the coaches who influenced me was Dean Smith at North Carolina. Dean, who's a friend of mine, was an innovator. He also cultivated what's called the "Carolina way"—which is nothing more than UNC's organizational culture.

Dean created the so-called four-corners offense, which he used so effectively to kill time in the late stages of games when the Tar Heels were ahead. He also pioneered the idea of substituting not just one or two players but an entire second unit. He'd pull his starting five out of the game and insert five new players. Because they were used to playing as a unit, and took pride in their role, more often than not the second five played well. Nobody really does it anymore, including UNC, but Dean made it work.

Dean also emphasized ball movement; his teams always shared the basketball. He recruited great athletes, and they all bought into Dean's team-oriented system. That's important. His players were very good, but the system was the star. (Why did Joe Montana achieve such success as an NFL quarterback, winning four Super Bowl titles? Yeah, he was talented, though certainly not the most physically gifted quarterback in football. He was also lucky enough to play in a superior offensive system, and for a brilliant coach named Bill Walsh.)

Dean, with help from great players and coaches, won two national titles. Only Bob Knight has won more college basketball games.

Dean created the North Carolina tradition, and when he retired in 1997, after thirty-six years as Carolina coach, people naturally wondered if the program could remain as strong. Who could possibly fill his shoes? It's a question that gets asked any time a formidable leader steps down.

Well, Carolina has carried on, and the reason is that, like all good organizations, they understand the importance of *continuity*. Continuity of standards. Continuity of excellence.

And the one key way you maintain continuity is to make good hiring decisions.

If you want to maintain a culture of winning, you have to hire people who embody the standards and values that helped establish your organization's success in the first place. To do otherwise is risky.

Look at the Boston Celtics. After the legendary Red Auerbach retired in 1966, the team hired Bill Russell to succeed him as player/coach. Russell, a Hall of Fame center, was a Celtic to his core. He'd won eleven NBA championships playing for Red, and knew what it took to win. Tom Heinsohn succeeded Russell, and he, too, played for Red and won championships. Tom's successor was Thomas "Satch" Sanders, another former Celtic player under Auerbach. Satch played on eight championship teams. That is continuity of values and tradition. Importantly, the Celtics kept winning after Red retired, at least for a decade.

The NBA has changed dramatically in the last fifteen years. There is less continuity in the game itself. Let me correct that: There is almost no continuity. Instead, there is constant player and coaching turnover. Nobody has any patience anymore—not the owners, general managers, fans, or players. It's all about winning and making money immediately. The pro game is still exciting. I still watch it and still like it, partly because a lot of former Huskies are in the NBA. But the league is always in flux, and the Celtics, like a lot of teams, have not managed change well. They've had too many coaches and too many mediocre teams over the last fifteen years. Still, the great

Celtics tradition hasn't dimmed, even though the hallowed Boston Garden has been replaced by the Fleet Center. As a kid from Boston, I'm betting that Danny Ainge and Doc Rivers, and the addition of Ray Allen, will restore a lot of the allure of the great Celtic tradition.

At North Carolina, after Dean retired, the school hired Bill Guthridge to replace him. Who better to carry on the Carolina tradition than a man who'd worked as Dean's assistant for thirty years? It was a wise choice: Guthridge only coached UNC for three years, but they were good ones. He took the team to the Final Four twice. And now Roy Williams is running the show in Chapel Hill. He played for Dean at Carolina. He's not a Dean clone—he's got his own coaching style and own coaching philosophy. But he knows the school, respects the tradition and the culture, and he won a national championship himself three years ago.

UCLA, Kentucky, and Kansas are the same way. Their winning traditions were established decades ago, and they all remain good programs. John Wooden won an amazing ten championships at UCLA in the 1960s and 1970s, and while the Bruins have been spotty over the last twenty years, they won a national title in the 1990s under Jim Harrick. Former Pittsburgh coach Ben Howland is now leading the Bruins, and he took them to the Final Four in 2006.

Adolph Rupp turned Kentucky into a powerhouse in the 1940s, 1950s and 1960s, and the great basketball tradition he created has been carried on over the years by such outstanding coaches as Joe Hall, Eddie Sutton, Rick Pitino, and currently Tubby Smith. (Tubby knows as much about fighting the beast of high expectations as any college coach in America. They take basketball very seriously in Lexington.)

Few basketball schools have a tradition that can match Kansas's. Former Jayhawks coach, Dr. Robert Naismith, invented the game of basketball. You don't get more traditional than that. Forrest "Phog" Allen, who coached Kansas from 1920 to 1956, won three national titles. He's a legendary coach, and like all these programs, the Kansas athletic department has had to hire special coaches to keep the program strong. In Larry Brown, Roy Williams, and now Bill Self, it has.

The "Connecticut Way"

LIKE THOSE PROGRAMS, MY assistants and I have built a tradition of excellence at UConn. We've established our own unique basketball culture—a "Connecticut way"—which I'm confident will succeed me after I retire. On the court, boiled down, it means playing hard-nosed, tenacious basketball for forty minutes. We emphasize rebounding, tough man-for-man defense, and an up-tempo offensive style, which kids like to play. Off the court, the "Connecticut way" means that we have a close-knit, family-style atmosphere, where everybody cares about one another.

As I've often said, we never think of ourselves as better than anybody else in college basketball. We aren't. But we do try to be special in our own way. And when everyone is invested in that idea, your standards will be adopted throughout the organization.

Former guard Kevin Ollie probably personifies Connecticut basketball, and my coaching standards, as well as anybody. Kevin, who played point guard for us between 1992 and 1995, was not the most gifted player I've ever had. He was a good athlete, not a great one. He was a good basketball player, not a great one. But he had—still has—a tremendously tough, determined attitude. He was a guy who played good defense, took care of the basketball, and was willing to work harder than other people. And he never quit trying to be a better player and trying to make us a better team. He's got the third highest career assist total in Connecticut basketball history.

After he left UConn, Kevin wanted to play in the NBA. But he wasn't drafted. So instead he went off to play for the Connecticut Pride of the Continental Basketball Association—the NBA minor league. Kevin played for the Pride for a year, then in 1997 was signed by the NBA's Dallas Mavericks. But he was soon cut by the Mavs, and over the next seven or eight years, Kevin was caught in his own version of *Groundhog Day*. He'd sign with an NBA team, play a little, and then get released.

In all, Kevin has been cut by eight NBA teams—*eight*—since he started playing professionally. But he wouldn't let the dream die. He kept at it, and after he was traded from Cleveland to Philadelphia in 2004, he signed a $15 million contract with the 76ers. Not bad for a journeyman reserve guard. That is competitive spirit and the Connecticut way.

I read a quote recently from Sir John Bond, the retired head of the global bank HSBC. Bond noted that one of his favorite sayings comes from Lao Zi, an ancient Chinese philosopher. He said: "When the best leader's work is done, the people will say: 'We did it ourselves.' " That is the essence of a culture of winning, and of a leader's standards permeating an organization.

I appoint captains most years, and I rely on them and other veteran players to communicate the program's values to our youngest players. I call it "passing down the gospel." It's clear to me that we've created something special, because a lot of my former players return to campus every year for our annual reunion game, including guys who are in the NBA, if they have the time to get back to Storrs. They're proud of the program.

When assessing the pro potential of some of our guys, a lot of NBA coaches seem to give UConn players the benefit of the doubt. That's because we've got a lot of former Huskies in the NBA and they're performing very well. Our guys give good value because they work hard, enhancing the reputation of the program. The success of Ray Allen, Richard Hamilton, and Cliff Robinson, to name three, has helped boost the draft prospects of more recent UConn players.

When Charlie Villanueva decided to leave the program early in 2005, he was initially projected to be a top-fifteen to top-twenty draft pick. He was drafted eleventh, which I took as a vote of confidence in our program by the Toronto Raptors. And Charlie had an excellent rookie year.

Be Forward-Looking

ANOTHER WAY TO PERPETUATE success is for an organization's leaders to keep their minds sharp and *keep looking forward*.

My tactical ideas about basketball don't change a lot from year to year, but I keep my head in the game every day by talking to other coaches, by attending coaching conferences and seminars, by running basketball camps in the summer, and by spending lots of time chewing the fat with my assistants. I'm still curious about the world, too. I read books about psychology and leadership to pick up motivational ideas. And I enjoy talking to people in other professions, which I do a lot because I give a couple of dozen speeches a year to outside groups. It helps broaden my perspective.

I try to stash my past accomplishments in the closet every day before I leave the office. It's not easy sometimes to forget about what you've achieved in the past. Concentrate on what great things you can do in the future. Look ahead, not behind.

As I tell my players: *The future is a blank slate. How you fill it out depends on what you do today.*

Planning is important to me. Every year we script out the first four weeks of practice—every drill for every day, for a month. My assistants also organize off-season workouts. I want to know when the kids are lifting weights, when they are running, and what the results are. If you don't stay on top of your operational structure—meaning the people who help you keep the screws tight—cracks will develop in the façade. And then there will be leaks.

ANOTHER KEY TO MOUNTAINTOP management is to *keep your hand on the wheel*.

I delegate a lot—giving my assistants a lot of responsibilities, ranging from recruiting to game planning—and yet I keep a tight grip on the program. I talk to my assistants constantly. We probably have more meetings than any college staff in the country. It's just the way I operate.

I'm always asking questions: Did we call that prospect? Have we made arrangements to travel to that AAU tournament? Is the Notre Dame scouting report ready? Have we mapped out tomorrow's practice and what we should be working on? I like *thinking* and talking about the program.

Confucius, the ancient Chinese sage, wrote: "Those who would be constant in happiness or wisdom must change."

It's a contrarian thought: Why change when you're content or happy? Why change when things are going well? Because contentment is one short step from complacency, and complacency can ruin a party pretty quickly. There is a thin line between excellence and mediocrity, and it usually separates those who are comfortable with change from those who are not.

I don't change my standards. But I also know that society changes, and so do kids, and you can't be a dinosaur. You've got to be ready to adapt. Just like everything else, college basketball today is different than ten years ago. Unlike in the past, the best high school players these days are fixated on the NBA. So are their parents and friends.

That's created new demands for coaches and their staffs. For one thing, we've got to make sure that the players aren't approached or distracted or by agents or "runners"—people who try to befriend players on behalf of agents—and various hangers-on. It's not something we had to deal with fifteen years ago, but it's an issue we must be aware of constantly these days. It's very important in every organization that the employees stay focused on the present. It's hard keeping pro prospects focused on college basketball sometimes, but we try. Distractions are never good.

More generally, it's simply tough keeping college teams together these days, because of the pro issue. It means my assistants and I have to spend a lot more time talking to players about their future, even when they've only been on campus for a year or two. I don't like it, but the siren call of the NBA can't be ignored. If you've got a stable staff that understands you and your standards, knows what you want and how you tick, you will be ahead of the game.

The Big Picture

HAVE I CHANGED MUCH over my career? My son Jeff, who played for me at UConn for four years in the early 1990s, thinks I've mellowed a bit. He contends my practices aren't as long or as intense as they were twelve or fifteen years ago.

But as I've reminded Jeff, he's not a player anymore. He's watched my practices from a seat in the stands, and practices never seem too difficult when you're sitting on your hands. Everybody thinks life was tougher back in the day. (I was pretty hard on Jeff, by the way, when he played for me, because I didn't want any of the other players to think I was playing favorites.) Jeff spends a lot of time around the program now. We talk on the phone at least once a day, and I value his judgment.

Jeff is right in one respect: My practices can be a *little* shorter sometimes, if we have a veteran group of players. But last year they were longer on average than they've been in recent years, because our Diaper Dandies, as some folks called our group of freshmen, needed a huge amount of work.

I vary the length of practices depending on what part of the season we are in, how we are playing, or how fresh or tired my players seem. Generally, we shorten our practices a bit as the season progresses because we don't want to burn out the players. Players are more focused when the sessions are fairly fast-paced and tightly structured. When kids get tired, their concentration wanes and their performance flags.

If I have mellowed, it's in these ways. First, the program's success allows me to keep the "big picture" in mind now more than I could in the past. The big picture is putting my team in a good position to win the Big East and NCAA tournament titles. You do that by trying to get the team to reach its peak near the end of the season when the conference and national tournaments start.

Don't misunderstand: I care a lot about the beginning, middle, *and* end of the season. Red Auerbach taught me that. Every game is important, especially in our conference. If we don't play well early in the season and in the conference over the course of the season, we risk being left out of the NCAA tournament. I hate losing, but I don't obsess over losses anymore. That's partly because we don't lose much.

In 2005–2006, our first loss was to Marquette in January. My point guard in that game was Marcus Williams, but it was his first game back with the team after serving an eleven-game suspension. Marcus was a key player for us, but not surprisingly, after missing the first month of the season, he was rusty.

I knew it would take Marcus a few games to get up to speed, and that it would take the rest of the team a game or two to adjust to his game. They'd been playing with backup point guard Craig Austrie for a few weeks, and he's got a completely different style. Either way, Marquette didn't care. One of their best players, Steve Novak, dropped forty-one points on us—made everything—and they beat us comfortably.

I didn't expect to lose to Marquette, but the outcome didn't distress me too much because I knew that we might have to go through a transition game or two until Marcus settled back in. I also knew that, once he did, we'd be a much better team, because in my opinion he was the best pure point guard in the country. After a long layoff, he needed to play, and play a lot. I threw him back into the fray, we got beat—but getting Marcus into the competitive flow again was my top priority. I knew that he'd come around quickly and we'd be on our way, and that's what happened. That's a big-picture viewpoint.

Earlier in my career, I didn't have that luxury. When I coached Northeastern, and during my first few years at Connecticut, we had to grind in every way, every day, to win games. Lots of things had to go right for us to get into the NCAA tournament. So every loss was big. When we got beat, I took it badly—and personally. It was a punch in the gut. If it was an away game, my assistants didn't want to sit next to me on the ride home. I didn't blame them. I wasn't in a pleasant mood. But that unforgiving attitude helped strengthen the program over time.

The big picture means keeping the team's spirit in mind over the course of the year. I don't want to wear out the kids. Unrelenting managers can tire a team, and a staff, if they're not careful, hurting performance. Even though college players are young, and seem capable of playing eight hours a day, every day, they can wear out mentally and physically.

And the college basketball season is long, upwards of thirty-six games if you go all the way to the NCAA title game. Very few of the games are easy. The schedule is demanding. Two years ago, we played fifteen Big East conference games, most of them dogfights. And our out-of-conference schedule was rugged, too. We played in the Maui Classic tournament to start the season, and beat a good Gonzaga team to win the tourney title. We also played and beat LSU, which was the best team in the Southeastern Conference, and went to the Final Four. We played Indiana at their place, which is always difficult.

In 2005–2006 Syracuse, which didn't have a great year and may have been an NCAA tournament "bubble team," beat us in our first Big East tournament game. They needed to win the game more than we did, and maybe that was a factor.

But Syracuse was also a good team, with a Hall of Fame coach. We beat them easily, twice, during the regular season, but the Orangemen won twenty games—and it's extremely rare to beat Coach

Boeheim and his kids three times in one season. And while we had a bye going into the Big East tourney game, Syracuse had already played and won a game.

I consider tournament "byes" to be a competitive disadvantage, because you not only have to play a solid opponent—like Syracuse—in the second game, but one that already has a game under its belt. And that's the way it played out. We came out flat, Syracuse started strong, and we lost a very close game in overtime.

If we're winning, the Big East tourney can mean playing three games in three days. Some teams spend a lot of energy winning their conference tournaments, and don't seem to have much left in the tank—physically or emotionally—for March Madness. We've generally not had that problem.

While I want to win every game, my biggest goal is getting the team to improve steadily as the season progresses. It's not easy. Almost all teams experience lulls during a season, and we are no different. If I think the team is tired, I might ease up on the gas pedal a bit, especially around the time of the Big East tournament. I don't want the team, or any of my best players, falling into an extended funk, and business managers should keep that in mind, too. Group morale is important. You want your people feeling fresh when you need them to be at their best.

In 1999, the day before the national championship game against Duke, we had our last practice at the Tropicana Arena in St. Petersburg. I'd planned to work out the team for ninety minutes. But after fifty minutes or so, I got a gut feeling to end the practice.

The session had been fine, but more important, I felt the team was in a good place emotionally. We were relaxed and confident, and let's face it, with only hours left in a long season, we weren't going to change. We were what we were. Our strengths were our strengths, and it was too late to fix our weakness.

I grabbed the ball, tossed it down the other end of the court, blew the whistle, and called the team together. I told the players, "You're ready. Let's go win the game." They were ready, and we did win the game.

We don't always win, of course. But when we do come up on the short end of the score, we've always been good about bouncing back with wins. At UConn, we've reached the so-called Sweet 16 eleven times in the last twenty years, and been to the Elite Eight seven times. So I feel pretty good about getting the team in a good position for the free-for-all that is the NCAA tourney. For all the frustration we felt after losing to George Mason, we were one missed shot away from another trip to the Final Four. I was standing about twelve feet from Denham Brown when he launched our final shot, a three-pointer, against Mason in the final seconds. I was sure it was going in. I'm not always right.

We have since tried to regroup. Last year we integrated a large group of new players into the "Connecticut way." We told them, and showed them, what our standards are, and while it was a tough year in some respects, *by our standards,* I was pleased with the attitude and work ethic of the players. They were gutsy. Not always good, by any stretch, but gutsy. And I expect good things from them in 2007–2008. They spent a year enduring the crucible that is Big East basketball, and that will either destroy a young player or make him stronger. I'm betting on stronger.

You need to be mentally tough to perform well year after year after year. I don't care if you're selling hairbrushes door-to-door or running Exxon Mobil. It's not easy keeping the pedal mashed to the floor when everybody is telling you how fast you are. There is a tendency to get lazy and hit the cruise control switch. Jim Valvano, the late North Carolina State coach, coined a phrase for how to get through the grueling NCAA tournament. "Survive and advance," he said.

That's a good motto for life, too, in a country as competitive as ours: Survive and advance. Success has a short shelf life. It comes and goes pretty quickly, leaving good memories but also creating new expectations and questions. Can you succeed again?

We all face a variation of that question every day. In life, as in sports, we are always being forced by circumstances to regroup, to reassert ourselves, to prove ourselves again and again.

Look at Tiger Woods. He's won twelve major tournaments. He's the best golfer in the world. Everybody assumes that he'll win every time he tees it up. But in last year's U.S. Open, Tiger failed to make the cut for the first time in his career. Maybe it was because he was still reeling from the death of his father, to whom he was extremely close. Tiger's dad taught him how to play golf, but also how to conduct himself with great maturity. That was evident when Tiger blamed his poor play at Winged Foot not on his grief, as he could have, but simply on his poor play. And so Tiger, as special as he is, had to regroup. He had to prove himself all over again. Did he? Bridging the 2006 and 2007 PGA seasons, he won eight straight tournaments! I think he reestablished his standard of excellence.

If you as an organizational leader understand that new challenges are *always* awaiting you and your group, and you have the courage and competitive fire to tackle them every day, you will remain a winner over time. So long as you remember what got you to the top of the mountain in the first place.

7

THE WOMAN IN SECTION 114

ON FEBRUARY 3, 2003, I announced that I had prostate cancer. It was two days after my worst loss as a UConn coach—a twenty-four-point defeat to Boston College. Prostate cancer is a common and treatable disease that mostly afflicts older men, but it can be deadly if it's not caught relatively early.

When my doctor gave me the news, I was shocked. Actually, I was scared. It's cancer. I don't like being scared—who does? So my first and strongest reaction was to get rid of the malignancy as quickly as possible. My doctor gave me the various treatment options, and I called my brother, Bill, for advice, too. He's a cardiologist, and he was very helpful in putting the disease and treatment into perspective. It helps to have a doctor in the family when there's a medical problem. They don't panic; hell, I'm not sure they even worry, because they've seen so much. Bill said I'd be okay, and that was good to hear.

Still, I opted to have surgery as soon as possible. Dr. Peter Albertsen, at the University of Connecticut Health Center, removed my prostate gland on February 6, three days after the announcement. I was released from the hospital three days later, and within days I was back at the office, running the program.

Then on February 22, thirteen days after the surgery, I walked—gingerly—back on the court in Storrs to coach the team against St.

John's. I was a little weak but otherwise raring to go. The fans gave me a standing ovation. That was a nice moment, and very humbling. I felt gratitude for the University of Connecticut. The administration has been great to me, and so have the fans. Three hours later, I was also happy about the fact that we'd beaten St. John's.

Basketball has been more than good to me. It's especially good after you win an NCAA title. In 1999, after we did, I spoke with President Bill Clinton. The team and coaches all later visited the White House. How many people get to do that? I was also invited to watch the final round of the Masters golf tournament in Augusta, Georgia, and then the next day I got to play a round on the course, with the final-round pin placements. That was incredible. I shot an 81—one of my proudest moments.

I've thrown out the first pitch at Fenway Park, a true thrill for a Massachusetts man. I've been on the *Late Show with David Letterman*, and I've been a guest at the White House Correspondent's Dinner in Washington. I received an honorary degree from Trinity College in Hartford. I have given scores of speeches to corporate and charity groups over the years.

Whenever I speak to outsiders, I make the point that I'm just one part of Connecticut's basketball tradition. The university has had a lot of exceptional players and coaches over the years. That was highlighted in February 2007, at the halftime of our game with Syracuse. The UConn Athletic Department honored thirteen former basketball coaches and players who helped lay the foundation for the basketball program. It was our inaugural "Huskies of Honor" celebration.

The inductees included former coaches Dee Rowe (1969–1977) and the late Hugh Greer (1947–1963), and one current coach, me. The former players included Vin Yokabaskas (1949–1952), Art Quimby (1951–1955), Toby Kimball (1962–1965), Wes Bialosuknia (1964–1967), Tony Hanson (1973–1977), Corny Thompson (1978–1982), and the late Walt Dropo.

Several of the first-time Huskies inductees played for me. They were Donyell Marshall (1991–1994), UConn's first consensus All-American; Chris Smith (1988–1992), our all-time leading scorer; Cliff Robinson (1985–1989); and All-Americans Ray Allen (1993–1996), Richard Hamilton (1996–1999), and Emeka Okafor (2002–2004). Marshall, who's thirty-three, unfortunately was the only active NBA player who could attend the ceremony. The others, Ray, Richard, Emeka, and Cliff were all playing games or on the road and couldn't make it. Each inductee got a plaque on the west wall of Gampel Pavilion. A tradition has started.

Most of the former players who were inducted were great scorers. Besides Chris Smith, Hamilton ranks second on UConn's all-time scoring list; Hanson, third; Allen, fourth; Thompson, fifth; Bialosuknia, seventh; el-Amin, nineth; Marshall, tenth; Okafor, sixteenth; Quimby, seventeenth; Kimball, nineteenth; Yokabaskas, twenty-fourth. We could have used a few of them last year.

As with so many recruits, Wes Bialosuknia and Toby Kimball came very close to going to other schools. Wes was ready to attend Syracuse. When then-coach Fred Shabel heard that news, he drove two hours to Wes's house, beat on his door, and offered him a scholarship. "By the time he left my house, he had me going to UConn," recalled Wes in a Jeff Jacobs story in the *Hartford Courant*. "He was a great salesman." Wes was known as the Poughkeepsie Popper because of his great shooting skill. He's the only UConn player ever to average more than twenty points a game in each of his varsity seasons.

Kimball was committed to attend North Carolina when coach Hugh Greer intervened and "convinced me to come to UConn," he told Jacobs. Toby led the nation in rebounding in 1966–1967 (twenty-one a game) and averaged eighteen rebounds a game during his career. His teams went to the NCAA tournament three years in a row, and in his junior year the Huskies beat Bill Bradley's Princeton team to make the Elite Eight. I remember Toby because he belted me with an elbow when UConn was playing my American International

College team. I got eight stiches in my face. Quimby led the nation in rebounds in 1954 with 22.6 a game—an amazing number. He remains UConn's career leader in rebounds.

At a luncheon to honor the inductees, I told the group: "We want to make sure that everyone realizes that what has happened at UConn didn't just emerge. It evolved. It evolved out of Hugh Greer. It evolved out of Fred Shabel. It evolved out of Dee Rowe. There are so many people it evolved out of. [They] set up the building blocks that have allowed us to be successful in recent years. I feel so overwhelmed and honored to be included among you. I also feel indebted to you for what you've given this university."

An Even Keel

THE CANCER SCARE MADE me realize how fleeting life is. It also made me thankful for the many blessings in my life. My success, as a coach and as man, is an outgrowth of the great support network I've had all my life. As much as I care about basketball, I care about my family, friends, and colleagues more.

Pat and I have been married for forty years, and she's always been a devoted wife and mother. She's kept me on an even keel in a business that can be very stormy. My sons, Jim and Jeff, have made me proud, and their wives, Jennifer and Amy, are the daughters I never had. I've remained close to my brother, Bill, and sisters Rose, Margaret, Kathy, and Joan, since I was a kid. They are all wonderful people. Any good qualities that I have as a human being can be traced to my mother and father, Kathleen and Jim, who gave me their complete and unconditional love. Any faults of mine are all my own. And I've been lucky to work with a bunch of quality people at Northeastern and UConn over the last thirty-five years.

It's not easy being in a coach's family. When we lose, when sportswriters or fans start shooting arrows, my family feels the negativity more than I do. We sometimes don't realize it, but spouses and children experience all the ups and downs of our jobs. They share in the joy and the heartache.

Leaders don't succeed in a vacuum. When the University of Connecticut hired me, the school made a firm commitment to get better at basketball, and that was the starting point. Making a commitment in part means investing money, and that's what we did. The university eventually built an on-campus basketball arena, upgraded the weight-lifting and locker room facilities, spent millions creating a life skills and tutoring center for all UConn athletes. Successful organizations are usually wise with their money, but they also know that you've got to invest to get ahead. That's why corporations spend significant sums annually to hire good managers, and even more on R&D, marketing, and advertising.

I, in turn, gave the university a commitment: that I'd spare no effort to improve the program. And one part of my commitment was to demand that our players make the same commitment that I did. There is a sign on the wall in our locker room which reads: *Connecticut basketball means commitment*. We take that idea seriously.

Molding Men

ALL COACHES ARE TEACHERS, in every sense of the word. We spend every day trying to turn youngsters into men. But we all play the games to win, too, and when you do that, you can't help but dream of grabbing that pot of gold at the end of the rainbow—an NCAA championship. You can see it, you want to get close to it, but it's always a lot farther away than you think.

One has to be realistic, and I am. At the same time, all genuine leaders have a desire to be the best, and that desire shouldn't dim with time. If I ever stop thinking about winning another national title, *then* it will be time for me to hang up the whistle.

I like the challenge, every year, of taking a group of individual kids—many of them still teens—and trying to mold them into a smart, tough-minded *team*. It's not an easy thing to do, as we learned last year. But when you succeed, there is nothing more gratifying.

Last year was one of the most frustrating seasons of my coaching career, and also one of the most exciting. We didn't make the NCAA tournament, which was disappointing. We have high standards, and we never like falling short of them. But we've missed the Big Dance before, and we may miss it again in the future. It happens to all programs. There are some years when you are rebuilding, and you have to be realistic.

We were certainly rebuilding last year. We'd lost six or seven of our top players from the 2006 team, including our three best underclassmen. Those big talent holes can't be filled overnight. We were almost at square one. We essentially had to build the team from scratch. It was like my first year at UConn, except that it was my twenty-first.

We had a large group of untested freshman and sophomore players, and had to work quickly before the season to evaluate them and decide which ones might be able to help us immediately. It proved to be a tough job. We had lot of young players with potential, and not surprisingly, their play was up and down all year. If you charted our play, it looked like the electrocardiogram of a man with a bad ticker— a line with extreme zigs and zags.

My assistants and I expected that, but we also hoped that the EKG would level out as the year progressed. It did, but it took longer than we'd hoped. We started playing better at the end of the season, but by then our record simply wasn't good enough to qualify for the NCAA tourney.

Defensively, we were good. We had a quick, athletic group of kids, and a big shot blocker inside, and we were tough to score on. Only one team in the country held their opponents to a lower average shooting percentage than we did. That was very encouraging.

But our offensive play was a different story. On offense, shooting and scoring were a big problem for us. There were games when we couldn't throw the ball in the ocean. We just didn't have enough guys with enough offensive experience to be comfortable with their roles and confident with their games.

The guys gave good effort all year, and they were coachable. The team's attitude was positive. We just couldn't find three or more guys who could play well together from game to game.

We tinkered with our lineup constantly, trying to find our best personnel combinations and build some chemistry. It was musical chairs. We couldn't settle on a point guard or on our small forward. We'd try one guy, and he'd play reasonably well for a game or two, and then regress—miss shots, commit turnovers, or just fail to make a strong impact on the game. We'd sit him down and try somebody else, and it was the same pattern: some positive play, followed by lackluster performances.

We thought A.J. Price would be the guy to run the team, but he was inconsistent and we ended up trying Doug Wiggins, and then Craig Austrie at the point guard position. They had their moments. Craig is not explosive, but he's steady and doesn't make a lot of mistakes. Doug is more athletic, but plays helter-skelter. Neither of them really seized the job. Late in the year we went back to A.J., and he was better. After a long layoff, I think he's starting to find his game. Point guard is a crucial position, and going into the 2007–2008 season, we need better play from the guys in that spot.

The number-three position—small forward—was also a mystery. We played Marcus Johnson and Stanley Robinson, and like everybody, they were inconsistent. Stanley has the potential to be a very good player, but he's got to work hard and do a better job of getting into the flow of a game. There were games when he and other freshmen would be on the court playing, but you'd hardly notice them because they weren't making enough plays. The bottom line was, with two weeks to go in the season, I couldn't tell you who the best five players on the team were. I could name three, but not five.

We have talent, and there's no doubt we'll be better, now that the players have a year of Big East competition behind them. The other coaches and I just need to keep pushing and prodding and molding them, and pretty soon we're likely to have some special players and maybe another special team.

That would be neat. There's nothing better than to watch a kid mature as a player and a person under your leadership. Hasheem, for one, is a big man who's going to have a big impact as he continues to learn the game. And Jerome Dyson is on his way to becoming a special player. He gave us some badly needed scoring punch late in the year, averaging about twenty points a game over the last six games or so.

I have seen a lot of freshman student athletes, and many tend to be a little immature and undisciplined, and perhaps even a little scared. Those things can cause some ripples in the player-coach relationship. But when you see a kid take your advice to heart, and start doing the things you ask, you know progress is being made. And then when it all kicks in and you see a once shaky kid become a confident, tough-minded player, there is no better feeling in the world.

I like making a difference in the lives of young men. I like helping them to get a sense of what it takes to be a winner on and off the field. The great thing about team sports, paradoxically, is that it fosters the idea of individual responsibility. A team is a reflection of the individuals who comprise it. Every single member of the team affects the group's performance.

Every coach's job is to take individual parts—the players—and use them to build a greater whole. That's only possible when every member of an organization, team, or corporate unit is fully invested in the success of the group, as opposed to his own success. That's why I constantly remind the kids: "When we succeed, I succeed."

And I like being a father figure to some players who may have grown up without one. We get kids from one-parent households, where Mom runs the show. That's okay. But young men need mentors, and my coaches and I can fill that role. That's why Caron Butler, a former Connecticut player who plays for the Washington Wizards, still calls me Pops. College coaching is, really, a laboratory for leadership every day.

The Woman in Section 114

MY COACHES AND I sometimes joke about the "woman in section 114." Who is she? No one—and everyone.

Section 114 is a seating area at the Hartford Civic Center, where we play several home games every year. It's where fans sit, people who love the Huskies but sometimes make observations and judgments about players or coaches, or the team, that can be superficial or a bit off the mark. Casual sports fans, as well as the media occasionally, make judgments about players, coaches, and teams that aren't always totally accurate. Because they don't see the players and the team up close. They simply aren't privy to what goes on inside the program, day to day.

Two years ago, the woman in section 114 probably thought we were a shoo-in to win the NCAA title. My assistants and I knew it wouldn't be so easy, because we saw our flaws as a team. We therefore laugh occasionally about how "the woman in section 114" would be surprised if she knew what really goes on behind the scenes in UConn basketball.

For example, the woman in section 114 might be surprised to know that I'm not really the hothead I'm reputed to be. Yeah, I'm intense. I still yell a lot during games. I have for nearly thirty-five years, and I don't plan to stop now. It's my personality. When I'm on the basketball court, I morph into Mr. Intensity. Most coaches do, and we yell a lot during games. For one thing, you need to, in a noisy arena, to get the attention of players who've got a lot on their minds. During those two and a half hours, I stalk the sidelines like a caged lion.

But two and a half hours is not quite one-tenth of a day. It's a pretty short time. And, believe it or not, I don't spend the other twenty-one and a half hours blowing my top. Like a lot of coaches, I'm more relaxed off the court than on it. I'm not a touchy-feely type, by any stretch, but away from the office I'm a husband, father, and grandfather.

Around the office, the atmosphere is businesslike, as it should be. There are, however, plenty of light moments. As in most athletic environments, there is a lot of good-natured needling. The players tease each other. The coaches tease each other. The coaches tease the players. The players *don't* tease the coaches. And I do more needling than anybody. Surprised?

I don't worry much about my image. In fact, I tend to have a bit of fun with it when I speak to outside groups, much like John McEnroe still cracks jokes regularly about the tantrums he used to have on tennis courts. In fact, as I've tried to suggest in this book, my coaching persona is a mixed bag—one part tough guy, one part mentor. And always, I hope, a leader.

When I go to a coaches' conference, I don't spend much time hanging out with other coaches. I much prefer to spend time with Pat, if she's with me. We'll go to dinner or a movie, maybe socialize with another couple. Or I might just read a book in my hotel room. If my sons and their families are around—I have six grandchildren—I will definitely be with them. I talk to one if not both of my sons every day. They are grown men with wives, careers, and families, but we remain close.

My sons tell people all the time that when they were growing up, Pat was the disciplinarian in the family. And she still is, to a large extent. She keeps the Calhoun family train running on time. I work long hours. I take my job very seriously. But I also try to keep a balance between my home life and my coaching life. I don't want my coaching life to intrude on my home life.

Does it sometimes? Yes, but I know the importance of keeping the two separate. If we lose a basketball game, I stew. But I don't go home and scream at Pat, or kick the dog, or punch a hole in the wall. I'm not smiling, but I don't take out my job frustrations on my family.

It's easy for an ambitious person to become obsessed with his job, but over time that's a recipe for burnout. Lots of people do flame out—they travel too much, suffer from too much stress, end up unhappy and divorced. You can't lose the balance in your life. If you want to be an effective manager or executive, work as hard at building a good, fulfilling personal life for yourself as you do building your career.

I've always tried to have a broad perspective on life, and to be a well-rounded man. I like to read history books and biographies: *The Purpose Driven Life*, coach John Wooden's *Pyramid of Success, Don Quixote, Final Rounds* by James Dodson, and Lance Armstrong's *It's more than the Bike*. I like to go to movies and plays. I also enjoy helping others through charity work. It has enhanced my life. My wife and I have donated money to the University of Connecticut Health Center, helping to fund what is now called the Pat and Jim Calhoun Cardiology Center. Given that both my father and paternal grandfather died of heart attacks, I couldn't think of a more meaningful contribution. Pat has spent a lot of time working on behalf of the American Heart Association. I've hosted a celebrity golf tournament in Connecticut for the last 9 years to raise money for the Calhoun Cardiology Center. Lots of my coaching friends and former players attend. Thanks to them, we've raised almost $3 million to help the Cardiology Center at the UConn Health Center in its efforts to fight heart disease. We've also given out more than 1.5 million Thanksgiving meals during that time, and my players are good about visiting area hospitals and Boys & Girls clubs a couple of times every year. We just recently held the first Cancer Challenge Bike Ride, which combines my passion for bicycling and my commitment to fight and to help eradicate cancer, and we raised more than $200,000 for the UConn Health Center Neag Cancer Center and Coaches vs. Cancer. It's all about giving back to a community that's given a lot to the university and me.

I don't confine my charitable efforts to Connecticut. In August of 2006, I traveled to Yokosuka, Japan, with a group of other NCAA basketball coaches to visit with American armed forces personnel in that country. It was part of a USO program called Operation Hardwood, which was started a couple of years ago to help bolster the morale of our troops.

Our trip was the third Operation Hardwood tour, and we had a terrific time. The other coaches included Edward Conroy of the Citadel, Darrin Horn of Western Kentucky, and two former UConn assistants turned head coaches, Dave Leitao and Karl Hobbs. I thoroughly enjoyed spending four days with Dave and Karl. It was a reunion for us. You can rehash a lot of old basketball stories during a fourteen-hour plane trip. Steve Lavin, the former UCLA coach who's now a basketball analyst for ESPN, was also in our group.

The United States has about 50,000 military personnel in Japan, many of them in the Navy. American troops are there to help provide security for Japan, and to protect our country's strategic interests in Asia.

We spent most of time in Yokosuka, Japan. I didn't know much about the place until I took the trip. Turns out it is America's most important naval facility in the western Pacific. Located at the entrance of the Tokyo Bay, about 43 miles south of Tokyo, Yokosuka is a big place. About 27,000 American military personnel and civilians are stationed there. The base has a new $35 million Activity Center, which includes a full-size gymnasium, food stores, and an Internet surf shop, among many other things. (We should all have the Pentagon's budget.) For troops who spend years on the other side of the world, it's home away from home.

We were in Yokosuka to hang out with the sailors and soldiers, tell some stories, and play a basketball tournament. Each coach got to lead two ten-person teams made up of military personnel selected from Navy ships based in Japan, and from nearby Army and Air Force bases, including Yokuta Air Force Base, about two hours from Yokosuka, and the Zuma Army facility.

Each base had a sign-up sheet, and then team participants were chosen by lottery. I got two teams from the USS *Juneau*, an Amphibious Transport Dock ship based in Sasebo, Japan, and named after the capital of Alaska. It's a transport ship for troops and landing craft, and it's home to 370 sailors and 40 officers. They call it "the Big J." It's one of seventeen major U.S. ships in Japan that make up the

Kitty Hawk Aircraft Carrier Group and the Belleau Wood Amphibious Ready Group in Sasebo, Japan.

The teams all had one practice, and we then played "pool" games for two days, followed by a championship bracket. Karl's team, from the Camp Zuma army base, beat my Big J team on the first day. I was not happy. But we rallied, won our next few games, and made it to the title game, where we got beat by Steve Lavin's AYG team. It was three days of great fun for us and the soldiers and sailors.

The USO sends a varied group of celebrities to our military bases all around the world, and I could tell from our trip that the visits mean a great deal to our service men and women in overseas countries. It was a special trip for me and the other coaches. Lots of the military men and women in Japan actually follow college basketball and wanted to talk sports. And many of them were eager to show off their basketball skills.

We also learned a lot about Japan. In our spare time, we visited a few historical sites, including the Great Buddha in Kamakura, said to be the second largest Buddha in Japan. It was built in 1252, destroyed by a tidal wave in 1498, six years after Columbus discovered America, and then rebuilt. I wanted to rub its tummy for good luck in the Big East Conference, but couldn't. Not too many Japanese play basketball, because they don't have the size. But soccer and baseball are extremely popular, and the people we met seemed genuinely pleased to have a few *gaijin*—foreigners—in their nice country. It was a great opportunity to meet sailors and soldiers, interact with them, and see what great people we have defending our country; and, politics aside, I truly support them all.

Three months earlier, in May, another large group of NCAA coaches traveled to Kuwait and Bahrain as part of Operation Hardwood. That group included Tom Izzo of Michigan State, Tubby Smith of Kentucky, Dave Odom of South Carolina, Gary Williams of Maryland, and several more. I heard they had as much fun as we did, too.

The Next Big Thing?

I AM OFTEN ASKED if I'm interested in coaching professional basketball. Some people assume that because I've been successful at the college level, I must have some interest in coaching in the National Basketball Association. It's the ambition factor: I've succeeded at the college level; therefore, I must want to move up to the pros. The truth is, while I've thought about it a few times, I don't see myself coaching professional ball anytime soon. I'm a veteran college coach. I like being a college coach, and I'm pretty good at it. Why mess with a good thing?

NBA coaches make more money than college coaches, and some people perceive the pro game to be more prestigious than collegiate basketball. I don't agree. Money and prestige don't equal happiness. And besides, my current job probably has a higher profile than a lot of NBA coaching positions.

Because UConn has a solid basketball program, I have more security than I'd have in the NBA. I run the UConn basketball program. We usually recruit well, and therefore we're usually in the hunt for the Big East Conference championship. And we're a regular contender for the NCAA championship, as well. UConn gets a lot of media exposure. Over the last six years, dozens of our games have been televised nationally. National reporters write about us regularly. It's all free publicity, which helps the basketball program and the university.

Two years ago, after Phil Jackson resigned as coach of the Los Angeles Lakers, team owner Jerry Buss tried hard to recruit Duke coach Mike Krzyzewski to replace him. The Lakers job is one of the best in basketball, and Mike apparently thought pretty seriously about accepting it, but ultimately turned it down.

Why? I don't know for sure, but my guess is that Mike concluded that what he has at Duke, and in college basketball, is too good to give up. He works at a first-rate university, he's built a great program in Durham, won national titles, and forged a gold-plated reputation.

And perhaps most important, he gets to help shape the lives of young men every year, like I do. That is a profound thing. Add it up and it's a lot to give up for a career change of pace, even one as lucrative and appealing as coach of the Los Angeles Lakers.

Jumping to the NBA is risky for an established college coach, because the pro league is unstable. No matter how good an NBA coach is—and the league is full of good ones—he is never far from the unemployment line. The season is long. The competition is intense, and owners and general managers can be impatient. Win quickly—or else. If you have one or two poor seasons, you're almost certain to get the ax. That's why the coaching turnover rate in the NBA is high. The league is a coaching merry-go-round.

After a very successful college coaching career at Providence and Kentucky, including a national title with the Wildcats, Rick Pitino tried his luck in the NBA. He was hired by the Boston Celtics to help turn around that storied NBA franchise. There was much anticipation and fanfare when he took the job, but it didn't work out. After five tough years, Rick left the Celtics and returned to the college coaching ranks. I'm guessing it was something of a humbling experience. Rick was a rival of mine years ago when I coached at Northeastern and he was at Boston University and then Providence. And now that he's coaching Louisville, he's a rival of mine again—only this time in the Big East. It's great to be competing against him again. And through our great rivalry, I've always had a great deal of respect for him.

I've never coached a professional team, but the challenges are pretty obvious. For one thing, there are a lot of things that are beyond the coach's control. That's something that would be hard to get used to. The players are all wealthy adults, and not always easy to motivate. If you, as coach, alienate a star player like Alan Iverson or Kobe Bryant, for whatever reason, he may stop playing for you, and then you and the team are in trouble. And general managers tend to value star players more than their coaches. That's not the case in college. I like kids who ask questions, but I don't want my players questioning my decisions, and those that do will wish they hadn't.

In college, my assistants and I decide who's on the team. In the pros, general managers typically make personnel decisions. The coaches usually have input, but not always. In fact, pro coaches and their GMs often have different ideas about whom to draft, which free agents should be signed, and whom should be cut. It's a recipe for tension.

My point is that the NBA is a risky business. Almost every coach who's been in the league has had his reputation dented. It goes with the territory. When you've spent almost thirty-five years building a nice house, you think twice about moving to a bigger house with a weaker foundation.

Don't get me wrong. I like the NBA. I watch pro games regularly, partly because so many former UConn players are in the league. The NBA has a lot of super coaches and GMs, many of whom I know. But it's not for everybody.

I'M ALSO ASKED OCCASIONALLY if I plan to retire anytime soon. The answer is no. I've been coaching for a long time and still love what I do. My enthusiasm for coaching is as high now as it was twenty-two years ago, when I took the UConn job. What's more, if I were to just hint to my wife that I was thinking about retirement, she'd run screaming from our house. As she tells people, I like staying busy. I get antsy when I'm not coaching or doing something related to coaching.

My family took a summer trip to France a few years ago, and we had an absolutely marvelous time. I had a truly wonderful time being with my grandchildren, my sons, and their wives, and of course Pat, but as my son Jeff likes to say about me, "A shark has got to swim," and the three of us did talk some basketball.

I sometimes suggest to Jim and Jeff that I might retire in a few years. They usually grin cynically in response. They never think that I'm serious, and they're right. They know I'm not ready for it, even if I could play golf every day.

The fact is, I'm still as hungry and competitive as I've ever been. I still enjoy working with the kids too much to retire. I still like chasing the brass rings—Big East and NCAA titles. I'd love for UConn to win another national championship, though that's not my number-one priority.

Asking and Giving

WHEN I WAS INDUCTED into the Basketball Hall of Fame, I gave a speech about my basketball life. Here is part of what I said:

"Basketball is a game that has blessed me. It's a game that's consumed me, that's given me so much. Basketball doesn't care what color your skin is; it doesn't care what language you speak or what religion you practice. It doesn't care if you're big or small, fast or slow. It just asks you to play, to compete, to lose with dignity, to win with humility.

"It asks you to make your teammates look good and to respect your opponents. The game asks that you work to improve, that you put something into it, and that you also give something back to it. The game has taken me to many places. I've traveled from Braintree High School to American International College in Springfield; from Old Lyme, Connecticut, to Westport; from Boston to Tel Aviv; from Dedham, Massachusetts, to Anchorage, Alaska; from Storrs to Sarajevo. I've experienced the noise of the inner city and the quiet of sleepy country towns. The game has introduced me to American citizens, families, and culture.

"To all of my assistant coaches: Thank you for your passion and for your commitment. It's been an honor to sit on the bench alongside all of you. Thanks to the fans, who welcomed me to UConn, who always cared about me and always believed in our players and our program. And lastly, and most importantly, thanks to all the players I've had the privilege to coach. You have filled my life with so many memories and treasures. No coach could ever be successful without the players, and I want all of you to know that I take a piece of each and every one of you into the Hall with me. You have dared to dream. You have enriched my life. And you made this game special."

That, as I said, was part of my Hall of Fame acceptance speech.

In the end, the thing that makes coaching special is the relationships that we build and maintain with so many people. After the Hall of Fame announcement was made, one of the first people who called to congratulate me was Rudy Johnson, who played for us from 1991–1996. Rudy was a backup player and even now describes himself as a "knucklehead" in college. There were times when he didn't go to class, and times when he broke rules. I sent him home once to think about his priorities. I was ready to kick him off the team.

As Rudy told Owen Canfield in a *Hartford Magazine* article, "Coach said if I wanted to come back, there were some things I needed to do. That was a crossroads in my life." Rudy did return, and he ended up getting his degree. "I think back all the time and wonder where would I be if I'd never gone back to school," Rudy told Canfield. He's now a counselor at a juvenile residential drug treatment facility in Connecticut, and I am so proud of him.

Donny Marshall, who was an excellent player for UConn from 1991–1995, grew up with a single mom in Seattle, Washington. He came all the way across the country to play for us, because his mom felt she could trust me to help Donny grow as a player and a human being. As Donny himself told Canfield, our relationship had a few tense episodes. "We argued behind closed doors and fought and all those things, but while we were doing that, Coach was instilling in me one big idea: That you always have to believe in yourself, and you always have to fight, because there's something better out there for you, if you're willing to go get it. As a coach, he never gave you anything. You earned it with him."

Donny wasn't the most talented guy to wear the Huskies uniform, but he was committed to maximizing his potential, and he did so. He played in the NBA for six years and then became a basketball analyst. He's an outstanding young man.

So is Brian Fair. Like Donny, Brian was also raised by a single mom, and he too traveled a long way to play for UConn. Brian grew up in Arizona. As he told Canfield: "I got into a little trouble my sophomore year. Coach called me into his office, and he had that look. I'd seen it before with my mother and my uncles. But Coach helped me through the problem and dealt with it like he was my father. He made sure my mother knew what was going on, and supported me like I was his own son. After that, our relationship changed, because we were able to talk about things more . . ." Brian is now a high school teacher and basketball coach in Phoenix.

Coaches influence young people. But the opposite happens, too. Young people often teach us about life. Back in 1999, the year we won our first national title, a guy named Joe McGinn spent a lot of time around the team. Joe was twenty-six at the time, and a special guy. At age three, he'd contracted a rare kidney disease that had a horrible effect on his body. He was five feet, two inches, maybe, and weighed 120 pounds. He had a four-volume medical history, but it didn't get him down. He had a personality to match his red hair. He was feisty, a wiseacre. He was happy to tell me or the players what was on his mind.

Joe spent some time at Northeastern University taking classes, and then transferred to UConn. That was his dream. He loved two things in life—UConn Basketball and the Boston Red Sox. Combine that with his personality and it's easy to see why we hit it off. Joe was a manager for us for three years, graduated, then went to work for ESPN.

By 1999, Joe was in a wheelchair. Both of his legs had been amputated the year before because of complications from his kidney disease. But Joe didn't feel sorry for himself. He wanted to be treated like an ordinary person, and that's what I did. If he called, I'd ask him: "What are you doing in bed? Get out of it and do something." He got a kick out of that.

Joe was excited about our 1998–1999 season. After we beat St. John's at Madison Square Garden to win the Big East tournament that year, he was in the locker rom with us to celebrate. He wasn't feeling well, but was joking with Scott Burrell and Ricky Moore and all the players. He was the last person to leave.

That's the last I saw of Joe. The next night, after the NCAA tournament brackets were announced, we talked on the phone. Joe liked to analyze the brackets, and he was happy that we were going out West to play. Joe did not make the trip. He died the next day. About three weeks later, we won our first national championship in St. Petersburg.

There is a tradition in basketball. When your team wins a tournament, you get to cut down the nets. Each player and coach snips off a cord, and then the last couple are saved for the head coach. I climbed the ladder in St. Pete and cut down the net, but I left one bit of cord dangling from the rim. "That's for Joe McGinn," I said. It seemed the right thing to do. Joe, with his courage, had touched my life and those of my players.

Write Your Script

YOUNG PEOPLE ARE ENERGETIC, curious, and intrepid. And some of them are curious about how to get ahead. Sometimes, when I'm around campus, students will approach me and ask about the basketball team. Occasionally, one will express uncertainty about his or her future.

My response is, "You've got every chance to be a success in life, if you treat it as a learning experience. I've been out of college for forty years, but part of me is still sitting in a classroom chair. Despite my gray hair and character lines—okay, they're wrinkles—part of me is still eighteen or twenty-two years old. When I was young, I had no idea what my life's script would be. I did know, however, that I wanted to find my mountain to climb. And through hard work and persistence, my summit ended up being basketball arenas in unlikely places like St. Petersburg, Florida, and San Antonio, Texas. Even now, every day I try to think of a new movie of my life that I want to produce. That idea has allowed me to love and have fun at what I do."

It's a message that resonates with young and old people alike.

The late Robert J. Hastings was a Southern Baptist minister for more than fifty years. He penned scores of sermons, speeches, and stories, including his boyhood memoir of the Great Depression, titled *A Nickel's Worth of Skim Milk*. He also wrote a well-known essay called "The Station," which means a lot to me. It reads:

"Tucked way in our subconscious minds is an idyllic vision. We see ourselves on a long, long trip that almost spans the continent. We're traveling on a passenger train, and out the windows we drink in the passing scene . . . of children waving at a crossing, of cattle grazing on a distant hillside . . . of row upon row of corn and wheat . . . of mountains and rolling hills. . . . But uppermost in our minds is the final destination. On a certain day at a certain hour, we will pull into the station. There will be bands playing, and flags waving. And once we get there, so many wonderful dreams will come true. So many wishes will be fulfilled, and so many pieces of our lives will be fitted together neatly like a completed jigsaw puzzle. How restlessly we pace the aisles, damning the minutes . . . waiting, waiting for the station.

"However, sooner or later, we must realize there is no one station, no one place to arrive at once and for all. The true joy of life is the trip. The station is only a dream that constantly outdistances us. When we reach the station, that will be it! we cry. When I'm eighteen, that will be it! When I buy a new Mercedes, that will be it! When I put the last kid through college, that will be it. When I reach the age of retirement, that will be it. I shall live happily ever after!

"Unfortunately, the station somehow hides itself at the end of an endless track. So, relish the moment. It isn't the burdens of today that drive men mad, it's their regrets over yesterday or fear of tomorrow. Regret and fear are twin thieves who rob us of today.

"So stop pacing the aisles and counting the miles. Instead, climb more mountains, eat more ice cream. Go barefoot more often. Swim more rivers. Watch more sunsets. Laugh more. Cry less. Life must be lived as we go along. The station will come soon enough."

I couldn't agree more. My message is to be ambitious. Set high goals. Be strong and positive. Learn how to lead. But don't let naked ambition consume you. A big part of being successful is setting the right priorities in your life—knowing how to balance your needs with those of people who are close to you. Never stop striving to succeed. But never forget that life is precious and fleeting. Don't take it—or your opportunities—for granted.